THE END
OF DAYS

THE END OF DAYS

Helen Sendyk

St. Martin's Press
New York

All photographs courtesy of the author

Design by Tanya M. Pérez

Library of Congress Cataloging-in-Publication Data

Sendyk, Helen.
    The end of days/Helen Sendyk.
        p. cm.
    ISBN 0-312-06962-6
    1. Jews—Poland—Chrzanów—Persecutions. 2. Holocaust, Jewish
(1939–1945)—Poland—Chrzanów—Personal narratives. 3. Sendyk,
Helen. 4. Chrzanów (Poland)—Ethnic relations. I. Title.
DS135.P62C53777 1992
940.53'18—dc20   91-38826
                                                                  CIP

First Edition: June 1992

10 9 8 7 6 5 4 3 2 1

For my children:

Zwika and Leah
Sharona and Alan

my grandchildren:

Rebecca Tamara (Rikki)
Daniel Ephraim (Dani)
Shlomo Yonatan (Yoni)
Shaul Elchanan (Eli)

and for future generations.

Remember the past and be wary of the future.

"Know whence you came."

Preface

There were many thousands of families shattered by the Second World War, and a large body of literature has arisen to describe the military, political, economic, and social repercussions of a conflict from which we are still recovering fifty years later.

Even though the immense tragedy that particularly affected the Jewish people has been recorded, there are those even today who deny the millions their deaths. There could never, therefore, be too many films and books to document the Holocaust, and to brand it in the memory of a forgetful world.

Let me offer, then, my own family. Let me paint these familiar, beloved faces on all the blank textbook pages and freeze-frame forms. I knew them, lived with them, shared their desires and their frustrations, their joy and their anguish, their moments of terrible dread and transcendent courage. I alone carry their lives in me. I cannot let them vanish without a mark, a legacy, a new family to carry on their memory.

Besides the precious few members of my own immediate family of today, my husband and I have cultivated an extended family of other survivors. Now that almost half a century has passed, few members of this family are left. I am one of the youngest survivors who was old enough to remember; I am now left a survivor of survivors. My drive to record, remember, and remind comes from a need to articulate what these silent victims could not. I have tried to tell their stories.

I am being gradually orphaned from my second family, leaving me all the more eager to reach out to my small biological family and to a new extended family of readers. You can be my survivors. Hear my story; take this great stone and pass it on to your children. Let my family be yours. And let no one forget.

Acknowledgments

I wish to express my gratitude to:

The Jewish Heritage Project:
Alan Adelson, director, for his constant encouragement.
Elaine Cohen for her cognizance and foresight.
Isaac Mozeson for his sensitivity and understanding.

Center for Holocaust Studies:
Bonnie Gurewitsch, librarian, for her optimism and belief
in me.

Silas and Antoinette Seandel for their prudent assistance.

My husband Abraham Sendyk for his love and devotion.

My niece Tova Farago and my nephew David Stapler for their enthusiasm.

St. Martin's Press:
Sandra McCormack, senior editor;
Cal Morgan, associate editor; and
Jordan Pavlin for their professional guidance and diligence.

THE END
OF DAYS

Chapter 1

If I did not write this book I could never forgive myself. I cannot let my family fade away and be forgotten as if they had never existed.

The leaves in my album still turn: there is my father, Reb Symche Stapler, serene, earnest, surrounded by his large family, famous for his good humor and storytelling. Beside him is my mother; born Sara Miriam Laufer, fondly called Surcia; a devoted wife and a tender, loving mother, she always looked worried and sad. The oldest of the children is Blimcia, classically elegant and bright. Shlamek, my oldest brother, is determination personified, and a heartbreaker with his athletic good looks. My second brother, Heshek, is the scholar; quiet, studious, meticulous. There is my sister, Nachcia, who is bashful and subdued but who shines with goodness; my third sister, Goldzia, with hair of gold and an angelic face and personality; my brother Vrumek, who never backed down from a challenge. Curious and talented Sholek is my fourth brother. That leaves me, the baby, Helcia. And now I must evoke the past and bring them all back to life.

The place of my earliest memories is Mickiewicza Street, where we lived on the ground floor of the Municipal Building. The offices of the town hall were upstairs. In back, at the far end of a large yard, was a detention cell used mostly for sobering up drunks overnight. Right in front, by the gate, was the police station. I was too young at the time to realize what an unusual living situation we had for a Jewish family in Chrzanow, Poland, in the 1930s.

Facing the street were several stores attached to the government complex; two of those stores were ours. Right behind the stores was our apartment, two bedrooms and a large kitchen, where we ate our meals. Adjacent to our yard was the public school and its yard. If I overslept, I would jump out of bed at the first bell and make it to school by the second bell. The bells we heard on Sundays were from the nearby church.

Afternoons I attended the Beis Yakov school on the Planty, the wide tree-lined avenue in the nicer, modern part of town. One of the most prominent Jews in our neighborhood was Zisme Kinreich, who lived in a big house at the beginning of our street. Most of the Jewish population lived south of the marketplace, near the synagogue, the *mikvah* (ritual baths), and other institutions.

Chrzanow's Jewish population was diversified, but the majority was Chasidic. There were many kinds of Chasidim, and *shtiblach* (houses of prayer and learning) for all of them. There were lots of Belzer, Bobover, and Sandzer Chasidim in our town; Papa was a Belzer Chasid. There was a picture of the Belzer Rabbi in our house. His face shone with grace and strength of character. He had a majestic white beard, and a tall fur Kolpak hat perched imperially on his head.

Jewish families knew each other in Chrzanow for generations. Traditions and family status, *yichus,* were very important, and children generally followed in their parents' foot-steps. An official, respectful distance was kept between Jews and Gentiles, but the Staplers had an unusually close relation-ship with our non-Jewish patrons. Policemen, clerks, and var-ious officials would come to our store for their soft drinks, sweets, and fruits. They would chat with Shlamek, Blimcia, or Papa and have Sholek and me run their errands.

Besides grocery items, the store carried mainly delicatessen. We were known to have the sweetest bananas in town, the juiciest apples, the freshest cherries and the fanciest choco-lates. Papa would travel to Katowice every day, where he would import the best and rarest fruits available in Poland. Our other store carried toys, also stocked by Papa with finds from the big cities of Katowice and Krakow. Shlamek sometimes traveled with Papa and also expertly arranged the showcase, having learned decorating and window display.

Come December, Shlamek would work all night on the showcase. Sholek and I loved to watch Shlamek work on an artistic winter scene of falling snow and gift-wrapped choco-late toys. The excitement peaked when Shlamek would pull up the gate of the display window in the middle of the night to check his work with a critical eye. Bathed in flashing lights, the scene would come alive in the stillness of the night. The next day passersby were drawn to the window, attracted by the imaginative display that had no equal in town. Children would dreamily flatten their noses against the glass, fascinated by the colorfully wrapped candies. Even adults would become en-chanted by the electric train running through tunnels and over bridges, carrying carloads of mouth-watering candy.

It was a quiet Sunday morning, when the Gentiles were attending church. In the Stapler household on Mickiewicza Street my big sister Nachcia was getting me ready for a birth-day party. She put a fine, freshly starched and pressed cotton dress on me, tied ribbons in my neatly combed braids, and got ready to walk me to my cousin Gucia's party. Having reached the age of seven, however, I considered myself old enough to walk there all by myself. I did not let Nachcia go with me.

Happily skipping along, my white dress shining in the sun,

I was stopped by a dark-haired woman in colorful skirts, who asked for directions to Yagelonska Street. Anxious to get to Aunt Esther's on time, I politely pointed out the direction and told the woman to make a right turn at the corner. The woman pleasantly insisted that I take her at least to the corner. She was a stranger in town, she said, and didn't know the neighborhood at all. I obediently walked beside her, annoyed at her numerous questions and her fondling of my pretty dress. She then remarked that my earring was open and that she would close it for me before I lost it. I wanted to get away from that dirty, smelly woman, but it was impolite to not help an old and poor person.

I then became very frightened when I noticed that the woman, instead of simply closing my earring, was removing it from my ear and quickly going for the other ear. Shocked, I realized that the woman was actually stealing my earrings, having led me to a deserted street. Frightened but determined not to be robbed, I grabbed my earring back from the woman's hand and fled home as fast as I could. Badly shaken, I wept in Mama's lap, telling her what happened, between heavy sobs. Nachcia could not forgive herself for exposing her baby sister to such an incident by letting her go out alone.

I remember Mama with an apron around her waist, kneading dough in the kitchen, hands all white with flour, pounding, squeezing, exerting all her energy and strength. Delicious long logs of cocoa cakes would be produced on that magic board, along with her expertly twisted challas. The logs grew longer and the challas multiplied, but we ate them faster than she could make them.

"A household of growing kids," she would sigh, "they need to eat. How lucky I am," Mama would say, "that all my children are grown up. Even my youngest, my Helcia, is off to school already, and Blimcia, my oldest, why she is ready for the marriage canopy." Blimcia was the prettiest of us all, very talented and respected by the rest of the family. Since Papa used to travel every day to Katowice to shop for the store, it was Blimcia who practically ran the store herself. Sometimes, when from the kitchen Mama would hear the clank of the bell

announcing a customer, she would go in to help Blimcia.
There were many fine customers that would frequent our store
for the delicious imported fruits and luscious chocolates.

"Good morning, Chrabina Kalinska," Blimcia would greet
her customer in a sweet, pleasant voice. "Will it be the regular
order? May I suggest some of these mandarins just arrived
from Italy?"

"Oh, if you think they are good, you may add some," said
the customer with a nod.

"I assure you, my lady, they are absolutely delicious; I
tasted them myself or I would not recommend them. What a
pretty dress my lady is wearing," added Blimcia.

"I had it brought from Paris," the Chrabina answered
proudly. "As a matter of fact, I am on my way to Krakow for
a fitting, and when I return this evening I will pick up the order
on the way back to the estate. And Blimcia, darling, will you
go to the stationery store and get me some ink and paper for
letter writing, for I have no time to waste."

"Of course, my lady, do not worry about a thing, and have
a pleasant trip to Krakow."

Blimcia would collect the order carefully and have it all
ready for the Chrabina. She knew exactly what her customers
wanted, and how best to handle them. She mostly attended to
the Gentiles, for her Polish was perfect and her accent clear.

The dark chocolates that the Chrabina favored were filled
with cream, the same ones I used to snatch every time I came
into the store. I knew perfectly well that I was not allowed to
take candy without permission, but being the youngest of
eight children, I got away with every trick.

"May I have a *chulenko*?" I would ask Blimcia—while pop-
ping the chocolate into my mouth before Blimcia could refuse.

"This child is impossible," Blimcia would complain to
Mama, but I knew that deep in her heart she loved me and did
not mind my occasional liberties. When Sholek came home
from school, Blimcia sent him to Langer's stationery store to
fetch the ink and paper she needed for her customer. The only
time a problem presented itself was when a customer wanted
Blimcia to prepare meats. These had to be obtained from a

Polish butcher. The problem was that Papa would never allow any member of his family to set foot in a nonkosher butcher store.

"Everybody knows that we buy meat for our Polish customers," Blimcia would timidly try to argue, eager to please her clientele. Papa, however, would not heed. He would bring up the law of *maras ayin,* meaning that a Jew should not do anything that might be misinterpreted as wrong. If someone saw Sholek go into Siersza's butcher shop, the argument went, it might get around that Sholek Stapler eats *treyf* (nonkosher) meat. There was no arguing with Papa, especially on a point of religious observance. Blimcia would have to find a non-Jewish child to run that errand for her. Mama would wait on the Jewish customers, with whom she would comfortably strike up a conversation in Yiddish. She'd known these people for many years and was sensitive to any change in their shopping patterns. When young Gitele came to the store, Mama immediately knew something was wrong.

"How is your mother?" she asked anxiously. "How come she sent you today for her order? Isn't she feeling well?"

"No, my mother isn't feeling well. She has been having bad stomachaches."

Mama would promptly pick up a jar from the shelf, dash some herbal tea into a paper, and hand it to Gitele. "When you get home, boil some water, put in a heaping teaspoon of the tea, and let your mother drink it. You will see, she will get well in no time."

Gitele collected her purchases in her basket. "How much will the tea be?" she asked.

"Oh, no," Mama responded, "there is no charge for the tea; it is for a *refuah sheleima* [total recovery] for your mother. Go, *gesunter heit* [go in good health], and please follow my instructions so your mother will get well soon."

When Sholek came home for lunch, he would gulp down his food and shoot himself out of the kitchen to run errands for Blimcia—but not before Nachcia, who was in charge of the kitchen, made him say grace after meals. "The Rebbitsin," the rabbi's wife, was Nachcia's nickname because she enforced religious observance in Papa's absence. Sholek was a wild kid, impatiently squirming in his chair, hardly able to control his impulse to get up and run before Nachcia allowed him to leave the table. Sometimes he would grab his Hebrew books and run before she had a chance to call after him, "Go straight to *cheder* [elementary religious school], Sholek, or else Papa will hear about it."

A little short in stature for his age, Sholek made up for it in talent what he lacked in height. Popular in both school and in *cheder*, he could memorize whole chapters of Chumash, the five books of Moses. On Sabbath afternoon Papa would say, "Come, Sholek, let me hear what you learned in *cheder* all week long." Sholek would recite the passages learned, giving Papa enormous pleasure. He would even be able to explain some commentaries, besting his older brothers. Papa would shake his head with pleasure and say, "What is your hurry, Sholek?" Later he would good-naturedly add, "Okay, go, run. Your friends must be outside waiting for you."

Then Papa would linger a while longer with Heshek at the table over a page of Talmud. Heshek, the slow, patient, studious one, was always anxious to find another solution to a talmudic problem. Nachcia, too, would stick around to help Mama clear the table.

"These are my two children," Mama would often say about Nachcia and Heshek, to her sister Esther. "They are both like me: quiet, subdued, and not impulsive. The rest are like Symche: quick, witty, agile, and spontaneous."

I had never seen Goldzia stand up or walk or even sit in a chair, for Goldzia was bedridden. When Mama talked about the younger Goldzia, however, you would see a beautiful child with blue eyes and flaxen hair. Growing up slender and tall, she absorbed every word taught to her in school. She read books like a grown-up and smiled like an angel. Skipping happily along, she would always come home from school with a story on her lips. She would climb all over Mama demanding attention.

"When I grow up," she would cry out while dancing and

laughing, "I will be a singer—no, a dancer—no, a ballerina." Bubbling with life and zest, she would fill the house with her presence. And then came the terrible day when Goldzia came home from school walking slowly, complaining of a severe headache. Mama touched Goldzia's forehead with her lips, feeling the fire of a high fever burning in her body. For days Goldzia lay there, her body consumed by the fever. The doctor visited daily, but Goldzia wasn't responding to any medication or showing any signs of recovery. The fever stubbornly wasted her weakening body. Mama sat nights at her bedside, putting cool compresses on her forehead, trying to ease her discomfort. She would pray and murmur, "My baby, my dearest, *mir zol zein far dir,*" I should endure for you. "I would rather suffer myself and see you get well." Papa would sit for hours in synagogue praying for his child's recovery.

As gently as she could, Dr. Szymerowa pronounced the verdict. "I am afraid it's polio," she said in a somber voice. "There is nothing I can do for Goldzia. My only suggestion is to take the child to Professor Alexandrowicz in Krakow."

It was not only Krakow that Goldzia was taken to: Papa abandoned the business, the source of his livelihood, and undertook a perilous journey, carrying Goldzia in his arms and attending to all her needs en route. In Krakow, he knocked on the doors of recommended physicians unrelentingly, to seek help for his sick daughter. He did not depend solely on the medical profession: his travels took him to the courts of the great rabbis of Belz and Bobov, where he asked for their intercession with the Master of the Universe, that a complete recovery might be sent to his lovely child. Tired and exhausted, he returned from his trips, carefully watching for progress. It failed to come.

He then took his child to distant Vienna, the capital of the once powerful Austrian Empire, the seat of the kaiser in whose army Papa had served. Papa had family in Vienna. His three brothers, Joseph, Heinrich, and Pinkus, and his sister Gusti had left the town of Chrzanow for a better life in this big city of immense opportunity. They all settled and married in Vienna, eventually becoming involved in the fur trade.

They would occasionally return to Chrzanow for a visit. Loaded with gifts for the children, Aunt Gusti would arrive with fanfare, stirring excitement in her wake. Dressed in her elegant clothes, she was the envy of the neighborhood. They all watched her arrive at her brother Symche's house, watched her fancy luggage being unloaded by her nephews. The children were curious to discover the contents of those suitcases, which often concealed interesting and valuable gifts.

Symche was now visiting his sister Gusti, carrying one precious bundle—his sick daughter. Gusti's house was spacious and comfortable. She tried to make her brother's stay as pleasant as possible, but Papa had not come for the pleasures of life in Vienna, he came to seek help from the great doctors of the city. Gusti, who felt at home in the salons of Viennese society, used her influence to get Goldzia into the examining rooms of the best physicians. They searched for effective therapy for the dreadful, crippling disease, but hope was scarce and progress nil. After several weeks' effort Papa returned home, beaten and distraught, carrying Goldzia in his tired arms. He laid her down gently in the bed Mama had prepared in the kitchen. As brokenhearted and distressed as they both were, they did not realize at the time the bitter fact that Goldzia was never to leave that bed again.

As the months and years went by, summer and spring, winter and fall, the only knowledge Goldzia had of the passing seasons came to her secondhand. We all adored her and loved her wisdom. We tried to bring the outdoors to her bedside: a snowball in the winter so she could touch the icy cold to her cheek, a flower in the spring to fill her nostrils with the sweet aroma of blossoming fields, a handful of sand or fresh earth to tickle her fingers. Much of our lives from then on was conducted in the kitchen in front of Goldzia's bed. She participated in every event and happening, aware of every bit of news.

The holidays, too, were celebrated with Goldzia in mind. On Purim a man was invited to come from the synagogue to read the Megillah, the Book of Esther, right there in the kitchen for Goldzia's benefit. Magically, the kitchen became transformed into a little shul (synagogue) where relatives and neighbors came to hear the reading of the Megillah. On the holiday of Passover the seder would be conducted right there in the kitchen, we children sitting on her bed and hiding the *afikomen* (a portion of the matzo) right under her pillow. On the festival of Shavuos (pentecost) we placed ornate greenery all around her bed, creating an imaginary garden. On Chanukah, the Festival of Lights, Papa kindled the lights for her while we placed a large board on her bed to play dreidel on. Only on Sukkos, the Feast of Tabernacles, was Goldzia left out. She would participate in making decorations, but she missed the excitement of running in and out of our *sukkah* (a booth roofed with branches constructed for the holiday) with hot soup plates spilling over.

Sadly, the trips to the *sukkah* were not the only things Goldzia missed. We could see the pain in Mama's eyes when she looked at Goldzia lying there limp on the white sheets as she made painful efforts to move her hands. Goldzia was slowly deteriorating. Her lovely white skin was unblemished, clean, powdered and fresh-smelling, yet her body was unresponsive to touch. Unable to command her muscles, Goldzia became totally dependent on Mama. Mama would tuck her in for the night, turn her from side to side, sit her up for feedings, and straighten her legs. Stoically, Mama stood by her child, feeding and washing her, combing her hair, attending to all of Goldzia's needs, never entrusting her care to anyone or letting anyone else get up at night when Goldzia called. Never did Mama go any farther than the store, always attentively listening for Goldzia's call. As Goldzia's condition worsened, Mama's determination to see Goldzia get well was slowly replaced by despair.

The best time of day for Sholek and me was the evening, when Papa would come home from his trips. After his dinner and evening prayers, there were the final chores that only Papa could do. Relaxing after a long day away from home, the day's stress would dissipate along with the last traces of anger, aggravation, or disappointment. His taut face regained its softness; the twinkle in his eye reappeared. Having looked over Blimcia's report and the bills from the store, Papa would spread himself out at the kitchen table to count the change and roll it up, rolling as well his daily supply of cigarettes. We would watch him skillfully fill the thin tubes of tissue with tobacco, stuffing it into the tissue tube by a handlebar on the gadget. The finished cigarettes, half filter and half tobacco, were then stacked in a box.

"Oh please, Papa, let me help," Sholek would beg. "Let me fill the cigarettes for you."

"Oh no, you may not touch that stuff," Papa would intone seriously. "I don't even want you to get close to this bad habit. It's bad enough that I got hooked on smoking; none of my sons smoke, and none are going to. So you better stay away from this smelly thing."

On seeing Sholek's sad expression he would then add, "Here, you can sort the change." And Sholek would happily set up rows of *grosze* (pennies), tens, and fives, handing them to Papa for rolling. I would jealously nag that I wanted to help too.

"But you can't even count," Sholek would tease me, angering me to tears. Eventually Mama or Nachcia had to carry me off to sleep under vehement protest.

Of my four brothers, I most adored Shlamek. Shlamek was handsome, athletic, and fun-loving. He would hoist me onto his broad shoulders and make me squeak with excitement by throwing me into the air. I would be so proud of my big brother when he would discuss sports with an acquaintance in the street. Shlamek would meet a Gentile fellow who would slap him on the back and say, "Hey, Stapler, watch out, for next time I get you in the Steinbruch, I will surely drown you."

The Steinbruch was a local lake where Shlamek used to go swimming.

"Don't be so sure, Janek," Shlamek would answer with a smile. "Remember how much you drank the last time you tried that trick on me."

Shlamek was widely respected and feared by the neighborhood Gentiles. They could not get over the fact that Shlamek the Jew was such a good swimmer, such an excellent football goalie, and such an outstanding runner.

Shlamek loved the outdoors. In the summer he would sneak away to the Steinbruch at every occasion. In the winter he would hire a horse-drawn sled and collect all the children in the family, and we would ride out into the woods. Soon enough a convoy of children with skis and ice skates would follow us. Among the large hollow trees, we would play games like hide-and-seek and get into big snowball fights. The goyim would not get too rough, knowing that Shlamek would not stand idly by.

But Papa did not appreciate Shlamek's behavior. We would hear Papa complain that he ran around with Gentiles and didn't study enough Torah. Papa never forgot that Shlamek served in the army. At the time, Papa wanted Shlamek to contract trachoma so he would be incapacitated and declared unfit for military duty. Shlamek could not conceive of infecting himself with a disease, and he preferred to serve in the army. Papa feared that the army would force Shlamek to discard his religious observance and that he would become assimilated. Shlamek countered that his military service did not infringe on his beliefs or hinder his religious observance.

Shlamek worked with Papa in the store and traveled with him on trips to Katowice like the devoted son he was. He never let Papa carry anything heavy or work too hard, and he had a good business rapport with Papa. Praying and studying with Papa, however, were activities he left to his brothers.

Heshek seemed to be Papa's favorite. He was the first one in the family to go on to higher education. He was an accountant, a very meticulous, studious fellow. Papa loved spending time with Heshek. They would sit and study or discuss the holy books together. Heshek was a deep thinker, calm, patient and scholarly. Heshek was closer to Vrumek than he was to Shlamek. Even though Vrumek by nature was a mixture of both his older brothers, he preferred to follow in Heshek's footsteps. Vrumek, too, finished business school, and Heshek was able to get him an accounting position in Bielsko, where he worked. The two brothers lived amiably together as roommates in Bielsko, a large industrial city several hours away from home.

Mama felt neglected and lonely having them so far from home. She'd be ecstatic when they came home for holidays and occasionally for Sabbath. She would cook them their favorite dishes, preparing extra for them to take back home with them, and spending hours just looking at her grown-up sons with tearful admiration.

Our weekday routine of work, school, and chores was broken on Friday. From early morning on, this day was the busy herald of the Sabbath Queen. Everybody rose earlier on Friday. Mama and Papa would splash water over their fingers with a cup and basin, and we'd all follow suit with the morning ritual that preceded our prayer, thanking the Lord for letting us wake up this day. Papa was in shul early, never failing to give the Creator his due in prayer and service. Mama would attend to Goldzia's needs, while Sholek eagerly watched his brothers put on their *tefillin*, their phylacteries, anxious to have a pair of his own.

Nachcia would wake me and help me get ready for school. She was plain-looking but she wore her dark brown hair pinned to her head like a crown, and she had lovely soft gray-blue eyes. Modestly dressed for her own kitchen work, Nachcia would dress me and say the morning prayers with me. I was Nachcia's personal possession, responding with affection to her love and care. I would hang on to her neck, and she would carry me in a mutual embrace into the kitchen. I was very aware of Mama's constant caring for Goldzia but was more than satisfied with the lavish attention I was getting from Nachcia. I didn't hesitate to turn to her for all my needs.

Nachcia would look over my homework and go to open-school night to see my teachers. With great pleasure she would report to Mama the progress I was making in school.

"The teacher says," Nachcia recounted, "that Helcia raises her hand too often and even answers without permission, not allowing anyone else in school to excel."

Nachcia was talented in many areas. She not only mended the family clothes but embroidered tablecloths, knitted woolen hats and gloves, and crocheted fashionable clothes for me. With all her energy and skills, Nachcia did not think well of herself. Nearsightedness compounded her inferiority complex. She wore thick glasses, and she wasn't very shapely; she thought of herself as fat and always wore dark, simple clothes. While she lacked self-confidence and pride in her accomplishments, Papa loved her for her religious devotion and her dedication to the family.

"She will make some young man a fine wife one day," Papa would say with pride in his voice.

On Fridays there was no afternoon Hebrew school for the girls or *cheder* for the boys, so when we came home from morning public school we would run errands. Sholek would impatiently wait for me at lunch while I dallied over my plate. Meanwhile, he would settle the pots that Mama handed him into a big basket. There was one big pot of *cholent,* the special Sabbath dish, to be brought to the bakery, and there were several small pots with meals that Mama prepared for the needy. One went to Miriam, a woman bedridden with arthritis who had two young children; how she coped all week long I do not know, but for the Sabbath she was included on Mama's cooking list. Every Friday for years Heshek, Vrumek, and then Sholek brought pots of hot soup, kugel, and *tsimmes,* a carrot stew, to Miriam's house. As Sholek was soon to graduate to other chores, he was grooming me for this task. There was also dinner to be brought to Grandma Chaya whenever she wasn't coming to our house, and to assorted widowers or ailing people who couldn't cook for themselves. Mama always had enough for everybody.

Blimcia was the last to rise on Friday. Papa did not travel on Friday, so he would open the store and let Blimcia arrive late.

"How long are you going to let her sleep?" the boys would ask Mama. "You would not let any of us sleep late on Friday," they would complain to no avail.

"Blimcia works hard," Mama would answer apologetically. "And besides, she came home quite late last night. She is so active in her organization, God bless her, and is such a smart and intelligent girl."

Indeed, Blimcia was a highly regarded, popular girl. She had plenty of girlfriends and a coterie of boys who gravitated to her. There was a fellow named Shmuel who was always around her; he lent her a record player so she could listen to records. Shmuel had a radio repair shop, and one day he brought a radio to Blimcia as a gift. Blimcia loved music and played the mandolin, but she could not accept something so extravagant. He tried convincing her how nice it would be for me, her little sister, for he marveled at the joy with which I would jump onto his lap and sing all the songs I heard on Blimcia's records. But Shmuel seemed to be only a friend, a good fellow and a fine neighbor. The fellows Papa had in mind for Blimcia had to be sharp in Torah learning. They had to be what Papa called *zu got und zu leit,* to God and man. Blimcia was already twenty-five years old, and Papa and Mama wanted to see some *naches* (pride and fulfillment in a family tradition, especially in the accomplishments of children).

An hour before sundown on Friday all activity in the store would cease. Shlamek would pull the iron gate down over the front of the store. It was time to get ready for the Sabbath, which would serenely reign over the workweek until the appearance of three stars in the sky on Saturday night. Papa gathered his sons and marched with them to the *mikvah,* the ritual bath, each one carrying his towel, soap, and fresh change of underwear. They entered the steaming bathhouse, where they greeted friends and neighbors. Sholek would bring home entertaining tidbits, especially regarding Papa's own tales and jokes, which usually made a big splash.

All cleansed, dried, and relaxed, they returned home and changed into their Sabbath garb to go to shul. Papa looked like a nobleman in his shining long silk *kapota,* (caftan) a *gartel* (belt) wound around his waist, and his seven-tailed fur *streimel* sitting proudly on his head. His face shone with pleasure at the sight of his entourage of sons, all in their long black coats and the small, round black caps of unmarried men. After services they would always come home with a stranger for the Sabbath table.

Back home in the brightly lit house, Mama was ready with

the festive meal. The girls were in their Sabbath dresses, their hair neatly combed, and their cheeks rosy with anticipation. After Papa sang his *shalom aleichem* (peace unto you) and chanted *Kiddush,* the benediction said over the wine, the atmosphere would shift from solemnity to gaiety. While Mama served the meal, Papa would engage the guest in conversation, eager to listen to new *zmiros* (Sabbath songs). Papa would often give Shlamek a nudge as a reminder to sing along rather than dream.

After a round of song, Papa would tell some funny stories for the benefit of the guest. One began with him humming, *"Ya, ba, ba, ba, ya . . .*

"I sit me in the train on the way home from Katowice," he would go on, "and since it happened that I got no time to *daven minchah* [recite the afternoon service] before boarding, I turned to the east in front of the window and prayed, disguising my prayer with the little *nigun* [tune] *'Ya, ba, ba, ba, ya . . .'* Just when I'm in the middle of *shemona esray,* the silent prayer which can't be disturbed or disrupted, in walks a goy. He turns to me immediately and says, *'Zydku,* Jew, move your suitcase!'

"When he gets no reaction from me, a strange, humming Jew, he becomes furious. 'Take your suitcase away!' he screamed.

"My situation was impossible. So what could I do? I kept humming, *'Ya, ba, ba, bai.'*

" 'You stinking Jew!' I heard him screech. 'I will throw your suitcase out of the window.'

"When even this threat goes for nothing, the angry goy opens the window and he flings the suitcase out. Then he slams the window shut and sits down on the seat like a king from the cossacks, spreading his legs wide and swearing through his clenched teeth, 'You stubborn idiot. You don't talk; now you don't have your suitcase.'

"I had just finished *shemona esray,* and with the *nigun* still on my lips, I tried to explain: *'Ya, ba, ba, ba,* the suitcase was not mine at all. *Ya, ba, ba, bai,* it belongs to *him,'* I say, pointing to a great big fellow standing at the entrance to our car hands on his hips and a face beet red from anger.

"You see, it just so happened that the owner of the suitcase, a giant of a man, was returning from the toilet—just in time to see his possessions being thrown out the window.

"The big one grabs the ill-tempered goy by the shoulders, picks him up out of his seat like he was a sack of potatoes, and smashes him against the door. He puts his face an inch from the fellow's. 'You bastard!' he growls. 'You son of a bitch! You go and get my suitcase back or I'll throw *you* out the window.' "

Some other Sabbath table tales of Papa's were about previous guests: "We once had a guest from the town of Tarnow, and I happen to know some people in Tarnow. So while the fish was being served I asked him, 'Tell me, how is my old friend Berish?'

" 'Dead,' was the simple reply.

"I was very upset and did not talk until the soup was served. Somewhat recovered from my sorrow, I asked, 'And how is Shulim the egg man?'

" 'Dead,' came the answer from the guest.

"My heart was sinking from grief; I couldn't eat anymore. At least our guest was able to enjoy his portion of chicken. I finally gathered enough courage to ask one more question. 'How is Moishe the shoemaker?'

"This was getting bizzare, but from his lips came the same answer: 'Dead.'

"I was devastated. I became gloomy; my Sabbath evening was ruined. I couldn't, I was afraid to say another word.

"When the guest finished eating he suddenly got talkative and began to urge me, '*Nu*, Reb Symche, let's hear a nice *nigun*.'

" 'I cannot,' I complained. 'I know it's Shabbes, but I can't stop thinking about all those Tarnower that I knew such a short while ago. To think that they are all no longer with us.'

" 'Oh, that,' the guest said with a wave of the hand. 'Don't give it a moment's concern. None of them is really dead. In the middle of such a delicious meal I can't have anything or anybody on my mind. When I eat, everything and everybody is dead.' ''

And so Friday evenings would melt away, with my older brothers and sisters disappearing to join friends in their respective organizations. Only Sholek and I were left to stay with Mama and Papa.

On short winter days, when the Friday night meal would be finished early, Mama would bundle up the children and sent them along with Papa to her sister, Esther. We would tramp through the crisp snow, its whiteness glowing in the moonlight. We arrived at Aunt Esther's with noses nipped red by the biting frost. In the brightly lit kitchen, Aunt Esther would unwrap our outer clothes so we could quickly join our cousins in play. Papa would settle down near the hot potbellied stove and warm his hands on a glass of steaming tea.

Uncle Pinchas Bromberger, Aunt Esther's husband, was in the middle of narrating his narrow escape from army service. Papa soon launched into a war story of his own, and the cousins would interrupt hide-and-seek to gather round and hear.

''It was in 1914 when I served in the kaiser's army against the Russian barbarians. We had no stake in the Austrian Empire, but we fought to keep from falling prisoner to the Russians, God forbid. We fought like lions, as if it were our own land we were defending.''

As usual, Papa's story soon turned into a joke, a funny anecdote that captivated everyone.

''This Austrian soldier stands guard on a dark, treacherous night, watching over a field of cannons. He keeps imagining that things are moving around in the darkness. Suddenly, he hears a strange noise. It doesn't sound like the howling of the wind or the crackling of branches. No, it sounds like dry leaves being crushed under heavy boots. It sounds like footsteps.''

The children on the floor hugged each other, sitting close to Papa, their mouths open with suspense.

''Suddenly, the Austrian soldier makes out a form approaching in the darkness. 'Stop or I'll shoot!' the soldier calls out. Putting his finger to the trigger, he thinks he hears a muttered swear from the intruder. But no! He realizes in astonishment that what he heard was the holy Jewish prayer of *Shema Yisrael*—Hear O' Israel. He automatically answers with the end of the verse, *'Hashem elokeinu, hashem echad'*—the Lord our God, the Lord is one. Lowering his rifle, he now approaches the stranger.

"Their embrace begins with *shalom aleichem*,—peace be unto you, and the answer of *aleichem shalom*, unto you be peace. The two soldiers not only find out that they are both Jewish, but that they are distantly related, even though they are fighting on opposite sides. The discussion develops, and each one tries to prove his loyalty to his army, his country, and his king. As a result, they conclude that they are obligated to kill each other.

"But how could they? What would their wives, who are distant cousins, tell all their children about their fathers? With emotions high but with national loyalties still strong, they search for a solution. They can't hurt each other and they can't convince their countries to call off the war. They therefore decide to desert together from the battlefield. They go into hiding, where they work long and hard on a joint letter begging for forgiveness from their respective kings, explaining the noble motives for their desertion. By the time the letter is finally ready, the Russians have invaded Poland. The two distant cousins now find themselves to be comrades in the same country, subject to the same authority, and finally able to fight on the same side."

The children happily clap their hands, satisfied with the wonderful solution to the problem. The adults smile and await Papa's inevitable closing commentary.

"The only problem that remains," Papa sighed, "is they are sure to meet other Jews on the next battlefield."

Everyone liked the story, and the adults went on to discuss how Jews are forced to fight each other for kings and lands that don't accept them as equals. The rulers then expel the Jews at will. The countries we shed our blood for will not protect us in time of need.

When the coals in the oven stopped crackling and the metal of the potbellied stove lost its red glow, it was time to bundle the children up again and return home. The streets were dark and cold, with only here and there a gas lamp lighting up the street. The marketplace, so busy by day, looked like a dark ocean, the empty stalls like abandoned ships. Unlike Sholek, I needed no encouragement to keep hold of Papa's hand.

"There is Uncle Nachman's stall," Papa would point out when we passed it, "and this one is Moishe the shoemaker's, beside Beila with her notions."

We wondered how Papa recognized every market stand in the dark without their occupants.

"When you grow up," Papa would explain, "and live in this town as long as I have, you will know it this well too. Even in your dreams you will walk these streets, like the rooms of your own home."

Aunt Esther, Mama's sister, would visit on Sabbath afternoons and try to distract Mama from her monotonous life of devotion to Goldzia. She would offer to stay with Goldzia so that Mama could go out, or offer to go out with Mama for a walk.

"Surcia, you have attained sainthood," Aunt Esther would say. "God will surely reward you with plenty of *nachas* from all your children."

But Mama would not listen, would not budge. Instead, she limited her horizon to Goldzia. A storm was brewing there. Goldzia's body was no longer obeying her brain, and her words were often slurred. Only Mama understood her. Calmly, Mama would stroke her golden head and assure her, "I know how you feel, my child, but I am perfectly content. I don't want to go anywhere. Here at home is my happiness, with Papa and all my children. I believe that our Father in Heaven is righteous in his judgment and will reward us when he finds us worthy. So we must believe and pray, and we shall live to see the coming of the Messiah."

On that note I would get very intrigued and ask Mama, "Is it true that when the Messiah comes there will be bridges of paper to span the oceans, and that Jews from all over the world will roll over these bridges all the way to the land of Palestine?

And will all the dead people really rise from their graves and roll to Palestine too?''

''That's right, my dear,'' Mama would answer.

''But how will there be room for all those people in Palestine?'' I'd ask.

''Because it would be the time of the Messiah,'' Mama would patiently answer.

The festival of Purim was fast approaching, and Vrumek was getting nervous. There was a play to be performed for charity, and Vrumek was afraid that his friends treated the project too lightly. Vrumek the director wanted his cast to transcend their daily lives and project themselves into the dramatic lives of their ancestors.

Vrumek was proudly responsible for costuming, staging, and casting. He was anxious to prove himself to his *melamed* (teacher) who had taught him Midrash, Talmud, and many tales and legends of the Jews, their joys and sorrows, their suffering and survival. Jewish heroes and heroines were models to him, and Vrumek wished he could have fought with Judah the Maccabee against the Syrian Greeks. He liked to live the lives of famous Jewish personalities through the different plays he put on during the various Jewish holidays. Vrumek's casting skills were keen enough to have his spoiled, dreamy little brother Sholek play Joseph.

The main benefit of the plays was entertaining the bedridden Goldzia, who rewarded Vrumek with an angelic smile. The Book of Esther was read at Goldzia's bedside when Purim arrived. Then everyone paraded down the street dressed in costumes. Blimcia was a Japanese geisha in a black robe embroidered with red, blue, and gold dragons. Shlamek, a black patch on his eye and a red handkerchief tied on his head, looked like a real pirate. Heshek, the traditionalist, wore Papa's long silk robe and *streimel* (fur hat), along with a beard pasted to his face. Nachcia, in a black dress and white cap of her own creation, looked like a perfect chambermaid. Sholek was gotten up as a paperboy; I was Little Red Riding Hood.

Vrumek was too busy with costumes for the play, but even Goldzia had her face made up as a clown.

On the morning of Purim, Mama busily prepared baskets of fruits, nuts, and goodies to be sent as *shloach manos,* gifts to relatives and friends, and *matonas l'evyonim,* gifts to the poor. Like bees, Sholek and I dashed around the neighborhood laden with baskets to deliver. With broad smiles we would sing, *"Heint is purim, morgen is ois; git mir a groszen un warft mich arois":* Today is Purim, tomorrow is not; give me a penny and then throw me out.

The streets were full of costumed children; Jews everywhere left their worries behind them to celebrate the triumph of good over evil, of Queen Esther and her uncle Mordechai over the villain Haman. Yet, centuries later, these celebrations were often disrupted by Haman's spiritual heirs: eager to disrupt the Jewish holiday, gangs of non-Jews would swell the streets looking to provoke a fight. And so that year a bunch of young thugs started up with two fellows dressed for a Purim party.

They began by calling the Jews ugly names, and when ignored, they proceeded to throw stones. They finally cornered the two Jewish boys in an attempt to beat them up. Badly outnumbered, the Jews had to fight their way out and flee for their lives, with cries of "Jew cowards" ringing in their ears. Panting heavily and with bloody noses, the two battered celebrants reached the party. Their friends washed their faces, bandaged their bruises, and calmed their fears. A heated discussion followed, because some felt they must go out to beat up the culprits and defend Jewish honor. Others said that those goyim were probably drunk, and they shouldn't be allowed to further disrupt the celebration.

"Swallow your pride for now," they said, "and wait for a more suitable time."

"Just when do you suppose the time could be more suitable?" came the exasperated response. The cooler heads prevailed.

On Christian holidays we had to lie low; that's when they were sure to be roaming the streets looking for trouble. On our festival of Pesach, Passover, we had to be extremely careful to stay out of their way. Passover was the traditional time when Christians would proclaim the libel that Jews use Christian blood in the baking of matzo. Those that used the big lie knew well that our religion forbids us the use even of animal blood. Our meat was always soaked and salted to extract the last drop of blood.

The Purim play at our house was set for four o'clock. In the afternoon chairs were set up in our big kitchen, with the stage facing Goldzia's bed. After a few typical mishaps the play concluded with a burst of generous applause. Vrumek, the producer-director, basked in his newfound fame. Goldzia was beaming with joy; Mama was serving *hamantashen,* traditional Purim pastry; Papa was keeping the last guests entertained with jokes. Great-aunt Channa and Grandma Chaya just sat there smiling contentedly. Channa praised Surcia in her sister's hearing for raising such fine children.

In the meantime Shlamek called his cousin Hania out into the yard, where they could be alone. He had adored Hania for a long time and was eager to look into those deep brown eyes whenever he could. Hania's heart was pounding, as she too was yearning for such a moment. But now, as she stood there facing him, she hid her hands behind her back. She was afraid she could not resist if he reached over and took her hand. "Shlamek, don't say those things," she protested, embarrassed at his compliments. "You are my cousin and are not allowed to act this way."

"But Hania," he protested, "I love you. What's wrong with being your cousin. I'm not going to listen to any old wives' tales about not marrying cousins. It's permissible, you know. I will not look at other girls. None of them have eyes as beautiful as yours, or hair as dark as yours, or a smile like yours that melts my heart."

She would not let him kiss her trembling lips, fiercely clinging to traditions that forbade such intimacy before marriage. "When will you finally see it my way, Hania," he pleaded, "and let me kiss you?"

People began spilling out into the yard. Given a reprieve, Hania left with her parents.

Chapter 2

Mama was at her station beside Goldzia's bed, a prayer book open in her lap. It was slowly getting dark outside. The men had gone to shul for evening prayers. Nachcia was out with her girlfriends in the B'nos organization. I was sitting close to Mama in the dim light of dusk, repeating after her: "God of Abraham, Isaac, and Jacob protect thy people Israel. Your holy Sabbath day is departing; may the new week greet us with good health and good fortune."

"If you will be a very good girl tonight," said Mama, "I will let you stay up. But you must not bother any of the guests that are coming to the house tonight."

"I will be as quiet as a mouse," I promised, "but who so important is coming tonight?"

"It is a fellow to see Blimcia, and you must stay out of his way."

I sat quietly in a corner observing Jacob, Blimcia's caller. I don't know if I liked him just then. He was tall but did not sit upright. His forehead was high, with a hairline somewhat receding. He had a sensual mouth, slightly protruding ears, and a high-bridged nose. The most interesting feature about him was his eyes. They were soft gray, with a sad look in them.

Blimcia wore a green dress to accentuate her emerald eyes. She was smiling, rosy-cheeked and as pretty as ever. Jacob looked her over, and Blimcia lowered her gaze. Silently presiding over the evening was an older man whom I later discovered was the matchmaker. Papa spent most of the time talking to Jacob, seeming very pleased. Mama was busy serving tea with lump sugar. Everything must have gone well, for Blimcia agreed to go on a date with Jacob.

What we did not know was that Blimcia had already met Jacob at her Mizrachi organization quite some time ago. I don't think Papa ever found that out. He was spared a lot of details that he was not supposed to know. Years later, for instance, when Heshek and Vrumek would come visiting from Bielsko wearing modern short tailored suits, the boys would quickly change into long traditional coats just to please Papa. And Papa, as smart as he was, so believed that his sons dressed traditionally all the time that he would even brag about it.

After Blimcia got married, everybody but Papa learned exactly how she had met Jacob. The true matchmaker was a Young Zionist meeting, where Blimcia was intrigued by a staring stranger. As soon as Blimcia arrived at the next Mizrachi meeting, her friend Srulek walked over to her with someone in tow. With a thud of her heart she noticed that it was the stranger who had been observing her so intently at the last meeting.

"This is Jacob," Srulek said, "a new member."

"Good of you to join," Blimcia said. "We need every person."

"Oh, I am sorry for not joining earlier, but we had a tragedy in the family."

"You shouldn't know any more tragedy," Blimcia said. No wonder he has such sad-looking eyes, she thought. It looks like those eyes have done some crying. His look is penetrating, yet soft and caring.

"It was Srulek who brought me in. We are neighbors," offered Jacob.

"You ought to know what a job it was," Srulek interjected. "I had to drag him all the way. But I think he'll stay."

There was a smile in Srulek's eyes, as if he knew something no one else knew. But Jacob knew it too, for it was Srulek whom he had asked for an introduction to the girl he liked.

Jacob was twenty-eight years old. Several of his sisters and brothers were already married, and only he and his kid sister Mila remained at home. His father had died years ago, and his mother wanted to enjoy his company for as long as she could. Babied at home, Jacob put his energy into studying and working. His mother had been his social life. When she suddenly died, he could no longer stand being at home. Now he needed to be with other people. When Srulek suggested he come with him to the Mizrachi meeting he gladly accepted after years of declining all invitations to social events.

Upon entering the room, it hit him like a wave. He felt then and there that God had consoled him for the loss of his mother. There on the opposite side of the room she sat. Her hair was brown like his mother's, combed to the side in a gentle wave. She wore small earrings, he later noticed, shaped like little violet flowers. He could not see her eyes at first, for her head was bent in conversation. Jacob sat on a bench against the wall, so intrigued with the girl on the next bench that he was oblivious to the evening's events. He knew he would have to talk to her. The meeting was coming to a close, and Jacob had barely caught her eye. Too inhibited to approach the girl himself, he decided he would get Srulek to introduce him.

At the next meeting, Jacob and Srulek conspired.

"So which girl is it?" Srulek asked.

"She isn't here yet," Jacob answered, trying to conceal his

disappointment. He sat uneasily for ten minutes, stealing glances at the door.

"There she is!" Jacob nearly yelled, grabbing Srulek's arm as Blimcia made her entrance.

"Come on, I'll introduce you right now," Srulek said. "But remember what I'm telling you. Her name is Blimcia Stapler. She will not put up with any nonsense, and neither will her father, Reb Symche Stapler. If you are really interested you are better off working with Reb Zisha the matchmaker."

But Jacob could not hear any of Srulek's mumbling, he was too eager to follow him to Blimcia's side. He was soon standing right in front of her. Blimcia was talking to someone. All Jacob could think of was that her eyes were emeralds, and her nose small and round. He suddenly became aware of his own long, straight nose.

It must be twice the size of hers, he thought in dismay.

Suddenly someone called Blimcia, and she excused herself and walked away. Jacob returned to a bench near the wall and sulked. She did not even notice me. Why would a popular girl like her have any interest in me? he asked himself.

He spent the rest of the evening brooding about his big nose, receding hairline, and slouched posture. He decided not to waste his time at these meetings anymore. He could have been home finishing his Shalom Aleichem book.

Yet on the next Tuesday night, he was eager to attend the meeting when Srulek came calling for him. Even observing her from a distance would be better than staying home thinking about Blimcia. Whenever he had tried to read, all he saw were her emerald eyes.

He gingerly strolled beside Srulek, hoping that he wouldn't bring up the subject of his interest in the girl. But Srulek was absorbed in the Zionist program discussed at the meetings.

"You heard the speaker from last week? We have to learn to work the soil. Without agriculture we will never be a true people. Farming our homeland is as essential to our physical survival as learning Torah is to our spiritual well-being. And do you think there is a future for young Jews here in Poland? You heard what happened to Herschel Sunday night, how they attacked him. It was three against one. He was lucky to have come away with his life.

When they reached the meetinghouse on Aleia Henryka, commonly called the Planty, Jacob felt a thud in his heart. Blimcia wasn't there. The Mizrachi members were seated in a circle with someone leading a discussion about Shalom Alei-chem. Jacob immediately felt at home and exuberantly offered comments on his favorite author.

When Blimcia came in she scanned the room and noticed an animated Jacob sitting in the circle with his back to her. There was an empty seat next to Jacob, but she thought it would be too obvious if she took it. Perhaps she should take a seat closer to her friend Srulek. She was curious about the new fellow. She had already missed one chance to meet him; she had been about to be introduced to him last Friday night when that meddlesome Rachel called her away. Blimcia finished deliber-ating and boldly tiptoed over to the empty seat near Jacob.

The discussion was lively. Jacob was talking about the au-thor's characteristic style. Blimcia was sure that this new fel-low was well read. For his part, Jacob was determined not to let her get away this time, not when she was so close.

When the discussion finally ended, Jacob turned to Blimcia and asked, "Have you read Shalom Aleichem's works?"

"Of course," she answered defensively, afraid that he might consider her an ignoramus.

"Oh, that's great," he said. "We must talk books some time, since he's my favorite author."

"So I can see," she said with admiration in her voice.

"I'm Jacob, and I know you're Blimcia; we were briefly introduced. So how come you are always late to meetings?" he inquired, desperate to continue the conversation.

"I help in my father's store, and there is always a late customer. It is impossible to get away on time."

"Isn't there anyone else in the store with you?"

Blimcia couldn't explain about the important customers pre-ferring her service and how Mama was busy feeding Goldzia at closing time.

"Well, I'm always the one to get stuck with the last chores,"
she simply said.

The two of them talked a long time before leaving with the
crowd. Jacob made sure to walk behind Blimcia and her girlfriends to get in a final good-night and to see where she lived.

When Blimcia turned in at the Municipal Building Jacob
was surprised. Srulek explained to him that the Staplers were
the only residential tenants in the building.

"You mean to say that you have never shopped in their
store?" Srulek asked, immediately regretting the question. It
was not a store for struggling families. Who else could afford
those ripe yellow bananas and exotic grapefruits and oranges
but northerners from the Planty and the Polish nobility? "It's
worth the trip to the Staplers' fine fruit and delicatessen store,
just to see all those goodies that they import," Srulek added,
making it sound exciting.

Once again Jacob was struck with self-doubt. Blimcia's family was surely looking for a better match than he would make.
He was an orphan who could barely make ends meet. He'd like
to join his sister and brother in far off Palestine, but he'd surely
have to see his sister Mila married here in Chrzanow first.
Even if he could get out, why would a girl like Blimcia ever
leave Chrzanow with a man like him?

Lying in bed that night, sleep eluded Jacob. His thoughts
were still with Blimcia. He remembered her straight posture,
and her waltzlike swaying from side to side as she walked. He
must ask her if she knew how to dance, and even more important, if she would go dancing with him.

Jacob attended every subsequent meeting of the Mizrachi.
He could feel that Blimcia was interested in him, yet she never
allowed him an opportunity to be alone with her. He knew
what he had to do. Even though he resented matchmaking and
considered it an antiquated institution, he knew he would
have to work with Reb Zisha the *shadchen*, the matchmaker.
How else could he formally "meet" and date a girl from an
old-fashioned family like the Staplers?

As for the professional Cupid, Reb Zisha was overjoyed with
the easy assignment. The client was already sold on his bill of

goods; he would only have to serve as broker. He immediately went to Reb Symche Stapler to fatten up the turkey.

"Reb Symche, do I have a *shiddach* for your daughter! Ai, ai, ai, a real match from heaven."

Reb Symche was nodding with interest, and so it was time to inquire about the dowry—and thus his commission.

"The most important question, Reb Symche," the match-maker said with a lilting melody in his voice, "is how much *nadan* [dowry] your daughter is going to come wrapped in?"

"A *nadan?*" Reb Symche inhaled with pride. "Why a most generous one indeed for my Blimcia. And a wedding I'll make that Chrzanow won't soon forget. The couple will have two years of *kest* [the gift of free board and lodging from the bride's parents] for full financial support, and we'll fix up an apartment as befits a Stapler girl. Now, Reb Zisha, tell me more about this fellow. Who is he? What does he do? How much learning has he got in his head?"

Confident that the big fish was on the line, Reb Zisha began enumerating Jacob's good qualities and assets. "This Jacob is from a fine family, and he's kind, sweet, tall, and healthy. And he can learn. Why, his room is a mountain of books. Yet his feet are on the ground; he's a good businessman."

"And what line of business is he in?" interrupted the prospective father-in-law.

"Oh, woven goods," Reb Zisha responded with satisfaction.

"It is his parents' store that he's in?" Reb Symche asked with keen interest.

"Unfortunately," Reb Zisha said with sorrow, "both his parents are now in the *olom ha'emes* [the World of Truth]."

"What a pity," Reb Symche said, pronouncing the benediction *baruch dayan emes,* blessed be the Judge of Truth. "Well, this is not the boy's fault and it is not to be held against him. God has blessed me with four sons; maybe it was meant for me to have five. So, *nu,* let me ask my daughter if she's interested in a meeting, and maybe we'll be lucky."

That evening, Papa went into the store at closing time and was soon alone with Blimcia. The gates were pulled over the front door, and no one could interrupt them.

"My Blimcia, I want you to know that Reb Zisha the *shadchen* was here today," Papa declared.

"Who is the fellow he's come for?" Blimcia asked with calm curiosity.

"You know, my child," Papa began, smiling and gazing at his grown child with adoration, "that I would not pick just anybody for you. I have turned away many suitors that I didn't even tell you about. But this fellow seems to be very special; you ought to give him a try."

"If you say so, Papa, I will."

She is so smart and good, Papa thought. "So I will set up a meeting in the house soon," Papa said with finality.

Papa came home from synagogue Saturday night long after the stars came out. He made *Havdalah*, the benediction at the end of the Sabbath, for us, ritually bidding farewell to the Sabbath Queen and blessing the coming week. Everyone was assembled in front of Goldzia's bed, listening to Papa chant the Hebrew, waiting in turn to smell the exotic aroma of spices from the land of Israel. Mama held the beautiful silver spice box close to Goldzia's nose, then turned up her fingernails to reflect the light of the *Havdalah* candle in Blimcia's hand.

"Raise it high," prodded her sister Nachcia. "You want a tall groom, don't you?"

Now that *Havdalah* and the accompanying song were over, each of us was getting ready to start the work week. The older kids, Nachcia, Heshek, and Vrumek were going out with their friends, while Sholek and I were getting ready for bed.

Only Blimcia did not leave. She wore her pretty green dress; her hair was neatly combed. She took out her mandolin and started playing a tune for Goldzia, trying to dissipate her nervousness while waiting.

She could not say no to Papa when he suggested this meeting. After all, what argument could she have not to want it? She was twenty-six years old already; it was high time she found someone to marry. She wished she could have gotten the message through to Jacob to *shadchen* himself to her, to have the matchmaker introduce him. But he was too modern to go through a matchmaker, as her father would want. She felt helpless. She couldn't just bring Jacob home and say she met him by herself. It wasn't done that way, not by Reb Symche Stapler's daughter.

"Who is he?" Papa would ask her. "Who is the family?" She couldn't answer Papa's questions. She was well aware that she liked Jacob, but she tried to repress her feelings. Surely Papa has someone interesting for me, and someone from a good family, Blimcia told herself. She trusted Papa's judgment. After all, Papa was the one who raised and provided for the whole family. He taught her everything she knew about running a store. Papa knew so many people and was loved by so many. Whatever Papa did was the right thing, and so, then, was this match.

Tense and apprehensive, Blimcia sat at the table when Reb Zisha came in. She was anxious to see who followed; it might be the man she was to spend the rest of her life with. The blood rushed to her face when she saw Jacob standing there. She almost jumped up to greet him but caught herself in time. She felt like a schoolgirl, her cheeks burning hot and her tongue in a knot.

Jacob was formally introduced and was seated across from her. Mama was busy serving hot tea with lump sugar, and Papa was talking to Reb Zisha. Jacob was staring into her eyes, his own deep-set gray eyes pleading, *Forgive me.*

Blimcia felt weak from all the tension and was relieved when they finally left. Papa was very impressed with Jacob's learning and knowledge of Torah, and patted Blimcia on the head when she consented to go out with the fine young man.

On their date, Jacob apologized for going to the matchmaker and then not letting her know. They both agreed, however, that it was the only way. "And I did need the chance to get to know you, Blimcia. Will you let me?" he added in a pleading tone.

"I wouldn't be here if I didn't want to," she answered, smiling. "There are a lot of Shalom Aleichem books you can introduce me to."

Over the books of Shalom Aleichem the relationship blossomed. The Mizrachi gave them the opportunity to work on the same committees. They went to a group outing in the forest, where Blimcia sang to Jacob and played her mandolin. He lay back, staring dreamily into her eyes, thinking, Is this wonderful girl going to be mine one day?

At night he would dream about her. She would be lying in the grass beside him, her head resting in his lap. He was caressing the soft brown hair that fell over her cheek. Her lips were so close to his. He could almost bend down and drink in her sweet breath. He woke up and pounded the bed. "Tomorrow," he pledged decisively, "I will announce my intentions."

"I cannot wait any longer," he said to Blimcia when they were next alone. "I am going to talk to your father about a wedding."

"My father is expecting it sooner or later," she said with a twinkle in her eye. "Better sooner," she added mischievously.

That night when he brought her home, he said, "I want to seal our agreement with a kiss." She let him kiss her on the lips for the first time. Gently, his soft lips touched hers for a sweet moment.

The church bells loudly rang for another Sunday mass. Blimcia awoke just as the sun peeked out from the rooftops. The air was fresh and brisk as she looked up into a sky that was blue with promise. It was about five o'clock when she woke me up.

"Wake up, Helcia, let me dress you. Remember you made me promise to take you along on our May trip. We must hurry."

I sprang out of bed, thrilled with my sister for keeping her promise. "I will dress myself," I said excitedly.

Jacob arrived before we were ready to go. Blimcia quickly finished packing her basket of fruits and goodies. In the street our carriage was waiting, its hood folded back to let the sunshine in. The horse was chewing feed from a sack hung around its neck. Blimcia slipped into the carriage, which was crowded full of her friends, and held me in her lap.

The driver shook the reins and the horse started his lazy trot. The driver flicked his whip several times, and the carriage clanked a bit faster down the cobblestones, the horse picking up more speed on the open road, among the golden wheat fields beyond the city. The young men and women in the carriage sang songs of wheat fields and orange groves in the promised land of Palestine. The songs promised a time of harvesting wheat in our own land, far from the alien corn of Eastern Europe.

The carriage stopped in a small village at the home of relatives of a young man in the group. This fellow, Manek, had arranged for the trip and for his uncle to provide lunch. We were all treated to a country feast on a large table in front of the house. Manek's uncle and aunt brought out baskets full of homemade bread. The cow that provided our fresh butter, cream, cheese, and milk was in the pasture, and I ventured out to see her. Everyone laughed and sang, enjoying the fresh-picked berries for dessert.

Manek took the opportunity to talk with his uncle. "How are things going, Uncle Baruch?"

"Not what it used to be, my boy," his uncle complained. "The crop was good, but more and more you hear them say, 'Don't buy from a Jew. Jews to Palestine!' Some of the older Gentile folks are embarrassed and make excuses for the Jew-hatred of their children. 'Ah, they are young,' they say. But we know the truth: the parents think the same way, but they do a better job of keeping it to themselves. We are not so worried about ourselves, but our children have no future here."

"Don't worry so much, Uncle Baruch," Manek said optimistically, "they can always come to Chrzanow. It's an industrious town, and there is plenty of work for everybody. Why would my cousins want to remain farmers anyway?"

"Farming, my boy, is the only thing they learned here, the only thing they know. It would break our hearts if we had to abandon all this that we worked so hard for. I know my children are welcome in Chrzanow, but by whom? By you, of course; not by the Poles. It's the same all over."

"Not true, Uncle Baruch," Manek argued. "Chrzanow is a big town. The Jews do business there and pay their taxes. The Poles know they need us. What would they do without us?"

"Naive, my boy. You have a lot of growing up to do. The Christians are not the same, neither our peasants nor your townspeople, since the new priests came on the scene. We never had the Garden of Eden here, but we lived and dealt with our neighbors well enough. Now every time they go to church they come out bloodthirsty. They are being fed wafers and poison, wine and Jew-hatred in the churches these days. Here they come from church now," Baruch said, pointing to a passing carriage.

As the carriage rolled by, the cold stare of enmity was unmistakable. The picnickers at the table didn't seem to notice, however.

When lunch was finished and grace said, we piled back into the wagon for the journey home. The sun was now falling behind the hills. The hood of the carriage was raised against the wind. The horse's hooves monotonously clip-clopped and the carriage wheels squeaked along in tune. Someone was telling a story. I fell asleep in Blimcia's lap.

"What a beautiful day it was! Thank you O God, King of the Universe, for granting us this day of pleasure," Blimcia added to her nightly prayers, her eyelids heavy with sleep.

Without delay, preparations began for Blimcia's wedding. A seamstress was summoned by Nachcia, and Mama unraveled rolls of linen cloth that she had been accumulating for just this purpose. The goods were measured, cut, and sewn into fine bed linen, every piece embroidered with a delicate design and Blimcia's initials. All the towels, nightgowns, and kitchen linens were similarly monogrammed. Dress designs were chosen from magazines brought by Papa from Katowice and Krakow. The seamstress and her girls busily made dresses for Mama, Nachcia, and me, as well as the wedding dress for Blimcia. There were new suits for the boys, and even Papa got a long black shiny new *kapota*.

Mama took some rare time out to shop with Blimcia for kitchen utensils. An apartment was rented for the new couple in an elegant new building on the Planty. Then came the hustle and bustle of preparing for the wedding itself. A caterer took a whole week to cook and prepare a multitude of delicacies, storing everything in our cool basement. The basement shelves were cleared of stock and used to store cooked fish, meats, browned chickens and ducks, sweet sponge cakes and honey cakes, stewed fruits and chilled wines. Early on the day of the wedding the household furniture was replaced by tables and chairs.

Blimcia had her fingernails clipped the day before in the *mikvah*. She now held court in our large kitchen–dining room in front of Goldzia's bed. Blimcia's hair was neatly combed beneath the veils that crowned her face. She was enthroned on a big soft chair, the folds of her white dress engulfing her slender body.

In the late afternoon the guests began arriving. They kissed Blimcia, admired her dress, and commented about her being pale from her prenuptial fast.

"God's presence is upon her," remarked Aunt Esther, "that is why she is a little pale and so beautiful."

"Yes," agreed Cousin Miriam, "that is what our sages teach us, that God's favor rests upon a bride on her wedding day."

Everybody was there. Great-aunt Channa, distinguished, matronly, and soft-spoken, embraced Blimcia and took an honored seat beside the bride. Great-uncle Moishe wore his fine Sabbath garb and greeted the guests from the doorway, wiping his tears with a big red hankie. He was so emotional that he wept like a woman.

When all the guests were present, a delegation was sent out to fetch the groom. Shlamek, the life of the party, called out, "Sholek, we are going to bring the groom." All three cousins named Sholek—one in each family was named after Grandfather Shaul—presented themselves to Shlamek. While Shlamek, the three Sholeks, and other male members of the family were gone, the guests stepped outside. Tension filled the air. The musicians were tuning up on their fiddles, cymbals, and trumpets. The desperate photographer attempted to gather everybody onto a bench set up for a family portrait. Aggravated, sweating profusely, and constantly peeking out from behind the large black cloth hood of his camera, he instructed someone to stand to the right and another one to stand in the middle. All the while, others would be getting up or turning away. By the time the photos were set up, there came a yell: "Wait, someone is missing."

Suddenly the tumult ceased. Everyone looked at the gate as the sound of distant clapping and singing was heard. The groom's party soon appeared at the far end of the yard. Slowly now, they approached the *huppa,* the wedding canopy. All the youngsters danced and clapped hands in front of Jacob, leading him to the canopy. Jacob looked serene yet exalted. On his serious face a slight smile revealed the joy he felt in his heart. Finally he saw Blimcia step over the threshold, his eyes lighting up as he watched her approaching. Her eyes were lowered, her ethereal face veiled. Mama and Aunt Esther held Blimcia's hands. With tall candles in their free hands, together they led Blimcia to the *huppa* and her destined one. Seven times they circled around the groom, Blimcia keeping her gaze on the ground so as not to dispel the sanctity of the moment.

"You are hereby sanctified unto me," pronounced Jacob, binding their lives together in accordance with the timeless code of Israel. Blimcia's dream of total happiness was surely being fulfilled. This man, for whom she had searched all her life, was finally becoming her husband, to love and protect her until the end of their days. And Jacob would no longer be a lonely individual, but half of a couple and head of a family.

The blessings were pronounced and the marriage contract read. A plate was now placed on the ground for him to shatter in commemoration of the destruction of the holy Temple of Jerusalem, for even at celebrations, the Jews are never to forget the sorrow of their dispersion among the nations. Greeting each other with the customary *mazel tov,* the guests were directed into the house to partake of the meal and festivities. The men followed Papa, encircling Jacob in a dance. The women embraced Blimcia, while Mama settled into her role of hostess.

The celebration went on until night. A *badchen* with his instant rhymes sang the praises of the bride and her family to the enjoyment of all assembled, clowning and entertaining them in various ways. The musicians, their heads light with wine, played enthusiastically. Great-aunt Baila, Papa's ninety-year-old aunt who had traveled all the way from Tarnow, amazed everyone with a *kosatska*. With ease she jumped up and down, throwing her feet in and out to the rhythm of the dance. Mama; her mother, Grandma Chaya; and Great-aunt Channa all danced with the bride in a slower circle dance, while from the next room came the voices of the men, with their exuberant singing and stomping.

The marriage celebration lasted for seven days. Finally, Blimcia was declared to be Mrs. Rauchwerger.

Chapter 3

The year was 1938. The school year was almost over, with the long summer vacation approaching. Mama was distressed. "What am I going to do with the child?" she asked Papa, referring to me. "She cannot play in the sand all summer long, or in the schoolyard next door. What can she learn from the children there? All year she has her friends from Beis Yakov Hebrew school, but in the summer, we can't have her run wild."

"I have a solution!" Papa exclaimed. "Vrumek just wrote from Bielsko that he and Heshek are not coming home for vacation this summer. Why don't I go to Bielsko to see what is keeping them from coming home and take Helcia along?

Maybe I will find that I can leave the child with them for a while?"

Mama nodded approvingly. "Good idea! But when do you have the time to travel to Bielsko?"

"Let me think about it," Papa said with confidence. "I am sure I can work something out."

It did not bother me enough to pay attention until the next Friday night's regular visit to Aunt Esther's, when I overheard Papa mention the trip again. Aunt Esther was enthused and had an even better proposal. She had a similar problem with my cousin Gucia. Since her other three children were already grown, it was only Gucia she was worried about. She would be delighted if she could send Gucia away to Bielsko together with me, especially since we were the same age and we were good friends from school. As for bringing us to Bielsko, she assured Papa that Mr. Barber, a traveling salesman she knew, could take us along. Papa was to write to Heshek and Vrumek and arrange to have them pick us up at the railroad station.

Gucia and I were ecstatic. It was the first time we would spend a vacation together, our first time traveling out of Chrzanow, and our first time in the big city of Bielsko. Papa wrote a letter to Heshek and Vrumek and got a response two weeks later. They would be very happy to have us for the summer. Between the two of them and with the help of friends, they should be able to devote enough time to me and Gucia, to show us the sights and give us a good time. The Hirschhorns, Vrumek's employers, offered to take us along with them to their summerhouse, where their own children would provide good company. They also offered their city apartment in their absence as a convenient base during our visit to the city.

The only thing that worried Mama was our getting lost on the way. "Make sure this Mr. Barber takes good care of them and does not let them wander away or get off at the wrong station," she said to Papa when he took us to the railroad station. She had a terribly worried look. Mr. Barber was a small, funny-looking man. He wore very heavy eyeglasses, his buttonlike eyes squinting all the while. As a matter of fact, he was known by his nickname "the Rabbit." He had a harelip, his upper lip split right in the middle, and his hair stood up on his head.

After taking leave of Papa, Gucia whispered in my ear, "Are we going to spend the whole trip sitting here looking at the Rabbit?"

When we told Mr. Barber that we would like to look around, he got red in the face and protested vehemently. "What for did I need this trouble? Why did I take on this responsibility?" he moaned. He started pleading with us not to leave. "Don't you see that I must bring you to Bielsko? I am not well, and I can not go chasing all over the train for you."

When he saw that his words had no effect on us, he swore that if we got ourselves lost, it would be our own problem. As soon as those little rabbit eyes closed for a moment of rest, we slipped out of the compartment. We wandered through the train, enchanted. The trees and fields rolled by with such electrifying speed that our heads began to spin. Giggling, we snooped around in different compartments, where peasants sat with baskets laden with luscious blueberries and cherries.

The old Poles smoked their heavy pipes. Their vodka-blurred eyes frightened us. We looked curiously at the terminals of the different towns we stopped in, running back after each stop to reassure Mr. Barber that we had not gotten off at the wrong station.

Finally we arrived in Bielsko. We held tightly on to Mr. Barber's hands as we descended the train steps, our eyes searching the crowd. Then we saw them; they were pushing through the crowd towards us. "Heshek! Vrumek!" we yelled in unison. In one sweeping motion we were whisked off our feet, tossed in the air, whirled around, and carried off the train. Gucia hung on to Heshek's neck and I was cradled in Vrumek's arms. We eagerly parted from Mr. Barber and thanked him for his help, at the same time complaining to Heshek and Vrumek how terrible the trip was, with the Rabbit watching us like a hawk. We told them how insulted we felt to be treated like babies and how we could have certainly made the trip on our own.

No sooner did we leave the railroad station then we started

asking questions. "Where are we going now?" "What is the name of this large street?" "Where would this trolley bring us?" "What is this tall building?" "Why are there so many smokestacks?" "How does the chimney cleaner reach that high?"

Heshek and Vrumek had decided to give us a dream vacation, even if it meant inventing some interesting tales about this large city. They described unusual-looking buildings as castles where princesses lived, and gardens as the real habitat of Snow White and the Seven Dwarfs. We were enchanted, eagerly drinking in all the stories with wide-open eyes.

In the Hirschhorn apartment the next morning, Heshek showed us the kitchen. He instructed us to be very careful with the gas stove, which if left unlit, emitted poisonous gas. Gucia and I looked at each other with dread, both too scared to handle such a monstrous invention. Yet, acting very grown-up, we would not mention a word about our fears to Heshek. When left alone in the apartment, however, we would stand in the kitchen and stare at the deadly oven, imagining ourselves falling asleep and inhaling the poisonous gas. Like Sleeping Beauty, we fantasized that we would be awakened by the kiss of a handsome prince. This gave us the courage to finally fall asleep at night.

Vrumek was lively, witty and quick, but he looked up to his older brother for his meticulousness, patience, and stability. Vrumek knew he could depend on Heshek and learn from him. They complemented each other in various ways, and living together as boarders, they became even closer than they had been at home. My two brothers and their two girlfriends, who were sisters, were determined to make our summer pleasant. At first we were somewhat jealous of the attention given to the sisters, Cesia and Mania, but once we got to know the girls, we found them to be sweet, kind, and fun to be with.

Early in the morning a slow carriage would take us through parts of the city. We would listen to Heshek describe the different buildings and the life stories of their occupants. The stories would always be intertwined with fairy tales. Vrumek would spice them up with descriptions of witches or monsters.

The carriage would then roll freely out of town, and sometimes the jogging horse would bring us to the famous Cigainer Wald, a fascinating park and nature reserve. We would take long wilderness hikes or bring hearty picnic lunches. We would go on berry- and mushroom-picking trips, make bouquets of wildflowers, or bake potatoes over campfires we built ourselves. On other occasions we explored surrounding forests, took boat trips on the Biala River, splashed in hillside streams, visited the private summer cottage of the Hirschhorn family, played with their children, and toured the soap factory where Heshek was the accountant.

We were tremendously impressed with my brothers' offices. They looked so official at their desks in their black half sleeves. We were thrilled to be in an apartment all by ourselves, where we were trusted with even that deadly gas stove. We returned home happy and content from this fine vacation, accompanied by Vrumek, who took a break from his bachelor life to savor some home cooking.

Summer was over and preparations began for the High Holidays. Mama was happily busy, with her sons coming home for Rosh Hashanah. Heshek had been invited to spend the holiday with the Hirschhorns but would not even consider spending the *yom tov* [holiday] away from his family. He told us how he missed Papa's Sabbath table, how he longed to hear Papa sing the *zmiros* in the familiar tunes. He even missed Shlamek's teasing.

"Why don't you ever play ball or run around a bit?" Shlamek would nag him. "Your muscles are like *shmattes* [rags]."

Heshek calmly responded that he had no desire to run aimlessly after a rolling ball when there was so much to learn. The old brotherly banter made Mama's eyes moist with contentment. Papa treated his returning sons like celebrities. He would not invite the usual guests from synagogue, as he already had honored guests for the holiday table.

On the day of Rosh Hashanah, Papa would not take his usual afternoon nap. "One is not supposed to sleep today," he explained to us, "for, God forbid, one might remain sleepy the whole year through. This day should be devoted solely to prayer, and to asking God for forgiveness. If we resolve to live better lives with complete sincerity, then we can hope to gain God's favor and begin the new year with a clean slate."

On the first day of the holiday, when the dishes were cleared from the table and the older children had gone out with their friends, Papa took Sholek and me to *tashlich* at the Steinbruch. The same lake that provided the populace of Chrzanow with recreational swimming and boating now served as the body of water in which the Jewish population would symbolically cast their sins.

When we reached the outer limits of the town, we could see men in their long black caftans and flat round hats standing on the edge of the water, reciting the *tashlich* prayer. Coming closer, we noticed a commotion among the people and saw four youngsters running from behind a big boulder. Instinctively, Papa took hold of our hands, pulled us away from the running boys, and rushed towards the crowds of Jews. Alarmed, we saw Reb Moishe lying on the ground with a bloody handkerchief on his forehead.

People were arguing as to what had happened and how it happened. Papa learned that it was four young Gentile thugs who threw the rocks and ran. The hooligans were aware of the holiday when Jews congregated at the lake, and they relished the chance to commit a little mayhem. Incidents of the sort always went unreported, the news spreading solely in Jewish circles. If reported to the local police, the event would only spur rumors that some innocent children playing by the Steinbruch were attacked by a large group of Jews.

Papa felt indignant. Since the police chief was a steady customer in our store, Papa spoke to him about the incident. With a crooked smile on his lips, Chief Kurek remarked, "Mr. Stapler, why do you have to worry about the whole town? You know I would never let anything happen to a member of your household. You are the safest citizen in Chrzanow, living right here under police protection. Do you appreciate what this is worth?"

So far, Kurek was right about our family's immunity from the anti-Semitism that raged in Chrzanow as it did throughout

Poland. The Staplers were seemingly safe at home, living right under the watchful eyes of the local police. We were not victimized by rock throwing, window breaking, beatings, or arson. On the other hand, these same friendly policemen and inspectors who generously patronized us would make sure that the store was not open a minute past its customary closing time. Similarly, the Sunday ban on business was rigorously enforced with us, but not on many other stores. The store was also favored by a multitude of inspections from the health, tax, license, and other departments.

"God gives each one of us his share of trouble," Papa would say, "so that we do not forget that we are living in *gules*, in exile. Some fare better and some worse. Like the tragedy that befell Uncle Nachman."

It happened late one Wednesday night. The children were in bed; only Papa and Shlamek lingered in the store. The gates were pulled down and closed, but suddenly they heard a violent pounding on them. Frightened, Papa jumped behind the counter to take cover. It was not unusual for stores to be broken into, yet it had never happened before here in the Municipal Building.

Sturdy, fearless Shlamek approached the door, shouting, "Who is there?" Papa was afraid that his son would get into a fight with some violent goyim.

From outside came a feeble voice, "Open, Uncle Symche, open!" Shlamek ran to the door and opened it. In tumbled Sholek, Uncle Nachman's son, white as a ghost, his mouth barely emitting a sound. He was in his undershirt, his hands clutching his unbuttoned pants. Shlamek poured him some water, but all Sholek could say was, "Fire! Help, water, water!" Shlamek thought Sholek wanted more to drink, but Sholek then began pleading, "Please, come help! Our house is on fire."

By now the whole household was up and on its feet. Vrumek and Heshek grabbed their clothes and quickly ran to Uncle Nachman's to help put the fire out. By the time they reached the house, a long line of people had already formed a bucket brigade. Men were furiously pumping water; buckets flew from hand to hand; bodies were soaked with water and sweat. But the bucketfuls of water seemed like thimblesful against the raging fire that engulfed the house. Its wooden planks cracked and fell to ashes.

All night they fought the flames, but finally neighbors and friends began to leave exhausted, their heads lowered in despair. As dawn broke on the horizon, Uncle Nachman and Aunt Lieba faced the charred skeleton of what had been their home and broke down, weeping. As they huddled together with their children beside the smoking ruins, Aunt Lieba lamented, "They burnt us out. They don't want us here. Where are we to go? This is our town, our home. This is where I bore my children, and where my mother bore me. It is the only place we know. This house is all we possessed. What are we going to do now? What can we do?"

Papa tried to console her. "God created us all naked and equal. God provides for all his children. He will provide again for you. Have faith, Lieba, have faith."

With help from the rest of the family, the Laufers managed to survive. Uncle Nachman went back to his fruit stand in the marketplace, saving every penny for a new home. They slowly started rebuilding.

"Where can I go?" Aunt Lieba would answer the sarcastic questions of her Gentile neighbors, who told her not to stay in the same place, in a house that was so unlucky. "This was my parents' home before it was mine. This is my town, my country, my place. This is where I first met my husband, where our children took their first steps, where we taught them right from wrong, and to respect their elders and live in peace with their neighbors. This is the language they speak, the flag they salute in school. Why should we have to search for a new place?"

Deep in her heart, despite her protestations, Aunt Lieba knew that her neighbors hated and despised us for being Jewish, and that no Jew really belonged. "Poland for the Poles and the Jews to Palestine" was the infamous slogan proclaimed more and more often. It echoed in the churches, schools, and government halls. There were Gentiles who quietly coexisted with Jews, but there were many who openly promulgated boycotts against Jewish-owned stores.

Uncle Nachman rebuilt his house on the same site, settling down to a familiar though precarious life amid animosity from his neighbors. Only in the company of his family and his fellow Jews could he feel comfortable and secure. The pain of his misfortune slowly vanished.

The summer of 1938 was over. Gucia and I skipped happily around. Vrumek went back to Bielsko after his short stay. But Papa was not the same. He was tense and upset. Always on top of events because of his trips to Katowice, he was aware of ominous developments. Jews were being evicted from their homes in Germany and were crowding the big cities of Poland. There were also many dispossessed German Jews in Chrzanow, where they had family to take them in or find apartments for them. The gruesome stories they told of German cruelty were unbelievable.

Papa remembered the Austro-Germans as polite, efficient, and kind, as opposed to the Russians, who appeared rude, illiterate, drunk, filthy, and cruel. In the First World War, Chrzanow belonged to the Austro-German Empire, and people were afraid of falling into Russian hands. So how could these same cultured, intelligent Germans change so radically in only twenty years? How had they been able to hide the beasts within themselves so well? Was the world going mad? Could it be coming to an end?

Marcus and Shaindele Landsman, Great-aunt Channa's daughter and son-in-law from Berlin, fled to their parents' home in Chrzanow. They were tired, penniless refugees who only months before had been respectable, well-to-do citizens. Now their only possessions were their two children, Izzy and Bertha. The first thought that came to Papa's mind was what if, God forbid, he too had to flee? What would happen to his wife and children? What would become of Goldzia? Friday nights were now spent at Great-aunt Channa's, where we all assembled to listen to Shaindele and Marcus. They told of how the Germans forced them to leave, how they barely had time to pack a few clothes and had abandoned everything else to the hands of the greedy German looters.

Now they were crowded in with their old parents, stripped of their home, their possessions, and their pride. Great-uncle Moishe wiped his teary eyes trying to console his sullen German grandchildren, who were further subdued by the language barrier between them and their Polish cousins.

It felt like Tisha B'Av, the day of mourning for the destruction of the Temple. Mama walked around the house wringing her hands, her eyes red and swollen from constant crying. Papa was unusually quiet, keeping his pain to himself. Blimcia, who felt physically ill, mustered all her strength to manage the store. She had just learned that she was pregnant but could not bring herself to break the news to Mama. How happy Mama would have been in better times! Sadly, there was no room now for her good news. Shlamek, an officer, was being called up to army service, and war loomed on the horizon. Mama was visibly suffering. Nachcia tried to sustain the family and kept us children occupied at home to keep us out of trouble. The streets were becoming dangerous, with rumors of spies being caught in town. The Poles, of course, blamed the Jews. With the threat of war so close, the Jews had a double problem: the war on one hand, and the wrath of their Polish neighbors on the other. Shlamek's leaving for the army was the first blow. For us World War II had begun.

When Papa himself was a soldier in the Austrian army in 1914 he was already a married man with children. He had to survive at any price. He bravely accepted all the abuse, as long as there was the promise of his eventual release from the army. His wealthy sister had convinced the officers in charge that a mistake had been made, that her brother was mentally disturbed and should not have been drafted into the army in the first place. A large bribe had been involved.

But Shlamek was a man with a mind of his own, not open to Papa's advice. "Papa," he would say, "this is not the Austrian army, and the Polacks are not as dumb as these Austrians you describe. And Papa, aren't you forgetting it is now 1939 and not 1914. The Polish officers are anti-Semites out to get us for being Jews, but I am going to show these pigheads that a Jew can fight as an equal."

"How is he going to survive with this kind of cocky attitude?" Papa would say. "When the bullets fly, don't be a hero," he begged Shlamek.

In his heart, Papa knew Shlamek wouldn't heed his advice, and this worried him. He prayed to the Almighty to keep his son under his wing: "Please, God, put him in your category of foolish ones who cannot protect themselves and are, therefore, subject to your protection."

"You should have listened to me," Mordechai said. "We could have all packed up and left for Palestine. There was still time when I first came here. I, unfortunately, did not have the money. But you, Pinchas, you are a wealthy man; you could have helped all of us. I begged you that we should leave. Now I am afraid it is too late."

"You are really talking nonsense," Uncle Pinchas would answer, all puffed up and defensive. "You want me to leave my house, the store, the warehouse, the merchandise, to take a suitcase, my wife and my children and go travel? And how in the world would I feed my wife and children for the rest of my life?"

"Don't get angry," Papa interjected. "The trouble is that you are both right. You see, Pinchas, Mordechai here is in a different situation than we are, having only his wife Rosa and daughter Annie. When the Germans chased him from his home in Hamburg, all his possessions had already been taken. What does he have to lose? The job he is looking for might well be in Palestine. With us it is altogether different. I wish I could go. The stores? *Nu,* I would leave the stores. We would start new stores there. I have sons who are strong and young. We would start a new life. Believe me, when I look at the *halutzim* [pioneers] I employ, I envy them. I wish I were as young and could go to Palestine with them to start a new life. But I also have a household full of women. And most important, there's my beloved daughter Goldzia. Where can I go with her? How could I travel with her? So we are staying here to meet our destiny. God is not going to forsake us. I have faith that our Creator will save and protect us. He has already given me my share of grief; perhaps what remains is only the good. So we will put our lives in his trust.''

''I believe in God too,'' Mordechai responded, ''but unlike you, Symche, I believe that God has given you life which he wants you to actively protect and cherish. And when you fulfill his commandment of self-preservation, he will be pleased with you and bestow his love upon you.

''I have seen the German beast in action when they dispossessed us in Hamburg. There is no good to be expected. These nationalists are not the Germans we have lived with all our lives. They are under Hitler's spell. They forgot all we did for Germany, our country—or so we thought, and just because we are Jews. They claim superiority as the Aryan race. They have *scientifically* legitimized their hate. God knows what else they are up to. A Jew can not trust anyone anymore in this world. If you believe that your Polish government is going to protect you, you are mistaken.''

''Don't you understand?'' Pinchas said in an apologetic voice. ''I do believe you. Your reasons are genuine and substantial. Still, you cannot compare your situation to ours. All my life I have worked hard, traveling every other day to a different marketplace, getting up in the middle of the night to get there on time and set up the stall. All day long, I'm on my feet, in rain or shine, snow or sleet, my eyes open for customers. All day long I'm without a decent meal, without a toilet till late at night, when I finally pack up my wagon and start my journey home. By the time I get home my kids are asleep, and I am too tired to eat.

''Still, all of it is a labor of love, for, thank the Almighty, I have established myself. My shoes are known in every town and surrounding village. They wouldn't buy from anyone else for half the price. My customers, the Poles, they keep coming back to me for their shoes, for shoes for everyone in their family. I have a name. I have a future here. I have my house, and my store is doing well in Chrzanow. One gets older, you know, and cannot always work so hard. Here I have a future for myself and for my family.

"Now how do you propose I take the hand of my wife Esther and say, 'Esther, my dear, let's leave all this behind. Let's take our children and go to Palestine.' People in that hot desert climate do not even need the type of shoes I make. They mostly run barefoot on the sand. I happen to know. The fund-raiser from Palestine is always a guest in my house when he visits. And then, of course, my Esther would never leave her sister Surcia or her mother. What would we do with her old mother? Shlepp her along at the age of seventy-two? She should live and be well till one hundred twenty. Neither could we leave her as an additional burden to Surcia. So you see, it is simply not feasible, not possible."

"Still, it looks like war, and I am worried," Papa repeated. "Mostly I worry for my Shlamek. The children nowadays consider Poland their country. But is it our country, our land, our people that he is out there defending? He would be defending those that persecute him, and for what? *Oy*, the children of today, they really think they can change the world. They think they can gain equality and recognition by serving. Silly children, if they would just look into our history they would know better."

And so the discussion continued until it was time to collect the children and go home. The sense of insecurity deepened.

Chapter 4

It was Wednesday, August 30, 1939, late afternoon. Someone came into the store all huffing and puffing. He was talking urgently to Blimcia. Blimcia went to call Mama. Sholek and I were out back in the yard when Mama called us to come inside. She was quite agitated. When Mama's cheeks became rosy pink, I knew she was frightened. Mama's words were unusually clear and strict.

"Stay near the house!" she ordered us. "There is trouble in town. There has been shooting in the marketplace. They say a spy has been caught."

Everyone was nervous. Sholek was dying to sneak out to the marketplace to see for himself. People were standing outside our store talking about the event. The mood was somber and uncertain.

Before the war had even been declared, the Germans flew into Poland and discharged a cargo of bombs. The municipal government ordered the citizens of Chrzanow to black out their windows and take other wartime precautions. A decree was posted saying anyone engaging in espionage would be punished by death.

Heshek came home from Bielsko the next day, but Vrumek stayed behind. This made our parents very uneasy. Heshek helped Jacob with the war preparations. Shlamek's absence was sorely felt, since he was handiest around the house. We meticulously covered all the windows and doors with heavy black paper or blankets. We pasted wide paper strips across the windows to prevent them from shattering. The building we lived in also housed the municipal offices, and although we had lived there a long time and were generally respected, we had to be extra careful. In this tense atmosphere, the Poles would not hesitate to accuse a Jew of treason if he did not adhere scrupulously to all the ordinances.

"You must not try to point out a target to the enemy, Mr. Stapler," the inspector arrogantly said to Papa, indicating a crack of light coming through a corner of the blacked-out window.

On Friday afternoon a faint sun was slowly tumbling down behind the slanted rooftops when I saw Sholek run towards us. I was playing hopscotch in front of the store with some friends, since I was not allowed to wander anyplace far from home. He was very excited and yelled out to us to follow him. We ran to the store with him, where he emphatically announced that Gdansk and Gliwice were in our hands.

"Where on earth did you hear that?" Blimcia questioned him.

"Out back in the yard," Sholek shot back. "There is a meeting taking place there right now."

I got very excited too. "Mama, Mama did you hear?" I screamed, laughing. "Gdansk and Gliwice are in Polish hands. Poland has won the war. Poland is victorious. Tomorrow I can go back to school."

Mama patted me on the head. Only a faint smirk danced in the corners of her mouth. "Good, good, my child, now go back and play outside."

"But, Mama," I protested, "you do not even seem to be happy. You were so worried about the war, and now that it is over you are not at all excited or pleased. Shlamek will come home now, and Papa can go back to traveling to Katowice. And by the way, where are Gdansk and Gliwice, Mama?" I asked curiously. I did not have time to wait for an answer, aware that Sholek had already vanished. I quickly followed him into the yard.

There was a lot of hustle and bustle in the yard. A general meeting of the police force had been called. The staff from the municipal offices on the second floor was there as well. The tall skinny inspector was talking to the crowd that formed a circle around him. This was Friday, September 1, 1939, the day Germany declared war on Poland.

"Our country is at war," the inspector general solemnly said. "Our country has been at war before and has been briefly partitioned in the past. But Poland will never surrender to her western enemy. The greedy Germans will not be allowed to stomp their boots on our soil. Not one fistful of land will they conquer, not one centimeter will we surrender. We will defend our country, my comrades, with our bodies and souls. It is our homeland, our fatherland. We will reconquer what they try to steal from us. Our Pomorze is what Hitler wants. No, my dear patriots, we will not give up Pomorze. As a matter of fact, we have Gdansk right now. This is what I am proud to tell you. We have just received the news, the good news, my fellow Poles. Gdansk is in our hands. And so is Gliwice, my dear gentlemen."

A loud burst of applause followed, drowning out the rest of his words. All the faces were smiling. The meeting started to break up, yet no one was leaving the yard. People formed small circles, enthusiastically discussing the war. It was obvious that the Germans were losing. It was clear that the Germans had no chance against our patriotic Polish army, which was fighting so gallantly.

Like field mice, Sholek and I were snooping around, attentively listening to all that was being said. Soon the officials got us busy running errands, as usual.

Someone prodded me. "Here, Helcia. Go get me a *krachel* of orangeade. Since there is no vodka in your store, we shall be forced to celebrate with a *krachel*."

Few, however, were satisfied to celebrate with soft drinks. They dispersed and went across the street to the tavern for some ninety-six proof. The occasion called for a bottle to be shared with friends. They sat around the table filling and refilling the glasses, laughing, enjoying, toasting the victory. Getting drunk always followed very good or very bad news. Today the mood was good, and the vodka flowed. This elated mood was not to last, however.

Before nightfall the windows were blacked out. At the Friday night meal, everyone was somber. Papa and Mama lamented Shlamek's absence and were worried about Vrumek not being home.

Heshek patiently tried to console Mama. "Vrumek is all right and will be home any day now. Believe me, Mama, he is safe in Bielsko." But Heshek did not sound too convincing.

The air in the blacked-out kitchen was stagnant; the light was dim. Nachcia, at Mama's side, tried to keep her composure. Papa hummed his *zmiros* quietly, mechanically, dutifully performing the Sabbath ritual he so dearly loved.

Suddenly the door opened, and in came Vrumek. An exhilarating scream of surprise and gratitude greeted him at the doorway.

"Thank God Almighty!" Papa uttered.

Mama wept. Nachcia, Sholek, and I jumped from our seats to hug him. Blimcia and Jacob made room for him to sit down. We all wanted to know how he was able to come home.

Weary and exhausted, Vrumek sat down at the table, but he was too tired to eat. He slowly began relating the events of the past few days.

"When Heshek left," he began, "I immediately realized

that I made a mistake not to have gone home with him. I was all alone, and the news was not good. People were leaving Bielsko, afraid that the big industrial city would be bombed. The trains were being taken out of service for military purposes. Whoever had a car or wagon was lucky. But I had neither. I packed my suitcase and went down to the railroad station. There were no trains running. I waited with throngs of people throughout the night. Finally, late in the morning a train came. People crowded in, squeezing into the compartments. But the train wouldn't move; it slowly inched its way ahead. Everyone was nervous and anxious. By five o'clock in the afternoon we had only reached Oswiecim. It was announced that the train was not going any further. I figured that from here I must make it on foot. When the sun started setting, I put all the *muktsah* [things one is not to use on the Sabbath] into the suitcase."

Papa managed a faint smile to show how pleased he was with Vrumek's behavior. "That is why the Almighty brought you home safely," Papa commented. "You will recite *birkas hagomel* [the benediction of gratitude] tomorrow in shul," he added.

We sat there till late at night, asking questions and thanking God for his divine guidance and deliverance of Vrumek back to the bosom of the family.

The next day was traumatic. People started leaving town. Whoever had relatives or even acquaintances out of town went to stay with them. People were frantically packing up anything they could haul along. They used cars, wagons, carts, anything on wheels. They left in haste without saying good-bye. Papa and Mama walked around the house, not daring to look each other in the eye. We all knew the sad truth. Where would we go? What would we do with Goldzia?

Aunt Esther came over on Saturday night. She did not sit, as usual, in the kitchen, beside Goldzia's bed. She went straight into the store, where Mama followed her. They agreed that we must all stay here in Chrzanow, and they talked about fortifying the house. Jacob was listening silently, but when Aunt Esther was getting ready to leave, he finally spoke up.

"You all know I have a sister in Krakow. I want to take Blimcia there. I know she does not want to leave you here, but she is my wife, and it is my responsibility to protect her. Please, Blimcia, for the sake of our unborn child, you must listen to me."

Blimcia was still reluctant. It was Aunt Esther and Mama who suddenly insisted that Blimcia and Jacob leave. Mama even came up with the idea that they should take me along. After long discussion, Aunt Esther went home with nothing resolved.

Sunday morning, September 3, I was sent away to Mama's cousin, who lived on the outskirts of town. Safely away from the commotion of the town, I played with my second cousins until Nachcia appeared. She called me to come home with her immediately. There was not a moment to waste, not even time to notify my cousin that I was going. She instructed the other children to leave word. I wanted to finish our game, but Nachcia insisted. We ran home together. On the way I learned from my sister that Blimcia and Jacob were ready with their bundles of supplies and waiting for me to join them.

We passed scores of people going down Krakowska Street with loaded backpacks. The atmosphere was one of panic. There were wagons, bicycles, and even baby carriages loaded with bundles. Blimcia and Jacob were indeed waiting in front of the store. Blimcia wore her coat even though the weather was still warm. Jacob carried a backpack. Mama came out carrying my coat on her arm.

"Here, wear the coat and go with Blimcia," she said earnestly. She helped me with my coat and gave me a brief hug. Then she quickly disappeared into the house, choking back her tears. Nachcia followed Mama, but there in the doorway stood Papa, Nachcia's coat in his hand. He threw the coat over her shoulders, delicately pushing her ahead and saying, "You go too, my child."

"But why?" Nachcia pleaded.

"It is for the best," he said, leading her out of the door. Blimcia and Jacob were already walking ahead.

"They are gone, Papa," Nachcia said, trying to come back into the house.

"Run after them!" Papa prodded her.

"I haven't even said good-bye to Mama," she cried.

"There is no time. I will say it for you, and anyway you will be back home soon."

Nachcia ran after Blimcia, holding on to my hand.

"Where are we going?" I demanded when we caught up with Blimcia and Jacob. "You are treating me like a baby," I said bitterly in an undertone.

They thought I did not understand the gravity of the situation. I knew it was war, and I was thoroughly frightened. I remembered the meeting in the yard, the enthusiasm, the cheering. I had thought that that was what war was like. There would be cheering when my brother Shlamek came home, dressed in his shiny boots and uniform, looking so handsome. And I would parade with him through the streets of town, so proud of my brother the officer. Now I realized that war was a terrible thing. War meant leaving Mama and Papa, walking as fast as you possibly can with people pushing all around you. I was hungry and I just remembered that we had not had dinner. I was not going to mention that to anyone, for I did not want them to think that I was a baby who could not go one night without a meal. Besides, what could they do about food here?

"We are going to my sister in Krakow," Jacob answered me patiently.

"It is far to Krakow. Papa used to go there by train. Will we be able to walk all the way to Krakow?" I asked.

"If you get too tired, I will carry you," Jacob said, trying to sound cheerful.

"I can walk as good as anyone," I boasted. "You will not have to carry me."

We walked on in silence, surrounded by crowds. People carried bundles, valises, all trying to push ahead of each other. Faces were somber, worried. Children were being dragged along, their tired legs refusing to keep pace, their small arms stretched out to hold their parents' hands.

It was pitch dark when we reached Trzebinia, a small town somewhere between Chrzanow and Krakow. Under total blackout, the town seemed like a quiet graveyard, the houses like silent monuments. Dark images, like ghosts, were moving around in the night with blank faces.

Jacob's back was sore from the heavy rucksack. Nachcia, who generally suffered from headaches, was dizzy now. Blimcia was nauseous from her pregnancy and looked worried and tired. I was fighting hard to keep my eyes from closing.

"We will have to find a place to rest for the night," Blimcia said.

"Yes, we will look for a place," Jacob agreed, seeing that Blimcia was unable to continue.

There were hundreds of people, all looking for a place to rest overnight. We knew that no one in town would let us into their house or barn. All the public places we tried, schools, churches, synagogues, were already crowded to capacity. Jacob was not a pushy man. He dragged us around town until we found a small Jewish study hall where there were still some benches available. Jacob pulled the blanket out of his rucksack, spread it on a bench, and made Blimcia lie down. I cuddled next to Blimcia on the narrow bench, while Jacob covered us with the coats. Nachcia squeezed underneath the bench on the bare floor, just to be out of the way of passing people. Jacob slept in a sitting position, resting his head on the bundle.

As soon as the first rays of light broke through the darkened windows, the commotion started. People were gathering their bundles and leaving. Jacob folded the blanket into his back-pack, and we marched out into the breaking dawn. Somewhat refreshed from the rest, we were able to keep up a steady pace and negotiate some distance before the sun became too warm for our tired bodies and heavy clothing. Before noon we took a break, going into the fields beside the road for a short rest and some food. Straining but determined, we continued on the asphalt road, passing wagons loaded to the top with bundles and children. People walked slowly, bodies aching, dragging their tired feet, changing heavy bundles from one hand to another. Some discarded possessions that became too heavy to carry. The road became littered with suitcases and bags. Coats and shoes that were too heavy and too warm were left behind; blankets and food containers were strewn around. Occasionally neighbors would pass each other on the road. There would be hurried greetings and inquiries about where is Rifka or Sala or so-and-so. Then the grim march would go on.

Suddenly the murmur of airplane engines was heard. In a wild scramble people tumbled down into the roadside ditches or fled into the fields trying to find shelter. We too ran down into the field, where we lay down under a lone tree. Covering our heads with our bare hands, we prayed. When the buzzing intensified, we looked up to see a German airplane. Huddling together, we awaited the impending disaster.

But the bombs never came. Instead, we saw five Polish planes in close pursuit of the enemy plane. A short battle ensued, and soon the German craft burst into a ball of flames, burning shreds falling like fiery torches to the ground. There was exhilaration and happy waving at the Polish planes, with some people applauding the Polish heroes who had just saved their lives. I was thrilled with this sight and was convinced that now the war was surely going to end, since it had just been won by the Polish air force. Enthusiastically, I asked Jacob if we could turn around and go home now.

"We are very close to Krakow," Jacob explained, "and we will have a good rest in my sister's house."

With renewed spirit in the wake of the air battle, we resumed our journey, and soon we were approaching the outskirts of Krakow. The crowds were thickening, the marchers slowing their pace. Eventually we realized that the columns were not moving at all. Bewildered, we found out that this was the end of the road. People were just piling up behind each other, for the gates to the city were closed. No one was allowed in.

"This is a dangerous area," Jacob told Blimcia. "We must get out of here. We are totally exposed to enemy bombardment. We will have to take the long way," he said decisively.

We turned and walked back into the fields, away from the

crowds. Avoiding populated roads, we found our way into the city through narrow passages near small blacked-out houses.

Soon it was pitch dark, and Jacob became disoriented in this unfamiliar part of the city. The search for street signs and house numbers was tedious. It was way past midnight when we finally stood in front of the house marked Brzozowa 16. Up the dark staircase we climbed, shuffling along a long balcony. We knocked on the door. Sleepily, Jacob's sister, whose married name was Petzenbaum, embraced us and welcomed us all into her darkened house. She immediately busied herself, searching for blankets and arranging makeshift beds. Other relatives were already huddled together here; the house was full of people sleeping two to a bed or squeezed together on the floor. Jacob's sister, a sensible woman, said, "We will talk in the morning. Get your rest now."

In the morning we found out that the city was bursting with refugees. There was a lack of food, housing, and other facilities. The authorities feared an outbreak of disease. There were thousands more at the gates pleading for entry.

Things were not much better in the Petzenbaum apartment. For Jacob, the reunion with members of his family was emotional; for Blimcia, Nachcia, and me, these were just a lot of people crowding together for elusive safety. Krakow had its share of air raids, with people scrambling into shelters and the back yards of buildings. Jacob's nieces and nephews, the Petzenbaum children, were busily scavenging the city for food to feed all these unexpected guests. When darkness fell, people would congregate in the back yard to avoid staying in their hot, blacked-out apartments. Solemn discussions were taking place as to the course of the war.

It was way past midnight when we were awakened by voices calling, "Petzenbaum, Petzenbaum!"

Jacob sprang to his feet and ran out to the balcony. In the darkened yard he saw some images. His eyes adjusting to the darkness, he could distinguish five people, some carrying backpacks. They were coming towards him now, two older figures leaning on the arms of three younger men.

"Papa? Heshek? Vrumek?" Jacob called excitedly, running

towards them down the long balcony, taking hold of Papa's arm.

"I am all right," Papa said. "Thank God we found you, for I would have perished."

Jacob was happy to see Papa, Heshek, Vrumek, Uncle Pinchas, and his son Chamek. He wanted to ask so many questions. Where was Mama, Goldzia, Aunt Esther, and the two Sholeks? Jacob's mind was feverishly working to figure out where to put them all. How was he going to tell his troubled sister that there were five more mouths to feed?

Papa looked around at all the people sleeping on the floor and sadly said, "Why did I listen to you, my sons? I left Mama and Goldzia. I should have had enough sense to know that this is not for me anymore. I am no youngster. I'm weak with exhaustion, and there is no room for us here."

Jacob made him lie down on his own spot, gently covering him with his blanket. Vrumek pulled out the blankets in his rucksack for Uncle Pinchas. Eventually they all found space to lie down, too tired to have regrets or complaints.

It wasn't until morning that we all hugged, kissed, and welcomed Papa and the others. We were anxious to know what had happened after we left Chrzanow.

Papa held me on his knee as he spoke. "The town started emptying," he told us. "The streets were abandoned. Whoever could walk had left. The panic was great. Rumors about the Germans taking away all males spread horror, and Aunt Esther came to the house pleading for me, Uncle Pinchas, and all the fellows to leave. I wasn't going to listen. I was not going to leave Mama and Goldzia alone. But Mama and Aunt Esther persisted. Finally, we came to a compromise. The two Sholeks, who are just boys, would remain. They would not be in danger and could be very helpful. Mama and Goldzia were to move to Aunt Esther's house, where they would be safer. Our Municipal Building was a prime target for bombardment. Mama's demands were relentless, so I gave in to her. We made it here in fifteen hours. There was no time to stop or rest. We had trouble finding this place."

Papa said he didn't see any possibility in staying when there was really no room. They must make arrangements to leave. Maybe they could go further east, away from the front.

Papa could not believe his ears when someone entered in the early afternoon to announce that the Germans were in Krakow.

"Are you absolutely sure?" he kept questioning the young man. "It can not be. You must have seen Polish soldiers." When the young man insisted that he heard them speak German, Papa went out into the street to be convinced. He could not conceive of the Germans taking the city of Krakow, the former capital and seat of the Polish kings, without a single shot being fired, without any resistance. Where was the Polish army? Were they fleeing like cowards? Where was Shlamek? Papa cringed at the sound of the German language coming from a group of soldiers in the street. He had no illusions now. They were Germans all right. He was confused and distressed. He regretted leaving his home, his wife, his child to undertake this treacherous journey to Krakow, only to find that the enemy had beat him there. Right then and there, he pledged to return home immediately.

All the refugees were similarly struck with chaos and confusion. The city was at a standstill. The stores were closed; people were afraid to go outside, not knowing what to expect of the occupying power. There was no public transportation whatsoever. Private cars or wagons were hard to find. But Papa did not rest, mobilizing even the Petzenbaums. Eventually a horse-drawn wagon was found to take us home. Ordinarily, of course, Papa never would have undertaken a trip like this on a Friday: he would never have risked desecrating the holy Sabbath.

Early Friday morning a man presented himself with his wagon in front of Brzozowa 16. We were all ready and waiting, having said our short, emotional good-byes. We eagerly piled into the wagon, and the horse broke into a trot. Papa sat up front, engaging the driver in conversation. Blimcia's nausea was aggravated by riding in the bouncing wagon. The impatient fellows would have liked to get off and help push the cart.

"Just a few more hours and we will be home again," Papa

said. "We should be very grateful and thank God for bringing us this far. When we get home, we will all pronounce the *birkas hagomel.*"

Distressed that he had not yet gotten a chance to recite his daily prayers, Papa was glad when the driver announced a stop for the horse to graze and get some rest.

Excitedly, Papa pointed to a building at the roadside and said, "Let's stop here. You can graze the horse while we go behind the building for a little while."

The man unharnessed the horse, letting it graze freely. Papa took out his *tallit* (prayer shawl) and *tefillin* (phylacteries) and said to the fellows, "This is perfect. Let's pray now, and we may still have time to eat something."

But the boys were tense. The building was actually a gigantic power transformer. If caught nearby, they could be accused of sabotage. The Germans were patrolling the roads. Who knew who else might be around? What made them most edgy was the sight of Papa wrapped in his *tallit,* swaying, absorbed in prayer. Behind the transformer, they were shielded from the road, but all around them were open fields. From a distance they could be spotted, identified as Jews.

"Papa," they pleaded, "we will pray when we get home. Let's not jeopardize our position here. Let's be inconspicuous. Let's get out of here, the sooner the better."

But Papa turned a deaf ear to his sons, and he and Uncle Pinchas continued their prayers.

The boys scattered in the field, strenuously keeping watch, alert to any movement in the area. Papa and Uncle Pinchas finally finished their prayers, just when the driver had harnessed the horse. Everybody climbed back into the wagon.

Soon we saw a man approaching through the fields. He was running, out of breath, his legs buckling under him. When he came near, we saw that his face was ashen. He fell upon the wagon, muttering something unintelligible, and fainted. We gave him some water and he came to. In a cracking, choked voice, gasping for breath, he managed to say, "*Yidn,* Jews, save yourselves, don't go there." Then he fainted again. We put him in the wagon, splashing water on his face. Once more he came to; with haunted eyes, he looked around. Urgently, he repeated his warning, "Jews, don't go there."

With Papa's prompting, the man recounted the horror he had just experienced. He was on his way home to Chrzanow, just as we were, when the Germans took him off his wagon. They brought him to a barn. There were other Jews already there, all seated on the ground. With no explanation whatsoever and no accusation of any sort, the Germans began shooting them. They were shot one at a time, so that the others might watch. Only two words accompanied each bullet: "Jewish swine." Somehow the man had managed to fall to the ground without being hit. The bullet just missed him. He made believe he was dead and crawled out of the barn when the soldiers had left. He began running, too petrified to look back.

He urged us not to continue, to turn back: there were Germans on this road.

For a short while, we just sat there. Papa and Uncle Pinchas tried to evaluate the situation. They were bewildered and could not decide which way to turn. Here we were on the way home, where Mama needed us. Should we turn back? To where? To what? To the Petzenbaums? We could hardly wait to leave—how could we go back?

Papa looked around. There was Blimcia, so weary, her beautiful face twisted in discomfort. Papa looked at me. My eyes filled with fear; I was afraid to ask questions, but I sensed the danger. Jacob, Heshek, and Vrumek were edgy. As young Jewish males, they were primary targets for the Germans.

"I have faith in our God," Papa pronounced. "We will not turn back. We will go forward, and God will protect us." Jacob, Heshek, and Vrumek were not so sure. They decided not to stay on the wagon. They took to the fields, taking Uncle Pinchas and Chamek with them.

The road went through the town of Trzebinia. The wagon had to pass the town. It was decided that the younger men would march through the fields around the town, avoiding the main thoroughfare. They would come out onto the road again on the other side of the town.

The wagon continued on the main road. Blimcia made Papa

slide down into the wagon, where he was hidden from view. Blimcia and Nachcia pulled big kerchiefs over their heads, peasant-style, lowering their eyes and hiding their faces. I closed my eyes and made believe I was asleep. In reality, I was too scared to look.

The wagon rolled through town. German soldiers were all over. The road was blocked by military vehicles, cars, wagons, carriages, and people. Slowly, we proceeded through town. No one stopped us. We saw a group of men sitting on the ground in the center of town. The sun was hot and the men, who appeared to be Jewish, were distressed. We glanced at them in fear. The Germans were too busy with these men to pay any attention to the three peasant women and the old driver. After a long while, we were out of town. The road was clear now. On the horizon we noticed the silhouettes of several men walking towards the road. These were our men. Relieved, they climbed back into the wagon. The sun was setting, and the horse picked up its pace. Soon we would be home.

This was the first black Saturday in Chrzanow, the first since the Germans marched into Poland. Twenty-five Jewish families in Chrzanow were notified to come to Trzebinia to bury their fathers and sons.

Our reunion with Mama was gloomy. Even though we felt fortunate to be home again, there was sorrow and fear in our hearts. We learned from Mama what happened after we had left Chrzanow. When Shlamek arrived at his unit, it was immediately shipped to the front. Before the soldiers even dug in, they were pulling back. Shlamek had a unit of soldiers who were his responsibility. Their retreat took them through his hometown. It was pitch dark when they reached Chrzanow. Houses and streets were indistinguishable. The men were exhausted. Shlamek settled them in the large marketplace, instructing them to stay put until he returned. Running through the dark but familiar streets, past the church and the school, he went home to see his family. How strange the buildings looked now, all empty and abandoned. Even the schoolyard, where he had spent his youth playing ball, was unrecognizable. The Municipal Building, where he had grown up, now appeared so

strange and foreboding. The gates were pulled down over the storefront; there was no sound or movement anywhere in the house. He checked all the doors and entrances. Shocked, he came to the conclusion that the house was indeed empty. There was not a living soul in it.

He stood there for a while, bewildered and frightened. "Where could they all be?" he asked himself astonished. Suddenly, he felt completely exhausted; he did not know what to do next.

Sadly, he walked away, going back down Mickiewicza Street to the marketplace, where the soldiers were waiting. He saw them sprawled on the cobblestones, but he did not stop. His legs carried him instinctively down Koscielecka Street to Aunt Esther's house. His eyes had gotten accustomed to the darkness outside, but he was not prepared for the internal blackness. He felt his way up the steps and lightly knocked on the door. Aunt Esther's house was a second home to all of us, so Shlamek knew exactly where her door was. Attentively he listened for any sound from within. Aunt Esther opened her door, then burst into tears. She pulled him inside, screaming, "Shlamek! It is Shlamek!" In a second everyone surrounded him. He was overwhelmed by the intense emotional outburst of his family.

There was Mama kissing his face, Aunt Esther embracing him, Hania and Gucia, our two cousins, clinging to him, and the two Sholeks pulling and tugging at him.

He wanted to ask questions but was met by their own queries: "Where are you coming from?" "Where are you headed?" "What is happening with the war?" "Are the Poles retreating?" "Is there going to be much more fighting?" "Will there be fighting here in Chrzanow?" "Where will the front be?" "Where are the Germans now?" "How long can you stay?" "Are you tired?" "Are you hungry?"

They told him how much they all worried about him, how they missed him, how they prayed for his safety and welfare. There was joy in seeing him, but it was a happiness mixed with sadness and anxiety. There was dreadful, tormenting worry, for they knew he was leaving soon.

He told them all he knew. He told them that the Germans were advancing. He voiced his disappointment that the Polish army was retreating in defeat. He was still hopeful for an eventual victory. He was certain that the army would regroup and put up a stiff resistance. In fact, he thought that right there in Chrzanow might be the decisive battle that would determine the destiny of the war. He was glad that Mama and Goldzia were there at Aunt Esther's. He instructed the two Sholeks to fill sand bags and put them up against the basement windows, so they could use the basement as a shelter.

There was crying when he told them that he must leave. He explained that he had a regiment of soldiers waiting for him in the marketplace and that he was not supposed to be there in the first place. He could not resist going through his hometown without stopping off at home, but now he really must go.

Aunt Esther hurriedly collected some foodstuffs for Shlamek to take along. Mama, beside herself, just wrung her hands in despair. Only Grandma Chaya, always ignored as a foolish old lady, now had words of simple wisdom for her grandson.

In a simple plea, she told him in plain Yiddish, "Shlamek, do not go back. Throw away the uniform and stay here. Put on your civilian clothes and stay. Without this uniform you are no longer an officer in the Polish army. You are nobody. Hide, Shlamek, and before you know it, the war will be over. The Germans will march in, and you will be a civilian like the rest of us. There will be chaos. No one will miss you when the Polish army falls apart."

"My sweet old Grandma," Shlamek said, speaking distinctly as if to a child, "this is not a game. If they catch me, I will be executed for desertion. It is wartime. I would be as good as dead if I stayed here. I cannot do that."

Mama and Aunt Esther desperately grasped at Grandma's idea. "Please, Shlamek, listen to us," they begged. "Stay here. We will hide you well. Can't you see the situation is not good? It will not last long. When the Germans come, you will be safer as a civilian. You are young, Shlamek, and know nothing about war. Please listen to us older folks. Don't be an idealist.

Save yourself. They will not notice you missing. They are too busy retreating.'' They could see how torn apart Shlamek was when he saw Mama's suffering face and Aunt Esther's anxiety and had absorbed Grandma's common sense. They could see that he wanted to stay, but had to leave. It was all so brutal. Tearfully, they all embraced Shlamek and clung to him for one last minute. They somberly kissed him good-bye, sadly watching him disappear.

On Monday, September 4, 1939, at five A.M., Shlamek and his army unit retreated from Chrzanow. That same day at noon the first contingent of German soldiers marched into Chrzanow. Without firing one shot, the Germans marched through Silesia, leaving the Polish population in chaos.

Except for Shlamek, we were all back home again. We were apprehensive about the future. The Germans' venom was immediately felt. The occupation began with the abduction of Jews in the streets of our town. People were randomly arrested and others forced to perform hard labor for the oppressor. The Germans were not yet skilled in differentiating Jews from Poles; they would grab whoever was at hand. But soon they learned to enlist the eager cooperation offered by the local population. The Jew-hatred that simmered in the Chrzanow population surfaced. They willingly helped the Germans identify and persecute the Jews. From the first day of occupation until the expulsion of the last Jew from Chrzanow, the Polish people presented the same threat to the Jews as the Germans did.

In the predawn hours, when Jews were on their way to synagogue, they'd be accosted and sent to dig trenches, clean the streets, and perform other kinds of labor.

Life became abnormal and uncertain, but life went on. The store was open, and even though there were no daily shipments of fresh fruit from Katowice and no Polish Chrabinas to patronize it, people still had to eat. Papa found other sources and was now selling more vegetables, along with staple groceries or whatever he could find.

One sunny morning bright and early a fat German marched

into the store. He grabbed Papa by his long distinguished-looking beard and asked, "Abraham, what is your name?" The Germans called all Jewish males Abraham and all Jewish women Sarah.

"Stapler," Papa answered shakily.

"I like you, Stapler," the German said. "My name is Schindler, Commandant Schindler. Remember that. I would like you to pack up some of these chocolates for me."

Papa understood the hint. The beard had to go, and Schindler could be bribed.

Papa hadn't been going out into the street for a while; even in the store he was extremely on his guard. Whenever he noticed a German approaching the store, he would quickly hide in the apartment. Schindler had caught him by surprise. The Germans would mercilessly tear out Jews' beards. The Chassidic Jews, pious people that they were, would rather hide than shave their beards. Some Jews could be seen with kerchiefs tied around their faces, hiding their beards. The Germans, wielding clubs or whips, would pull off the cloth disguises, relishing in cutting or ripping out the beard to the agonized cries of pain from their victim.

Only after Commandant Schindler's warning did Papa reluctantly cut his beard, losing his sense of dignity with the falling clumps of hair. He felt humiliated, reduced from a God-fearing Jew to an ordinary man. A short, trimmed beard did not conform with Schindler's standards, so, after a second warning from the commandant and pleading from the family, Papa finally gave up. His clean-shaven face was listless. He looked like an old man, every wrinkle showing.

Poland surrendered, and the Germans occupied the country. The defeated Polish soldiers were either coming home from the battlefield or sending home messages from prisoner-of-war camps. There was nothing at all from Shlamek, as if he were swallowed up by the earth. Several Chrzanower soldiers returned, some of them Jewish, but no one knew what had happened to him. No one had yet come home from the prison compound at Oswiecim, so that going there was the only way to find out if Shlamek were there.

It was a risky trip, and it was brave Vrumek who undertook the perilous journey. Avoiding the watchful eyes of the Germans, he rode to Oswiecim on his bicycle. The camp in Oswiecim was heavily guarded. For hours he circled the camp, trying to make contact with the prisoners, endangering his own life: if caught he would have been arrested for spying. He eventually came close enough to speak to the prisoners. He asked questions, but there were no answers.

Vrumek dreaded coming home to his brokenhearted parents with no news of Shlamek. So he lied. He told us that Shlamek had been seen in a hospital in the town of Sanok. We eagerly grasped at this proffered straw of hope.

One morning I woke up and promptly ran to Mama, happily telling her about the dream I just had. In my dream I saw Shlamek. He could not hoist me onto his shoulders the way he used to because he was ill. Both his legs were heavily bandaged, and he could not walk. But he smiled at me and assured me that he was getting better, that he would come home soon all well again. My dream was so vivid that I laughed and happily tried to persuade Mama that Shlamek was indeed alive and well.

But Shlamek could not recover or send home any messages because he was dead. He was wounded by a bullet to the head in the town of Sanok near the river San. Weeks later, Papa found someone who knew exactly how it had happened. The bullet hit him just below his helmet in the back of his neck. With hospital treatment Shlamek could have lived, but there was no help available on the battlefield, where the wounded were left to die.

So for my wonderful brother Shlamek Stapler, life ended on a cold battlefield. In agony, Papa said Kaddish, the prayer for the dead, for his first-born son. And Mama, she could not forgive herself. "I had him right here," she cried. "Why did I let him go?" No one could console her.

Chapter 5

Goldzia's life was pure misery. As a victim of the dreaded polio, she'd been bedridden now for eight years, and her inactive muscles had deteriorated. Once intelligent and talkative, her speech had slowly become too slurred to be intelligible. She still had a lot to say, but she knew that others became impatient when she struggled to communicate. She would restrict herself, but we knew how she suffered. We stood by helplessly, until talented Vrumek constructed an alphabet board. When Goldzia wanted to say something, we would place the board in front of her and she would point her finger to the letters, spelling out what she wanted to say. This manner of communication was much easier for her. With tears in her deep blue eyes, she kissed Vrumek's hands to thank him for his invention. Goldzia could comment on any subject and give sound advice. When the war broke out, our concern for her welfare became a debilitating obsession.

In one of the house searches, the young German SS officers who came into the apartment were quite intrigued when they saw Goldzia's radiant face, milky white skin, deep blue eyes, and blond hair. They stopped by her bed to ask questions about her. Goldzia motioned to Mama for the board. Goldzia proudly spelled out in perfect German, which she had never formally learned, *Ich war in Wien:* I was in Vienna. The Germans stood there mutely staring at Goldzia, struggling with their emotions. After momentarily being caught in the act of being human, they began yelling and throwing things about in the usual German fashion. Goldzia, well aware that she had stirred the inner feelings of humanity in the soldiers, defiantly smiled at them, as if daring them. The Germans made a lot of commotion but quickly finished the search to get away from Goldzia's haunting gaze.

Unfortunately, it did not work out the same way in our future meetings with the enemy. It seemed that in the beginning the Germans did not quite know what they were supposed to do with the Jews, but as time progressed they became better skilled at persecution. They found new ways to abuse, torture, and inflict their wrath upon the Jews. While performing subsequent house searches they were more destructive and cruel, and Goldzia was lucky to be ignored.

New decrees were imposed daily. Jews were shut indoors in the early evening with a strict curfew. They were to wear white armbands on their sleeves, ten centimeters wide, with a blue star of David clearly imprinted on them. Failure to wear the armband was punishable by death. Jews were not to congregate; this meant no walking in pairs or stopping to talk to anyone in the street. Jews were forbidden to shop in non-Jewish stores, which meant that an important source of food was eliminated.

Fat Commandant Schindler kept visiting the store as long as there was enough chocolate to satisfy his expensive appetite. When the supply was exhausted, his visits diminished. With his visits went his promise of protection. Schindler was on hand when the Germans eventually made us clear out of our apartment and store. His pink, hanging cheeks creased in a broad smile and his fat belly heaving with every chuckle, he stood there carrying out the evacuation orders. Our world had suddenly caved in on us.

Luckily, Blimcia had her own apartment; disorganized and distraught, we quickly moved there. Papa was frantic about moving his store. From his prestigious, elegant store on Mickiewicza Street, which he had built so laboriously and with such pride, he relocated to a tiny, dilapidated store on Koscielecka Street at the other end of town. We were targeted for this displacement because it was inconceivable to the Germans that Jews should be allowed to remain in the Municipal Building complex.

Meanwhile, new ordinances were announced daily. Jews were not allowed to possess radios. Jews were to turn in all their valuables, including furs. There were quotas of gold and silver, which they were to submit to the authorities. Large sums of money were also requested of them. A daily contingent of males for hard labor was demanded. Hostages were taken from among the prominent Jewish citizens and members of the Jewish community council.

Food was scarce. The lines in front of the few bakeries that functioned were long and dangerous. One had to stand on line for hours to obtain a quarter loaf of bread. One quarter loaf could barely feed two or three people, and surely not the large families that huddled together. People lined up before dawn, since there was not enough to go around. The angry Poles claimed that the Jews were taking away their bread. They would start fights, pretending that a Jew pushed ahead of them in line. They would complain to the Germans, who would eagerly punish the Jews. The lines also yielded young Jewish males whom the Germans picked up for slave labor.

Sholek and I became our family's only lifeline with the outside world. We scavenged the city for food every day. We would stand on separate lines for bread, so as not to be recognized by Polish neighbors, who would readily report to the

Germans that a brother and sister were bringing bread back to the same family. Sholek cleverly cut holes in his coat lining. After sliding each portion into his secret compartments, he quickly ran back to the end of the line to wait for another portion. I would follow suit. Together we were able to keep the family from starving. Sometimes, though, the Poles discovered our ruse and started a commotion. We'd have to run for our lives.

Blimcia's apartment near the Planty, at 1331 Slowackiego Street, belonged to Uren Hochbaum. Uren and Malcia Hochbaum had supplied fruits in Katowice for Papa to import. The apartment was situated in an elegant five-story building, one of the newest in Chrzanow. It was surrounded by a garden and bordered by a large park and the castlelike Lebenfeld house, a city landmark. Before the war the gates to the Lebenfeld's private park were always closed to the public. When the chestnuts were ripe on the trees, the servants would open the gates and let the neighborhood children go picking.

Now, in wartime, we had the early evening curfew to contend with. The fence between the Hochbaum house and the Lebenfeld park had been carefully cut to allow postcurfew passage and secret contact with the neighboring houses. The park offered a place to hide from German eyes and a haven for smuggling food and information.

March 17, 1940, was a blustery clear and cold day. Blimcia had not slept all night, and by five o'clock in the morning her pains were coming at regular intervals. She went quietly to the bathroom, not to wake anyone. But Mama, always the light sleeper at Goldzia's beck and call, heard Blimcia and went to her daughter's side. By the time the rest of the family had awakened, Blimcia's hair was in disarray, her forehead was covered with cold sweat, and she was sprawled exhausted on her bed. Mama cleared everybody from the room and spread some clean sheets on the bed. She sat next to Blimcia, wiping her brow and squeezing her hand when the pains came. I was scared, sitting glued to the closed door, waiting for Mama to come out with some news. All I could hear were the sounds of my older sister groaning in pain. Mama ordered Sholek to run

and summon Mrs. Koniecpolska, the midwife. She also instructed me to open all the cabinet and closet doors in a super-
stitious effort to unblock Blimcia's birth canal. Nachcia put up
water to boil on the stove and took care of Goldzia. Mama did
not budge from Blimcia's side throughout the day-long ordeal.
After dusk, when the sun was hidden behind the rooftops, a
baby's cry was heard from behind the room's closed door.
Mama opened the door, smiled faintly and said, "*Mazel tov*—
it's a boy."

There were no lively cheers, only a desperate sense of relief.
Papa and Jacob, who had been reciting psalms all this time,
put their prayer books aside. Papa shook Jacob's hand, wishing him *mazel tov*.

"Our first grandson," Papa said to Mama when she emerged
from the room.

"May God bless him and keep him under his protection.
May he live to know happiness and freedom from bondage,"
Mama said. She shed tears of relief, tears of hope for the
baby's future, drawing from her own agonized but unshakable
belief in the Almighty.

Mama called Jacob into the room to see his wife and son. I
squeezed in right behind him. Blimcia rested on her bed, covered with a white sheet. Her face was pale, her eyes closed in
exhaustion. She slowly lifted her heavy lids, looked at her
husband and said, "Forgive me, I am so tired."

"Rest, my dearest. Rest and gain back your strength," Jacob
said. "We have a son! I am so happy."

Blimcia dozed off while the midwife skillfully turned the
baby on its stomach.

"Oh God!" I exclaimed. "He has a head like a cucumber."

The baby's skull was elongated, but Mrs. Koniecpolska
smiled and assured me that there was nothing wrong with the
baby. She tied a kerchief over the baby's head, babushka style,
tightening it around the baby's chin.

"By tomorrow," she declared, "his head will be normal like
yours and mine."

I got up early the next morning, curiously watching the

midwife unwrap the baby's head. Sure enough, the cucumber had rounded into a tomato.

Papa was attending daily prayers in our building's make-shift synagogue, where a brief, quiet *bris*, the circumcision ceremony, was held. The baby was named Yitzchak after Jacob's father. There was no respite from the German oppressor, yet the thriving baby was our solace and our resistance.

Chapter 6

Blimcia's one-bedroom apartment became even more inadequate for the two families, but space was not the reason why we moved again: the Germans fancied the elegant building at 1331 Slowackiego Street.

It was before dawn on a Friday morning. Mama was busy cooking, preparing for Sabbath. A hot soup was simmering, made from a small, bony chicken that was smuggled in from a nearby village at much risk. The now rare aroma of the soup caused hunger pains in our shrunken stomachs. A small fish in another pot was an additional piece of costly contraband obtained to honor the Sabbath. Sholek, our lookout, suddenly burst inside to announce, "The Germans are coming!"

Mama's face flushed with panic. The Germans were making

these sudden searches very often now. They might announce that they were searching for hidden weapons or gold, but one would certainly be arrested for harboring an illicit chicken or the possession of an unregistered fish. Even worse, one's husband or son might be abducted for a labor detail—for a job that never ended. Mama had to desperately hide the illegal food she'd been cooking. The chicken might have brought disaster on us all, but that's not what the Germans were after this time.

"This house is to be evacuated, abandoned, cleared out within three hours. You will take only your personal belongings with you."

Not a stick of furniture was to be removed. The Germans stationed themselves in front and in back of the house, blocking the exits. Now began the mad, nerve-wracking race against time. The tenants of the building had but three hours to move their households. Mama was so nervous that everything kept falling out of her hands. Blimcia started madly bundling clothes and linens, throwing pots and pans into any receptacle she could find. Nachcia and I were rapidly dispatched to get Papa and Heshek from the store, and to summon the help of Aunt Esther's family.

All the tenants were frantically running in and out, up and down the staircase, bumping into each other with heavy bundles, carrying whatever could be grabbed, remembering the soup ladle and forgetting a hidden watch, an heirloom. As people ran through the streets of town, trying to reach relatives and friends or to find anyplace to stash their worldly possessions, the oversize bundles burst open and scattered articles like some botanical miracle. The desperate chaos continued as a constant stream of people were thrown into the street, men, women, children, and elderly. With the world out of kilter, Mama concentrated on saving the food she had so laboriously prepared for the Sabbath.

A commotion erupted at the side of the house, where the terraces faced the Lebenfeld park. Mrs. Korngold, an immaculate woman on the third floor whose household was her kingdom, could not take the sudden shock of the German decree. She could not tolerate the thought of losing her exquisite household and becoming a homeless pauper. She ran out to the terrace, ready to jump to her death. Her husband and daughter restrained her, her little daughter bursting into wild screams. "Mama, Mama," she cried, "please don't leave me! Mama, you have to live for me, for Papa. Mama, please! Mama, I will die without you! Mama, don't leave me alone!"

The Germans flocked to the side of the house to watch Mrs. Korngold hanging over the railing of the terrace, trying to free herself from the grip of her husband and her child.

Sholek, alert to the opportunity, quickly grabbed a table and chairs and stuffed them into a storage shack just before Mrs. Korngold was restrained and the Germans came back. That was it. A table and four chairs were saved. Nachcia used the opportunity to smuggle out the basket of food that Mama had prepared.

Mama stood there in the house near Goldzia's bed, shocked and confused, contemplating Mrs. Korngold's suicide attempt. "Maybe Mrs. Korngold is right," she said. "What is there to live for? To be reduced to thieves stealing our own food and furniture?"

It was her children who packed and carried and grabbed whatever came to hand. Mama just stood there unable to function, looking down at her daughter, her helpless child, her Goldzia. Where was she to take her? Into the street? Yet she could not even consider Mrs. Korngold's option: she lacked the strength, the courage, and the time to go kill herself. She had Goldzia to worry about.

Before noon the Germans made their rounds to make sure that all the inhabitants were cleared out. *"Raus schnell!"* is all the former occupants heard now, as they lingered in the street, remembering a photo album they had left, or that they had nowhere to go.

The family was now scattered between Aunt Esther's and Grandmother Chaya's house. A futile search for a place to live began. Sholek, on the other hand, was absorbed in plans to salvage the table and chairs from the storage shack.

On the next Monday, Vrumek and Sholek ventured into the yard of 1331 Slowackiego Street. They tiptoed to the storage shack, loaded the chairs onto the table, went out through the ripped fence, and swiftly vanished into the Lebenfeld park. In the park the going was easy, for they were hidden by the bushes and trees. Eventually they had to come out into the street. They were just two houses away from the house of Kalman Klein, their prewar neighbor, where they intended to hide the furniture if they encountered a German patrol.

"Wohin gehst Du denn Abraham, mit diesem Tisch?" the German asked. Where are you going, Abraham, with this table? The blood clotted in the two brothers' veins, and a cold sweat dripped down their backs. Before they could mumble an explanation, they were led into the police station, table and all. The table was identified as an article missing from Blimcia's apartment. Vrumek and Sholek thought that this was the end for them, but miraculously the Germans were more interested in the table and chairs, which matched the rest of the furniture in the apartment, than in the two fellows. They were made to carry it back and got off cheaply this time, with only some lashes. Beaten and empty-handed, they returned to their scattered family.

Eventually a small one-bedroom apartment was found on Kadlubek Street. The house belonged to David Stapler, a cousin of Papa's. Symche Stapler's family now crowded into this tiny apartment, the children being sent away at night to sleep in relatives' houses. For two months we suffered in this uncomfortable little apartment we called home.

The Germans continued their searches and persecutions. The house on Slowackiego Street, number 1331, stood empty and abandoned. The Germans decided to then play a devilish trick on the Jews. They notified the Jewish community council that the original owners of the apartments were allowed to come back. At first there was apprehension and fear. This was the better part of town; surely the Germans would not let the Jews live there for long. But there was so little to lose. Even if we had to move again, Papa preferred living there even a short while to our present situation. We had no furniture to move back anyway. Our only possessions now were some chairs, a table, a bed for Goldzia donated by Aunt Esther, and some sacks of straw for the rest of the family to sleep on.

And so the family moved back to 1331 Slowackiego Street. Slowly, other neighbors began coming back too, for all were in the same crowded predicament and preferred the bare walls of their own apartments. There was some cheer in the reunion of old neighbors, but life did not return to normal. On the contrary, every day brought harsher decrees from the oppressor. Food got scarcer, searches continued, and more men were sent away to forced labor camps.

The long hard winter of 1940 had come to an end. With the coming of spring came fond memories of our previous existence. The days were longer, the trees in the Lebenfeld park found their green garb, and the shrubs and flowers smelled sweet. The sun was so much warmer, but its rays could not penetrate the tiny apartment where we were now all huddled together.

Before the war, we would rise with the first rays of the sun on a morning like this and go hiking into the woods with our cousins. We'd pick berries and mushrooms or play hide-and-seek in the old hollow trees. We might go to the river to wade and splash, taking along baskets of fresh fruit. But things had changed. There was no use getting up with the sun, for we were not allowed outside at curfew time. No one carried picnic baskets anymore, for there was nothing to put in them. What little food one could obtain outside a breadline had to be well hidden and well paid for.

Food shopping for the family was now mostly entrusted to Sholek and me. On Thursdays food was accumulated for the Sabbath, so that's when I ventured into the marketplace. Dressed in a light cotton peasant dress, my light brown hair gathered into two long braids, I tried to look as Polish as possible. Jews were not permitted to shop in the marketplace, where the merchants were local peasants. Ordinarily, I would remove the armband that identified me as a Jew, make my quick purchase, and vanish through an alleyway.

Today, however, I was not lucky. I had only succeeded in

buying one miserable bunch of beets, which I slid deep into my cloth bag, pressing the bag close to my body to conceal its contents. Convinced that the bag was flat enough, I tried to squeeze through the stalls to make a quick getaway. Suddenly, I heard that bone-chilling "Sarah!" I continued walking, ignoring the shout. Having pretended not to be Jewish, I must not acknowledge that I was the one who was called. While trying to quickly disappear, I found my path blocked by a tall uniformed German. He pointed to my bag with his club, smiling sarcastically. In a shrill voice, he asked, *"Was hast Du denn da, Sarah?"* What do you have there, Sarah?

I felt that I was going to collapse upon jellied knees. My tongue stiffened in my mouth. "Nothing," I dared to say.

The German, his threatening rubber club in hand, made me open the bag. There were the incriminating beets. I wished I could become invisible under his stone-cold gaze. I twitched each time the club thumped into his open hand. The German, relishing my fear, took out a pad and pencil. "You know, Sarah, you are not allowed to shop here. You must be punished. What is your name, Sarah?" he demanded.

I was terrified. I knew that once a German records your name, you are in trouble. The Germans could then deport the whole family. But I had no time to contemplate.

"You will pay a fine of five marks," the German said while writing down my name.

Devastated, I handed the five marks over to the officer and ran as fast as I could. I was too scared to tell Mama what had happened, and besides, I did not want to worry her. I was worried enough myself. I could not sleep at night, feeling responsible for any fate that might befall my family. Every German action, every knock on the door, every crunch of German boots, sent shivers through my body. I suffered headaches, and my pillow was soaked with tears of anguish.

In May of 1940, curfew was set in the early evening, when it was still broad daylight. The tenants of 1331 Slowackiego Street would sit out in the garden; they were not allowed out the gate. They would talk about their situation, share the news of the day, and search for ways of easing their pain.

There was talk about people getting away from the Germans, seeking refuge in the Russian-occupied zone. In our family Heshek and Vrumek decided to risk the move, walking forth into the darkness of the night with only some extra clothes in their backpacks. While reluctant to leave the womb of our family, the risks of staying were too great for young Jewish men. For Mama it was a traumatic experience to have her two sons vanish this way when she had not yet finished mourning the death of her oldest son, Shlamek. Two of her other sons, her pride and joy, would now be lost to the unknown. Even Papa had nothing to console her with, his once joyful spirit now broken.

Blimcia wanted her husband Jacob to join her brothers, for he was young too and could withstand the rigors of travel. If they could sneak through the border, there was hope for their safety. But Jacob would not listen to any of her pleas. "Blimcia, my dearest, how can you even conceive of my leaving you? I would perish with longing for you. We are man and wife. No force in the world will part us."

It was the nights that were safe for travel, when one could hide in the shadows of the forest. Joining a small group of refugees, Heshek and Vrumek marched through the forests, hiding out during daylight. Their heavy backpacks weighed them down, and they often lost their direction. Through battlefields and burnt-out villages they trotted, catching short naps, faithfully watching out for one another. Eventually they reached the border of Russian-occupied Poland. All day they lay low in the high wheat fields, observing the movements of troops. They noted the changing of guards, marking the time intervals. Finally, in the stillness of night, they made their move. Bent low to the ground, often crawling, they crossed over to the Russian side. At dawn they could make out the *rubashka* tunics worn by the Soviet soldiers, and they knew they were safe in the Russian zone. With exhilaration they hugged each other, hardly able to believe that they had really made it. They were free from the clutches of the Third Reich.

For hours they waited for the crowded train that brought them to Lvov. Now their task was survival in a strange city far from home and family. The two brothers, devoted to each other, swore to strive together to overcome the crises of war and to return safely to their family. Having lived together away from home before the war, even if in far better circumstances, prepared the brothers somewhat for this predicament. They rented a small room near the many other refugees who were crowding the city. The next most pressing issue was earning money. They had no legal documents and could not count on anyone hiring them. The alternative was to go into business. From Papa they had picked up a talent for trading. Into the marketplace they went, buying and selling all kinds of goods. They started with soap and sugar; then it was matches and kerosene lamps, which were much-sought-after products. Business was done out of the coat pocket and constantly on the lookout for approaching police. Since they were foreigners, refugees and illegals, they were vulnerable to arrest and deportation to the German side. Even in the freedom of the Russian-occupied zone people were assaulted and threatened. There were searches performed for illegal refugees, and here too life was stressful.

Chapter 7

The resumption of our family's life in Blimcia's apartment on Slowackiego Street was short-lived. After a couple of months the Germans again showed up at the front door to announce our eviction. Once again we had no more than three hours to clear out. This time it went more quickly, for our possessions were now quite meager after the three previous expulsions. For Goldzia these evictions were torture. Her bones were deformed from inactivity, her muscles were soft, her back was bent to the cavity of her mattress. She had to be transferred into a series of strange beds and suffocating rooms. Every expulsion, every German search, every new order or decree made her cognizant of her unique helplessness. We all felt Goldzia's terror, but we knew that there was no way to help her or change her destiny. We were all condemned, all of us vulnerable to the fury of the bestial enemy. With full faith we entrusted our fate to the divine mercy of our Almighty God, unconditionally believing in his power to rescue us.

It had hardly been a year since the Germans occupied Poland. The world of nature seemed to proceed at its own pace. The summer was coming to a close. The evenings were cooler now, and the trees began shedding their coats of green. No one dared to steal into the Lebenfeld park to pick chestnuts. The Germans lived there now. No one even thought much about the holidays. It was the Germans who celebrated victories over us, the innocent, unprotected Jews. Jews were being punished for fictitious crimes. They were arrested for behaving unlawfully, buying from a Gentile, possessing a forbidden article, or congregating in the street.

Somehow the Germans always found Jews who misbehaved, disobeyed the law. These Jews were detained, jailed, and then shipped away, never to be heard from again. Israel Gerstner and his two sons were arrested when a Pole informed on them for allegedly baking bread illegally. The Pole claimed he saw smoke coming from their bakery's smokestack, which, of course, was a lie.

Shaye Malach was caught with illegal onions in his possession. Seven such criminals were not sent away; it was here in Chrzanow, their hometown, that the Germans put them to death in a big spectacle attended by the whole town. On Krzyska Street, right beneath the windows of Shaye Malach's home, was a big old tree that must have held plenty of fond memories for him. Now there were seven ropes tied to the tree. Earlier in the day German troops drove around the town in their military vehicles with bullhorns and loudspeakers, announcing the event. Seven Jews who disobeyed the authorities were now going to be publicly hung. All Jews of all ages were to present themselves on Krzyska Street. Everyone's document would be stamped at this time; anyone later found with an unstamped document would be punished by death. This way the Germans avoided going into every Jewish home. The Jews obediently came.

The Germans dressed in their best uniforms, like for a ball or celebration. They came trailing fat Commandant Schindler and Gestapo Chief Lindner with pomp and fanfare. The Poles came uninvited. They came to enjoy the spectacle.

For hours we stood before the gallows. I stood close to Mama, clutching her hand. I felt Mama's agony. We had to leave Goldzia home alone. I shivered at the sight of all those Germans with rifles and clubs. Blimcia, tears rolling down her face, clutched her baby to her breast. We had been brought here to witness the bloodthirsty Germans at their game of murder. It was traumatic for the children, gruesome for the women, and intimidating for the men. Of course, the mass execution was a merciless torment for the families of the unfortunate victims, who were brought out of a truck with their hands tied behind their backs like criminals. Their only crime was being Jewish.

Their faces pale and unshaven, they looked down the vast expanse of spectators. The downtrodden Jews, the wrathful Poles, the sadistic Germans were all assembled for a spectacle befitting the savage ancient Romans at the Coliseum. The victims were looking for help, for a miracle to happen, but none did.

The ropes were slowly placed around their necks, the vicious German hangmen delaying the final torture, prolonging the poor victims' suffering. The sun shone weakly through pale clouds, but there was no rain. The heavens did not cry with us. Many of the onlookers fainted, unable to endure the anguish. But even the faintings had to be hidden from the Germans, who watched the crowds, making sure everyone was attentive. With their loudspeakers they repeatedly proclaimed that dirty, disobedient Jews must be punished.

Finally, the hangmen kicked the stools from beneath the seven men's feet, leaving them to hang by their necks. Mama placed her hands over my eyes while in my ears rang the loud scream of *"Shema Yisrael!"*—Hear O Israel—which pierced the air. The last words of the seven sacrificed martyrs echoed in the square, while their faces twisted and turned blue in death. Until the curfew at dusk, the Germans kept the suffering Jewish populace at the gallows, watching our brethren twist from the tree. Exhausted and shaken, we returned home before nightfall to an uncertain future that dangled from a frayed rope.

Chapter 8

The Germans were not satisfied with Jewish gold and silver, furs, and radios. Now they wanted Jewish bodies for labor in concentration camps. The Jews had to fill quotas of young men for labor. The Jewish community council asked for volunteers.

Chrzanow's Jews formed a solid community, where mutual trust and cooperation reigned. The community in Chrzanow always took care of its sick, old, and poor. Families knew each other for decades, even centuries. They survived in the hostile, Gentile world thanks to their unity, and this same unity was maintained in these hard times of war. When the council asked for volunteers, the town's young men enlisted, to save the community, to save their families. The Germans got their quotas filled.

In our household Sholek was the only son left. Only fifteen years of age, he knew he must go. Mama's back was bent with the pain of losing her last son. Papa suffered silently thinking of his intelligent Sholek, the only son left to say Kaddish for him. Would he be able to survive, this young, still-growing, always hungry boy? With his beard gone, Papa's hollow cheeks were sinking deep as graves. Courageous young Sholek, my closest brother, my confidant, my valiant protector, would have to go. Always ready to spit in the devil's face, he had nervous cramps in his stomach and goose pimples when he marched into the marketplace. I recall the last glimpse of his pale face in a flock of males that was herded to the railroad station. They were shipped to Katowice, where he had always wanted to go with Papa on his prewar business trips.

We learned from his subsequent letters that he was thrust into a dark bunk, wakened before dawn, and brought into a stable. Sholek was given a pail and brush and told to scrub the horses. He had no idea how to reach their backs or how to make them pick up their legs. He had to be quick, efficient, and thorough, as the German guard was ready to whip him for being a lazy Jew. His stomach growled with hunger, his soul with disdain. His letters did not reveal all his suffering because he did not want to worry us or provoke the censor. Sholek composed a song and promised to sing it to us when he came home. Meanwhile, missing Sholek and worrying about him added to the misery of the German occupation.

The Jews were chased out from the Planty and Mickiewicza Street; they were forbidden not only to live on these streets but also to walk by. A ghetto was created. Attending school was prohibited. The Jewish population everywhere was harassed and abused, their lives constantly threatened. The Jewish community council did its best to care for the poor and the elderly. Schooling for children was arranged, and trade courses were instituted. All able-bodied persons had to either be employed by the Germans or shipped away to camps.

I was now thirteen. My schooling interrupted, Mama sent

me to attend a course in millinery work. Not that anyone cared which hats would be fashionable next season, but the women who could teach dressmaking, corset making, or other useful trades had already been shipped away to camps. It happened to be a hatmaker who was left in Chrzanow, and so she taught us what she knew best. It was the best time I can remember during the war, all of us sitting together in her apartment creating beautiful hats. The atmosphere was one of concern and friendship. We would all bring our family's stock of old hats, for there were no new materials available. With the help of our teacher, the hats were completely refashioned. We learned to apply ribbons, feathers, flowers, and other ornaments to produce beautiful new hats. There was even an exhibition attended by our parents. People even bought hats, to promote our work and encourage us. We were all thrilled. We lost ourselves in the creative, painstaking work of patiently steaming and pressing the old felt into the contours of the dummy heads, reshaping hats as ardently as we would have liked to reshape our lives. We dared to be imaginative, happily forgetting, gossiping, and singing with our work.

Mama grew morose lamenting Shlamek and worrying about Heshek and Vrumek—and Papa, God forbid the Germans should ever get hold of him. She never cared about herself. "After all, what could they do to an old woman with a sick daughter to care for?" she would say. During all the searches, she would try to hide Papa and the children, exposing only herself and Goldzia. In one of the searches, I was the only one home with Mama and Goldzia in our tiny one-bedroom apartment on the ground floor. Mama could not find anyplace to hide me, as the Germans were right outside the house. Desperately, Mama pushed me under the steps, where I crouched into a small ball. Mama quickly covered me with some rags and sacks. Soon the Germans were in the house, and I felt the heavy steps of their boots on my head, which was pressed against the wooden steps. I pressed my hands to my heart to stop it from pounding so loud. I trembled and prayed. My limbs ached. The moments hung like hours. The Germans searched the house, methodically climbing up and down the staircase, going in and out of the house. They poked around in every nook and cranny, every hiding place, their heavy boots banging on my head as I cringed there right under their feet. They never did find me. I was convinced that my prayers had been answered.

Nachcia, who was at Aunt Esther's house at the time, was spared too. She was hidden with Aunt Esther's family in their family bunker. One bedroom in Aunt Esther's house had been converted into a hiding place by placing a large wardrobe against the door leading to that room. The wardrobe had a false back door, covered with garments, through which you could get into the room. When they found out about the search, Aunt Esther piled everybody through the wardrobe into the hidden room, remaining herself to wait for the Germans. Silently they all sat listening to the Germans enter their apartment. They could hear them shout at Aunt Esther, questioning her as to the whereabouts of her family. They pressed their ears to the door to catch what was going on in the next room. Their hearts stood still when they heard the Germans open the door of the wardrobe.

Pale and exhausted, Aunt Esther finally opened the hidden door when all was clear and the Germans were gone. They cried and laughed hysterically. They had outwitted the Germans. They were saved. It was a joy tempered by pain, for having survived one search did not mean being free of danger.

But it was actually the Germans who were besting the Jews: first they took away their victims' valuables, then they beat and killed many of them, then, for the promise of some relief, they succeeded in getting the cooperation of the Jewish population. They had been filling their quotas of male Jews with volunteers for the labor camps; now they claimed the women. The Jewish community council asked for volunteers, and every family gave up one of its lovely, cherished daughters to serve as a slave to the German oppressor. The girls cooperated as the boys had, to spare their families the collective punishment that awaited them if they were caught holding out.

In our household it was Nachcia who went. Nachcia was not a strong girl; she often suffered severe migraine headaches.

Mama always protected her, making sure she didn't work too hard and that she ate well and slept enough.

Now they were taking my sister away. Who would care for her? How could she withstand the ravages of long days of hard labor? Mama was distraught. Nachcia tried to allay Mama's fears, even though she was scared to death herself. But Nachcia, like all of us, knew she had no alternative. She had to go.

With some clothes and articles of food in her backpack, she joined the line of girls at the marketplace. We wondered when we would hear from her again.

Sholek's letters were heartrending. He was, after all, a young boy, burdened with the care of these huge, unfriendly beasts. He was also mistreated and kept hungry and scared by an army of two-legged beasts. All his talent, wit, and agility were of no consequence in his dreadful situation. Eventually, one of the horses ended up kicking him in the shin, which swelled up and hurt badly. His leg, inflamed and oozing pus, was getting more painful every day. The Germans hit hard to make him perform his daily chores, but finally Sholek was unable to work. Useless to the Germans, he was sent back to Chrzanow. The happiness was indescribable when Sholek, sick and limping, came home. Papa took him to Dr. Ritter, who discovered much scar tissue deep in Sholek's flesh. But at least he was home alive.

The Germans sent their quotas of Jews to the labor camps. There were promises that the rest of the population would be left in peace, but the raids at night and the searches during the day did not diminish. People were stopped in the street, arrested, and shipped away for no reason. Only landing a steady job with the German authorities provided a measure of security. The majority of these jobs involved cleaning the streets, digging ditches, or otherwise serving the Germans.

Jacob was lucky to have such a job. By nature Jacob was very handy, orderly and immaculate, and the German he worked for was satisfied with his performance: the man's boots always shined like a mirror, the bushes in his garden were neatly trimmed, and his floors were kept sparkling. Jacob was issued a pass that permitted him to come and go freely, even in areas forbidden to Jews. It was a tremendous advantage, even if it had its hazards. He would still be at the mercy of each individual German. Sometimes an officer would capriciously ignore Jacob's pass and arrest him anyway. It took Blimcia's ingenuity and his employer's intervention to have Jacob released.

His freedom of movement, however, enabled Jacob to establish contact with an old Polish acquaintance named Malik, who lived on the Planty. Malik had done business with our family before the war. He was free to travel to the big cities of Krakow and Katowice, where he purchased sorely needed staple items. He would resell these to us, and Papa, who had given up the store some time ago, was now conducting some business from the house.

Jacob established the contact but could not endanger himself by carrying any of the groceries home. It was Sholek and I who were the runners, as children were at lesser risk. In constant jeopardy, we would remove our armbands and carefully make our way to the Planty and the Malik residence. Once there, we would hand over the money and pick up the bags that were prepared for us. The Maliks, too, wanted the transaction to be as quick and unobtrusive as possible. The bags of different foodstuffs were quite heavy; still, we had to be able to outrun a German if spotted, to jump a fence, to hide under some bushes, to sneak through yards and gates. Sholek's leg hadn't fully recovered, but he was still as quick as a squirrel. I nimbly followed Sholek, able to take his wordless orders. An expression on his face, a blink of his eyes told me exactly what to do. Sholek and I were our family's sole link with the outside world. Papa's face would shine with relief and pleasure when he would finally see us both home. Papa did not go out into the street anymore; it was too dangerous.

Life was harsh, but it went on. Mouths had to be fed, money was needed, and Papa's financial resources were depleted. Papa would unpack the bags for which we had risked our lives, glad to find in them beans, barley, hard cheeses, whole pepper, sugar or flour. We never knew what was in them. Whatever the Maliks could find they would smuggle in. Anything edible was precious.

As cautious as we were in our work, as swift and as daring, we still needed God to protect and guide us. One Thursday afternoon, we returned home with beating hearts and bursting lungs only to encounter the Germans right in our building. They were searching our house just when we arrived. Sholek, alert as always, noticed the boot of a German soldier in the doorway. He pulled me away from the threshold just in time. We quickly hid the bags in a pile of rubbish in the back yard, put our armbands back on, and waited impatiently. Only after the search was completed did we retrieve the bundles and go upstairs. Papa promptly had us recite the blessing of *birkas hagomel,* and Mama could not stop praising the Almighty for the miracle of our safety.

Receiving our supplies was only half our daily battle—now came the second part, selling the merchandise. Much of it was going to other cities, where food was even more scarce. Jewish women who could pass as non-Jews risked their lives traveling as Gentiles. These women, even young children, would dress as peasant girls and come shopping in Chrzanow to smuggle food back to their families and towns. Only young, slim blondes were good candidates. They wore special corsets with long tubular pockets that could be filled with grains. Tied securely to the waist, the corset would be covered with layers of wide, loose dresses or skirts, with a big shawl covering it all. The girls who came in slim as a beanstalk would walk out as large, fat peasant women. God forbid if someone should but touch them. Every week we would anxiously await them, distressed when some were missing. Too often we'd hear that Frania or Bronia or Cila was picked up and sent to a camp. These common tragedies slowly destroyed our resistance and threatened the frail intercity Jewish network.

Having babies was the ultimate act of resistance. Little Aiziu, as we affectionately called Yitzchak, was growing and developing. On March 17, 1941, his first birthday arrived without celebration. Jacob came home too tired from his day of demeaning hard work, and Blimcia was too absorbed with the daily struggle for survival. Papa was depressed, with no chance to get a job.

New work opportunities arose in the summer of 1941. The Germans sponsored two plants, a rubber factory and a tailor shop, where Jews would have the opportunity to work—aiding the Axis war effort, unfortunately. In the rubber factory, boots, tire tubes, and other rubber products were made; in the tailor shop German army uniforms were sewn. The shop was to be organized, run, and maintained by Jews. Chrzanow had always had a large clothing industry and boasted well-qualified tradespeople. The Germans allowed tailors to bring their own sewing machines into the shop. There was a need for other than machine tailoring, but only skilled people had a chance for such positions. My millinery course turned out to be a valuable investment. My teacher attested to my ability with needle and thread, making me eligible for a job in Rosner's shop. My certificate of graduation from the millinery course was presented as proof of my skill with a needle. I was placed on the floor to sew buttons on military jackets, working the night shift.

The shop was located in a former old-age home, and the rooms were small, crowded, sweaty, and stuffy. In a dingy corner I would sit through the night energetically pushing a needle through hard buttons and into heavy jacket material.

Every night my eyes grew red with sleeplessness, my fingers were pricked by the needle, and my hands and muscles ached from handling so many heavy garments. In the pale morning, I'd return home exhausted and downcast, but I would perk up upon seeing Mama's glowing face. Mama was so happy to know that her youngest, her thirteen-year-old daughter, was working at such an important job. Mama's happiness would recharge me for the next night. At least in the shop I felt secure among Jews, away from German clubs. In the constant clatter of the sewing machines and the suffocating heat from the steam pressers, among the close company of the other button sewers and buttonhole makers, I could block out the ravages of the outside world. During supper break we would talk to each other and share the burdens of our anxieties.

Even though Sholek was dismissed from the equestrian labor detail because he became disabled, his unemployment was a dangerous provocation to the authorities. Papa's influence with his old acquaintances landed Sholek a job in Rosner's tailor shop as well. I was ecstatic to be working together with Sholek on the same shift. We would come and go together and share supper breaks. I felt safe being close to my brother, who had always protected and guided me. Sholek was placed as a floor boy, so he was all over. Sholek had Papa's gift for telling jokes, along with a pleasant singing voice. He was able to compose songs and poems and to perform them to everyone's pleasure. Never timid and always smiling, he would climb on one of the tables at suppertime and a crowd would soon assemble around him. Everyone would applaud enthusiastically and beg for more. Sholek would run through the shop, alert and lively, quickly producing his own quota of work and always making time to help others. He was always the one picked when a scout was needed to go outside and check on the Germans. Even now with his ailing leg, he could still outrun a German pursuer. Sleep was at a premium, since our nights were spent in the dingy shop and our days in constant pursuit of adequate food to sustain the family.

As troubled as our lives were, we missed Heshek and Vrumek and wished they were back with us. We knew that they were in the town of Lvov in the Russian compound zone. We knew little about their lives there but prayed and hoped for the best. We only found out what happened to them later on and so were unable to be of any help to them.

Vrumek's and Heshek's lives in Lvov were hard and perilous too. They had difficulty sustaining themselves and were persecuted as foreigners and illegal refugees. In one of the actions aimed at illegal refugees, Heshek and Vrumek were arrested and loaded into trains with hundreds of other refugees for deportation. Heshek accepted his fate, too tired to fight it. He sat calmly among the closely nestled crowds waiting for the train to move. Not so Vrumek. Of a more fiery character, he was unable to submit to being trapped. Energetic and ready to fight for his life and freedom, he could not sit idly by. He paced the train cars and alertly watched what was going on. He was able to find out that they were being shipped deep into Russia. He whispered into Heshek's ear, ''We have to get out of here! We must escape.''

Heshek, being the older, more serene one, tried calmly to persuade his younger brother that it was too dangerous to attempt escape. They had made it so far. They would continue to survive only if they stayed calm and stuck together. ''The guards outside are armed,'' he reminded Vrumek, ''and will not hesitate to shoot.'' He reprimanded Vrumek for being reckless and asked him to sit tight.

Vrumek, convinced that his brother was not going to listen, was becoming nervous. He absolutely could not just let himself be carried away deep into frozen Siberia. He and his brother were young; he saw the possibility of living free only in escape.

The train was moving now, and Heshek was still unconvinced. Vrumek was wrestling with himself. He did not want to leave his brother and fought fiercely to make Heshek see his point. But Heshek looked around at all the other people huddled there in the train. He had faith in God; he had no desire to go against the tide.

Vrumek restlessly looked out the window and saw the fast-disappearing city. In one moment he made his decision. He looked about, then jumped, rolling down into an adjacent field, where he lay for a while, catching his breath. Eventually he got up and ran back to Lvov, where the people were calmly going about their business. Only now he felt like a branded animal, as if everybody could see a sign on him labeling him as a refugee and escapee. He went back to the apartment where he had lived, finding it empty, abandoned. He felt forlorn, lonely, unsafe. How could he stay there? Frantically Vrumek began searching for a new place to stay. He tried a small village but soon found out that he was even more exposed to danger there, for there was no way to get lost in the crowd. It was imperative for him to return to the apartment in Lvov so that Heshek could stay in touch.

Eventually a letter came saying Heshek was in Siberia, not far from the town of Omsk. Between the lines Vrumek understood that the situation wasn't good at all. Although a poor and a wanted man, Vrumek felt that he must help his brother. He went back to the marketplace and traded with all his energy and resourcefulness to send Heshek a package of necessities. With doubled determination he worked diligently, all the time avoiding capture.

Chapter 9

Before Heshek knew it, Vrumek was out the window of the moving train. A cry of *"Shema Yisrael!"* escaped Heshek's throat. It was already too late to see what had happened to his beloved brother. The train was rapidly picking up speed, wheels clacking, shrill whistle shrieking, and the scenery was quickly being sucked into the irrevocable past.

Vrumek's jump tore at Heshek's raw nerves. He sat back in the crowded slave train bound for Siberia, his thoughts going back to those last days in Lvov with Vrumek. It was a dog's life, with a city full of refugees seeking food and a roof over their heads. The kindness of the Stern family provided them with beds, while the brothers spent their days in the dangerous business of buying and selling on the black market. Together they struggled, longing for the day when the war would be over and they could return home.

Then came the announcement that all refugees were to report to the police. They were to be issued legal documents and resettled where they would be allowed to work and earn a normal living. Heshek, like most of the refugees, chose to present himself to the authorities rather than attempting to stay illegally. With food in one's stomach it would be much easier to wait out the war. But Vrumek did not trust the Russian promises. He was too hot-blooded to sit it out, to wait and see where fate and the Russian railway would take them. Heshek now contemplated his brother's chances. He worried about where Vrumek would be able to hide.

It was dawn when Heshek woke. The train was standing still and people began to stir. The air was cold. Mothers cuddled their youngsters closer and fathers covered their sons with an extra coat. Heshek wished Vrumek were there to talk to him, to calm him or even to scold him.

It was dusk before the train started moving. The whole day they had watched soldiers marching back and forth. The refugees looked at each other anxiously, listening to every murmur. Rumors were spreading from car to car.

"We are being sent to Kiev," someone proclaimed. "I heard them talking with my own ears."

"Kiev, shmiev!" another voice grunted. "You must be crazy. The Russians would never send foreigners to a big city. They are going to settle us in a remote village where we can be watched carefully."

"They will send us to Siberia," a woman cried, "where we will freeze to death. Who knows if we'll ever see our parents again?"

"They are bringing food!" someone shouted. Hot coffee and bread were distributed, and as people ate, their mood improved. Now they were speculating about the kind of lodging they would get. Would they be in large barracks or small cottages? Families were planning out their lives, assigning chores and roles, considering the various eventualities. But Heshek could envision no possibility, no future.

Night fell and the train moved again, slowly increasing its speed. Soon, renewed snoring was heard in the car. A numbing cold permeated Heshek's body. He sat crouched for warmth, his eyes closed, but he could not rest. His chattering teeth woke him from sporadic naps.

With another day came more questions and no answers. The rumors and fears grew with the length of their journey. It was clear to all that the Russians did not want these foreigners near the border; it was obvious they were being shipped deep into the interior. But where?

Again the next day the train would run for a while and then stop for hours. Rumor had it that the train lines were needed to ship soldiers, supplies, and the wounded to or from the front. The passengers became more uncomfortable and restless. Many had several layers of clothing on them, along with all their possessions. On and off went people's coats and jackets. Many sprawled on the floor, propped on their shapeless bundles. Some had meager food supplies, while others depended entirely upon the token provisions supplied by the Russians.

Heshek slept on his small bundle, alongside Vrumek's bag. He woke before dawn to find the train had stopped. Officials came aboard, ordering everyone to disembark. When all the passengers were out, the train started up, leaving them to be whipped by the wind in an empty field. Hours passed. Parents sheltered their young ones. Another train eventually arrived, a string of cattle cars with tiny barred windows. The refugees had to help each other climb into the darkened boxcars; the air inside was stagnant and they could barely discern the wooden benches against the walls. The train moved on, and the exhausted travelers settled in for another night.

A week after the journey began they reached a small railroad station, where they were allowed to disembark. They were in a village deep in Russia. As soon as the local peasants saw some money flashed by the strange refugees, they scrambled back to their farms and returned laden with milk, bread, butter, and some fruit. After the welcome break, the passengers were loaded back on the train for the night.

In the tedious days and nights that followed, the only change was in the scenery, as rolling fields studded with small villages gave way to endless, thick forests. It was obvious to all now: they were deep in Siberia.

It was late afternoon when the train finally stopped. Wardens led the way on an hour-long trek down a muddy road. Before nightfall they reached a clearing. Distraught, the refugees looked at the godforsaken forest, thick and foreboding. They were led to several roofless, shaky barracks. Exhausted and bewildered, the travelers collapsed and slumbered till dawn.

Heshek found a corner, tucked his own and Vrumek's bundle under his head, and silently said his prayers before falling asleep. He was drained emotionally and physically, and now he found himself challenged spiritually. Throughout his life Heshek had been a religious man, who never questioned his faith or his God. He loved God unconditionally and joyously observed God's commandments. He was convinced that his own devotion would help speed up the redemption of the Jewish people and promote the coming of the Messiah and a better world.

Now Heshek felt that he and his people must have sinned greatly to have been punished so severely. And why had he escaped the Nazis only to battle the Russians and the elements in this brutal country? He felt utterly alone. True, he was among fellow Jews, but everybody else had someone, a family member, a friend, or neighbor to share their misery.

People began getting organized. Families settled into specific corners of the barracks. Men went into the woods and dragged back planks and branches to make dividers for privacy, and a communal effort was started to rebuild the barracks' roofs. But Heshek remained passive, crushed by the long journey and its dreadful destination.

A fragile man of medium height whose dark beard was sprinkled with gray came over to Heshek. "Young man," he began, "my name is Reb Moishe Spitz. Maybe you would be kind enough to help a little. You see, my wife here is pregnant and can't be of much help. If you would just hold these planks for me while I knock in the wooden nails, we could have a partition. You would have your own room, and I would have some space for me and my wife and the children."

Heshek's sense of decency was immediately aroused, and his listless body sprang back to life. He thought of Papa and Mama, who looked as vulnerable as Reb Moishe. He looked at Reb Moishe's pregnant wife and thought of Blimcia, who had been expecting a baby when he last saw her.

It must be the will of God, he said to himself. I am here for a purpose, and God is reminding me that I am on this earth to help my fellow man, not to sit and beg for salvation.

Extricated from his gloomy fog, he embarked with new energy on the projects at hand. Into the woods he went with a borrowed saw, sawing trees into short logs, then splitting them into planks. Reb Moishe sat on a rock chopping wood into small splinters to use as nails. Together they built the walls that formed a large room for the Spitz family and a small one for Heshek.

Heshek became more a friend than a neighbor, a resourceful helping hand for Rabbi Spitz, who was unaccustomed to physical exertion and handiwork. Reb Moishe was a deep thinker and provided stimulating company for Heshek. Jewish teaching always surfaced while they were busy working.

"When God commanded Noah to build the ark, he too lacked tools and nails. Still, the ark got built, and they survived the Flood."

"That is so," said Heshek, "but in Noah's case, God instructed him exactly how to build the ark. His intention was to save Noah and thereby rebuild the world. God, however, does not seem to be instructing us here. From the looks of this vast wilderness, this endless war, and our Russian friends, who knows if God intends for us to survive?"

"Heshek, Heshek, you are talking like a nonbeliever, which surprises me after hearing about your background. Can't you see? It is clear that God has given us all the traveling and physical labor that we tried to save by not going to Palestine after the Great War. And after this Great Flood, this world war, the goyim will be weak from destroying each other. All these trains and ocean liners and airplanes that the Almighty allowed this century to invent will hurl us back to our promised land. Surely we are in the period of great destruction that was prophesied millennia ago.

"And Heshek, don't despair over the many tragedies that befell our families and hometowns. Each victim of the cruel enemy is a holy martyr, a merit for us in heaven, another stone in the Third Temple, may it be built speedily and in our days. There is no answer—in this world—to the question of why so many have perished. But why, Heshek, are you and I alive? We all just went through three weeks of unbelievable tribulations, yet we are here building our ark. Surely it will carry us on the stormy waters to our redemption."

Reb Moishe's optimistic vision was invigorating. Although burdened with his pregnant wife Gittel and two daughters, Sheindle and Shprintza, none of whom could really work, he constantly saw the positive side of things. His infectious spirit gave Heshek and others the faith and will to persevere.

"When the Germans came to our village and began their ruthless expulsions, I was the first to leave," Reb Moishe stated. "My estate was not rich, my house was not large, so I quickly gathered my precious possessions, my wife and children, and fled. They burned the town to the ground, I was told. People lost fortunes, homes, stores. I was merely a poor *melamed* [teacher]. My wealth is my ability to teach Torah, which I always carry with me and which cannot be stolen or burnt."

Heshek's childhood belief in God was replenished by Reb Moishe. In these bleak circumstances, he felt it was God's grace that placed him next to this outwardly fragile but inwardly invincible man.

Heshek stayed close to Reb Moishe as they were assigned their labor contingents. They were to work in the woods cutting trees for lumber, hard manual labor to which neither of the men was suited. The meager portions of food were allocated by priority. Able-bodied workers received one hundred grams of bread daily, while nonworking inmates got only half as much. Some potatoes, cabbage, or beans were also dis-

tributed according to priority. Food was withheld for disobedi-
ence or for not filling quotas. Workers who produced above
quota were awarded an extra slice of bread.

Heshek worked feverishly to provide Reb Moishe's household with adequate food. "You know I have no one to cook for
me. I am better off taking my meals with your family," Heshek
said to his neighbors.

Heshek pretended to be helplessly in need of their hospitality, when in reality, the Spitz family would have starved without his major contribution. Gittel would heat some water on
the open hearth that the men built for her, crumbling some
black crusts of bread into the pot to make them a hot broth for
supper. Reb Moishe and Heshek would come from the forest
exhausted, carrying firewood on their backs. The girls found
employment cleaning the barracks of the Russian wardens and
would sometimes be rewarded with little bundles of tea, barley, or grain. Gittel would trek into the woods to find berries,
mushrooms, or wild beets.

While Reb Moishe prayed the evening service with Heshek,
Gittel would busy herself at the "stove." After meals, Heshek
liked to linger for a discussion of the holy books. Not that they
had any books with them, but Reb Moishe spent his life with
Scripture, the commentaries, and the codes of the Law and
could even quote much from memory. These shared spiritual
and intellectual moments rescued Heshek from his life of brutal labor and gnawing loneliness.

It was only several days after his arrival that Heshek went to
the commandant to inquire about sending a letter to his family. "Is there any possibility of getting some writing paper and
ink?" he inquired politely of the Russian.

"Sure there is," the Russian boisterously replied. "Here in
Russia there is no such thing as 'We do not have.' If we do not
have it here, we issue a request for it from elsewhere."

Well aware of how long it took them to get there from Lvov,
Heshek understood why receiving the paper and getting his
letters back to civilization was a matter of months.

One letter he addressed to his brother Vrumek in Lvov, and
another he mailed to his parents' home in Chrzanow. He

wanted his family to know that he was alive, resolving to tell them that all was well. He spared them concern over his dismal situation. Using his imagination, he told them of the beauty of the land he now lived in. He described the enormity and richness of the vast woods. He wrote of the white night, when the moon shone so brightly that one could read by it. He told them of his conversations with his Russian warden, who assured him that in Russia there was no lack of anything. When he told the man that in his hometown they had a store with citrus fruits like grapefruit and oranges, the warden answered, "Oh, yes, of course, oranges. We have huge factories of oranges in Russia."

Since his arrival in the Siberian work camp, Heshek had been studying Russian and was now able to write his address in Russian. He brought his correspondence over to the commandant, who made him read the letters out loud and translate word for word. Impressed with Heshek's colorful and glowing descriptions of Siberia, he promised to mail the letters out with the next week's delivery wagon. From then on the commandant engaged Heshek as a translator every time anyone wanted to mail a letter. Heshek learned fast, picking up the Russian language and script in a short while.

The only news of the outside world arrived with the food wagon. People were anxious to hear what course the war was taking. The news that filtered through the Russian guards was always the same: Mother Russia was winning the war.

"If so, why can't we go home to Poland?" the Jews would ask.

"Because there is no more Poland," the Russians would answer. "It is all Russia, like it is supposed to be. You are home. This is your land. You are to love it and serve it. You are to be dedicated Communists. You are to love our Papa Stalin, who is so good to you. This is the land you are to live for and die for."

It was March of 1942. "The sky is all snowed out," Gittel said one evening. There cannot be anymore snowstorms. I could never have believed that there would be so much snow in the world; surely now it is finished."

No sooner had Gittel finished speaking when a fresh snow started falling, the flakes soft and large as stars falling out of the sky.

"Not again," she groaned. "God in heaven, have some mercy on us!"

She was expecting the baby to come soon and was hoping for a way to be brought to the hospital in Omsk. With new snow falling, even the combination nurse-doctor-midwife who usually visited the camp would not come. She would be left alone to bring a child into the world, with only other women inmates to help.

Prompted by Gittel's predicament, Heshek volunteered to go to Omsk with the next contingent in the hope of summoning some professional help from town. With dawn the group of travelers rose, bundled up with whatever was available, tied themselves into a caravan, and set off.

The leader of the snow caravan was a young fellow who had made the trek twice before. A lantern in his hand, he led them through deep snow and howling winds. The piling snow began to form drifts on their brows and mustaches. Their breath froze in midair. When someone slowed down to rest, the others would tug at the rope because stopping was dangerous; one's extremities could get frozen off if he remained inactive.

When they finally reached town Heshek directed himself immediately to the *shochet's* house, having obtained the address from Reb Moishe. The *shochet,* the ritual slaughterer of animals for kosher meat, could only provide a promise that if the newborn was a boy, then he, a *mohel* (circumciser) as well, would come to perform the ritual circumcision, entering the newborn into the covenant of the Patriarch Abraham.

The next day, as Heshek went to collect his bread rations, he saw through steam-filled eyes a woman standing in line in front of the counter. He could not guess her age, for she was bundled up in several layers of skirts and shawls. Even her head was swaddled with a heavy woolen shawl, from which a few locks of brown hair escaped. He could not see her eyes because of the steam, but there was definitely something familiar about her face. He was amused that he could imagine one of his family or friends in this remote part of the world. He caught glimpses of her face as she turned towards him. Suddenly it was clear, and a deep, choked moan escaped his throat. "Cesia!" he called out. "Cesia!"

Startled, she left her place in line and approached him, her eyes straining, trying to identify the man who had called her name. As soon as he pulled the rags off his face, she, too, was dumbfounded.

Positive that it was indeed Heshek, she threw her arms around him, burying her face against his chest and weeping uncontrollably. She clung to him like a hurt child, as Heshek contemplated the miracle that God had performed for him. He kept pronouncing her name, pressing her face to his heart with awe and disbelief.

For a while they stood motionless, unaware of the people around them, who were staring and whispering.

"Who are they?"

"Maybe a brother and sister who just found each other, or maybe a husband and wife who were lost from each other."

"Heshek . . . Where . . . ? How . . . ?" Cesia whispered. She could not form the questions that pressed her so urgently.

He led her to a bench in the corner. "I know what you want to know," Heshek began. "I also want to know how you got here. But all this must wait. The most important issue at hand now is to get you to my camp."

She told him how she came to Omsk with a contingent from her own work camp to pick up food. She told him in which direction her camp lay, how far away it was, and who the commandant was. She held his hand for a long while, unable to part from him and wanting to hear again his promise to come for her. Then she had to leave. He stood and watched her slowly disappear, melting into the white vastness.

The next day his team was ready to return to camp. He now trotted energetically, driven by his new purpose, and immediately upon arrival he went to see the commandant.

"I need a pass to visit the town of Tomsk," he stated with urgency.

"And what kind of speculating are you going to do in Tomsk?" the commandant asked distrustfully.

"I would like to bring home with me a woman to marry," Heshek answered with determination.

The commandant laughed heartily. "That seems to be a good reason. You come tomorrow and we will talk about it."

Eager to hear what news Heshek brought, Reb Moishe waited for him outside the barracks.

"Were you able to contact the hospital, Heshek?"

"Unfortunately, there is no way to bring Gittel to Omsk, or a nurse to us. But there is still good news," Heshek added. "The town's *shochet* is also a *mohel,* and he promised to perform a *bris* (circumcision ceremony) if the baby is a boy.

Reb Moishe kept calm and collected. "We are in God's hands, and he will help us. May he grant us a healthy child, girl or boy, who will grow up in a world free of this bondage, and who will experience the full redemption."

Relieved that his failure to help Gittel was taken in stride, Heshek continued to talk. "I have more good news to tell you, concerning myself."

"We all need good news badly. Come, Heshek, sit down and tell me about it."

Finally able to relax, Heshek sat down next to Reb Moishe. "I had the most marvelous encounter today," Heshek said, beaming. "In fact, I can hardly believe that it is true. I met a friend, a girlfriend, the girl I'm going to marry soon."

"Heshek!" Reb Moishe exclaimed. "You seem so sure. How can you know you are going to marry a girl whom you just met?"

"Rest assured, Reb Moishe. It is not just a girl. This is the girl I have loved since I worked as an accountant in Bielsko before the war. That is where I first met Cesia. She, just like myself, came to the big city to work. She and her sister Mania lived in a modest apartment, saving part of their salary to send home to their parents. I liked Cesia from the day I met her. If it weren't for this horrible war, we surely would have been married by now. When the war broke out and we each had to go home, my heart was broken. The future was so uncertain that I lived in constant dread of losing Cesia forever.

"My arrival in Siberia destroyed the last shred of hope I had of ever seeing her. And yet, there I was, coming into the bakery at Omsk to pick up bread rations, and she is standing at the counter! I could not believe my eyes. I was sure it was a hallucination, a snow-crazed dream. Only when she threw her arms around me did I know she was real. I am reborn, Reb Moishe! I believe now that I was sent here for a purpose, that the Almighty is watching over me and steering me in the right path. Now I will survive, for I have my beloved Cesia."

Reb Moishe was still confused. "What do you mean you have her? So where is she? I don't see that you brought anybody with you."

"Oh, don't worry, Reb Moishe. I have already requested permission from the commandant to bring her here to our camp. I do not see any reason why he should deny me this small privilege. After all, what difference does it make to the Russians which camp Cesia is in. She is now in a work camp near Tomsk. Tomorrow I am to speak to the commandant again and fill out applications for her transfer."

Now Reb Moishe became cheerful. "So let it be with *mazal!* [good luck]. You should marry by the Law of Moses and Israel and build a faithful house in Israel. You should know freedom soon, and we should all be set free from this bondage."

Heshek did not sleep much that night. His mind kept churning like a whirlwind. He thought about Cesia, the miracle of finding her, the tragedy of their life, how she had looked so much older bundled up the way she was. Even though he never had the chance to tell her, with the war catching them by surprise, he had meant to declare his intention to marry her in Bielsko.

And now what? Which family members, which guests were available to dance at their wedding? Then again, his thoughts returned to Cesia and how he was grateful for this second chance to share his life with her. He feverishly planned all the details involved in bringing Cesia to his camp, where they could be married.

Early the next morning he presented himself to the commandant. He spent several hours there, his spirits soaring and plummeting with the commandant's various questions and comments. He filled out papers, applications, and declarations, unsure if these would help or hurt him.

Russian promises, like Siberian winters, take their time. As Heshek waited, he resumed his work with renewed effort and determination. The snowstorms slowly subsided, and soon even the snow on the ground began to melt. Heshek tried to spruce up his living quarters for Cesia's eventual arrival. He built another cot, and collected fresh straw to soften up its rough wooden planks.

Five weeks passed. Heshek's optimism was dwindling. When Reb Moishe's daughter Shprintza came running towards him in the woods at midday, he could only think of an emergency involving Gittel. He couldn't imagine why the girl ran up to him instead of to her father, who was working nearby.

"Come! You have a visitor," she called out breathlessly.

He ran back to camp with Shprintza. His heart stood still for a moment, for there, in front of the supply wagon, stood Cesia, with a bundle at her feet. Heshek approached, and she threw her arms around him. He led her to his room in the barracks. Hardly able to restrain himself, he closed the door, yearning to greet her alone in his own room.

Just then they heard a piercing groan from nearby. Gittel was screaming for help. Heshek dispatched Shprintza to summon some of the experienced womenfolk, while Cesia rolled up her sleeves to help. Heshek was in a daze. He went out to sit on the barracks stoop, not believing what had happened to his long-awaited moment of bliss with Cesia.

Women were flying past Heshek carrying bed sheets, towels, rags, and pails of hot water. Stewing in frustration, the neglected Heshek prayed for Gittel's easy and speedy delivery. Finally a baby's cry was heard. Cesia stood in the doorway, proudly announcing the birth of a boy. Heshek then swept the brown-haired midwife off her feet and carried her into his room.

"This sure is cause enough to celebrate, but we have as much to celebrate ourselves."

She embraced him and whispered, "Yes, it is a good sign for us. A new life has come into the world, and a new life is beginning for us too."

"You will be my wife," he said.

"I am so happy," she whispered in response.

The *shochet* who was also a *mohel* came from Omsk to perform the circumcision. "It was sure worth my trip," he said when immediately after the *bris* he performed a marriage ceremony. In the presence of proper witnesses, Heshek placed a plain metal ring on Cesia's finger, pronouncing the ancient vow, "With this ring I thee wed, according to the Law of Moses and Israel."

They were all just beginning to settle in when the announcement came: Hitler had marched his armies into Russian-occupied Poland. The Polish general Anders, under the auspices of the Polish government in exile in London, was forming an army. They would fight on the Russian side to free Poland from the Germans. All Polish citizens were free to join the army of General Anders. Many of the non-Jewish Poles in camp joined immediately.

But when Jewish Poles wanted to enlist, the old anti-Semitism raised its head. Even in Siberia the slogans echoed: "Who needs you Jews? Jews, go to Palestine."

The work camp was instantly dissolved. Like many others, Heshek and Cesia walked together as far as they could until they reached a small village, where they managed to rent a room and find jobs. They had lost touch with the Spitz family and were entirely on their own. Having mastered the Russian language, it was easier for Heshek to get work than for others, yet working did not guarantee their survival. Heshek's market trading was limited in their small village, so Cesia helped out by sewing and selling her handiwork. Sanitary conditions were abysmal and lice became a major problem. The lack of

The author's mother and father, at the time of their engagement in 1908.

The author's grandmother, Chaya, with her children: Standing in the rear are Surcia (the author's mother) and her brother Nachmann; in the front are Abraham and Esther.

The great synagogue in Chrzanow.

The site of the Stapler family shop as it looked in 1988.

The Stapler family gathered in 1938 for the wedding of their daughter Blimcia. The author, Helcia, is at center foreground.

Blimcia and her fiancé, Jakob, in 1938.

Sister Blimcia with her baby son Aizu in 1941.

Heshek Stapler, an accountant, in 1938.

Corporal Shlamek Stapler in his Polish Army infantry uniform, 1937.

Learning to ride a bicycle—the author with her brother Vrumek in 1938.

Vrumek Stapler, who also survived the war. The photograph was taken in Palestine in 1945.

No photo exists of Helen's brother Sholek, who was killed by the Nazis when he was fifteen years old.

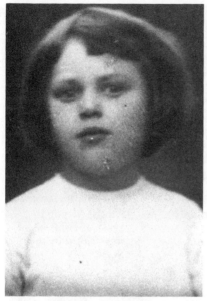

Sister Goldzia.

The author, Helcia Stapler, in May of 1946, one year after the end of the war. The photograph was taken in Palestine for the required identity card as an immigrant.

Nachcia, who survived the camps with her sister. Photo taken in 1937, when she was twenty-three.

Sister Blimcia.

Simcha Stapler, the
author's father, in
1939.

Heshek hauling his
kerosene lamps to
market in Lvov.

Simcha Stapler in
1940, after his beard
was shaven by the
Nazis.

Jewish men of Chrzanow, forced laborers, digging ditches for the Nazis in
1940.

vitamins and proper nourishment resulted in lost teeth and weakened bones. Lung disease was rampant and contagious typhoid was spreading.

"The winter is almost over," Cesia cheerfully said to her tired husband one evening as he returned home from the day's struggles. He had been in a low mood for several days now, uttering complaints that he usually kept to himself.

"How long is this war going to last? Who knows if we will get out of here? When will we know how our families are?"

"Aren't you happy, Heshek? I am your family now. I am here with you and will be with you forever."

When they sat down to their meager meal, Cesia noticed that Heshek wasn't eating. "What is it, Heshek?" she asked anxiously.

"You are suffering enough without having to worry about me," he said. She soon found out that he had injured his leg and had kept on going to work in spite of immense pain.

For two days Heshek wasn't himself. Feeling weak, sweating uncontrollably, he attributed it all to their prolonged captivity and deprivation, but finally he had to admit to Cesia that he was not strong enough even to go to work. He woke the next day burning with fever.

Cesia was distraught. Here they were, deep in Siberia, destitute and alone. Heshek was her pillar of strength. What was she to do? Where could she seek help?

She tried some home remedies, compresses and herbal teas offered by peasant neighbors, but none seemed to relieve Heshek's distress. She bathed his body in rags soaked in cool water. But Heshek was growing weaker. He called her name deliriously or just moaned unintelligibly. When days passed without improvement, Cesia resolved to seek medical help.

It was the last day in May. The sun shone with new light, yet Cesia's world was dim. In the early morning she asked her neighbor to look in on her sick husband while she went to Tomsk to get a doctor. She looked anxiously back at her beloved Heshek. Again, the inner struggle tore her up. Should she leave him in this condition. Should she stay by his side?

No! She concluded that she couldn't help him by sitting idly by.

Cesia left the cottage, walking for hours, sometimes urgently quickening her pace and sometimes slowing down with exhaustion. The sun was high in the sky when she entered the forbidding forest, and it was dark when she finally left the woods to see lights flickering in the distance.

Hungry and exhausted, she finally reached a cottage, where a compassionate old woman spread some straw on the floor so Cesia could spend the night. Early in the morning she inquired about a doctor. She could not see him immediately, she discovered, because he was at the hospital, which would not allow her in. Squeezing her throbbing head in the palms of her hands, she sat waiting for hours. With pleas, cries, and some bribe money, she eventually convinced the doctor to give her a prescription. She then ran to the druggist, only to be told that she would have to wait several days for the rare medicine. But sure enough, after shelling out the last of her money, a small bottle appeared on the counter. It was too late to begin the trek home, so Cesia stayed another night at the old woman's cottage. Before dawn she rose and set out on her return trip, with the precious bottle held tightly in her hand.

By late evening she stood exhausted in the doorway of her hut. The cottage was dark and quiet. With trembling hands she lit the lamp to see Heshek's pale, white face against the straw mat. His eyes were closed. She came close and rested her head on his chest to listen for a heartbeat. It was weak and sporadic. With tears choking her throat, she poured the precious liquid slowly into a spoon, held his lips open, and poured the medicine down his throat. She stared at his face, waiting for a miracle to happen. She wanted him to open his eyes and look at her. She was sure he would say, "My poor Cesia, my dearest one, you are so exhausted. You went so far to bring me this medicine. Only your love could have brought me this healing. It brought me back to life. It brought me back so I could love you and care for you forever and prove to you that I am worthy of your love."

But none of it happened that way. Heshek's face remained

pale. She sat there watching his face and listening to his heart-beat. She felt the warmth of his feverish body with her own flushed face. She patted his head, fed him more medicine, and changed his compresses, fighting her own exhaustion.

Before dawn Heshek opened his eyes, looked at Cesia, and weakly pronounced her name. And then it was over. She saw the color draining from his face. She embraced him and felt the chill of death in his body. She wanted to scream, to call to him not to leave her, but no sound escaped her throat. It was an hour before dawn, June 2, 1942, when Heshek's young soul returned to his maker.

Chapter 10

Several months passed with no communication from Heshek, and Vrumek began to doubt that his package had ever arrived. When a letter finally came from Heshek, Vrumek was overjoyed to read that Heshek had received the food package. Heshek thanked his brother and discreetly praised Vrumek for being courageous enough to have escaped. Heshek wished he had listened to his younger brother and had done the same. Vrumek learned from the letter how bad things were for Heshek. The letter gave Vrumek the strength and will to struggle on. Whatever he could accomplish or acquire was for the two of them, he felt.

Meanwhile the war took a dramatic new turn. The Germans, ignoring the nonaggression pact they had made with Stalin, suddenly attacked the Russians in June of 1941. Vrumek now found himself again under German occupation there in Lvov. The chance of surviving under German rule for a young Jewish fellow with no friends or relatives seemed bleak. Vrumek decided to try and return home to Chrzanow, to his family, but this would not be easy. Luckily, he still had his original documents that showed he resided in Chrzanow. Through some local Jews, Vrumek was able to contact a smuggler, a local peasant from a neighboring village. For a sum of money, this man provided Vrumek with additional documents.

Once he had the documents, Vrumek started out on his perilous journey. Travel by train was too risky, since the Germans were everywhere, checking papers. Vrumek bought a bicycle, stuffed some food into his pocket, and started his trip home early in the morning. To avoid suspicion, he didn't carry any luggage. He rode all day, carefully avoiding the Germans because his documents identifying him as a local laborer would not clear him so far from Lvov. Nervous and tense, he pedaled his bicycle with all his strength, trying to cover a great distance as quickly as possible. He stopped only at night, sleeping in abandoned buildings or in haystacks. When he had to stop to buy food, he'd watch the store for a while first, then quickly make his purchase and leave before any questions could be asked. He had to be wary of every dog that would bark to announce a stranger. As much as being labeled a renegade Jew, he had to worry about local peasants mistaking him for a thief.

By the sixth day he knew he was close to Chrzanow: he was exhausted but excited at the prospect of seeing his beloved family once again. His reverie was shattered by the sight of a German patrol. His body stiffening with terror, he barely managed to turn off the road, almost toppling over as he made the sharp turn.

Peddling fiercely, he tried another approach to Chrzanow, but once again he saw German soldiers. Finally, he managed to make his way into town without being stopped. There were many more Germans around than when he'd left, especially near the house at 1331 Slowackiego Street. From a distance he

could already tell that no Jews lived there anymore. He saw
Germans coming and going and guessed they were living
there, naturally having occupied the nicest homes in town.
Had he come all the way from distant Lvov, overcoming so
many dangers and obstacles, to find himself unable to locate
his family? Instinctively, he rode down to Aunt Esther's house
and slipped inside, carrying his bicycle on his shoulder.

Vrumek ran up the stairs and knocked on the door, un-
nerved by the unusual silence within. He knocked again and
listened. His family and Aunt Esther's family could be anywhere, he feared—or nowhere, God forbid. Why had he taken
it for granted that everything was going to be the way it had
been before he left? Who knew what his family had endured
in his absence?

The self-torture ended when he heard a few tentative steps.
The door opened, and there stood a frightened Aunt Esther.

"My God, it's Vrumek!" she gasped. "Quick!" she said,
pulling him into the house and shutting the door. She dragged
him into the next room. "Help me move this wardrobe," she
said urgently. "For God's sake, Vrumek, the Germans are right
here in this building. There is an action going on. We don't
know who they are looking for this time, young people or old
people, but if they see you, God forbid, we are all lost. This
bicycle, it could be our end: Jews have not been allowed to
possess bicycles for a long time now."

Vrumek helped her move the wardrobe that hid the door
leading to the secret third room. He pushed through the narrow space, pulling the bicycle with him into the hiding place.
He then pulled the wardrobe back into place from the inside.
In the darkened room he could make out Uncle Pinchas sitting
in a corner. Sholek, Chamek, Hania, and Gucia embraced him
in absolute silence, freezing in mid-embrace when they heard
rapping at the outer door. They listened to the thumping German boots. They could hear the Germans question Aunt Esther
as to the whereabouts of her family, and her stuttering response that her husband was at work. Barely daring to breathe,
they heard the Nazis opening closets and cabinets, knocking
furniture around. Their hearts skipped a beat when the Ger-

mans opened the wardrobe that concealed the door to their hiding place. It seemed as if the Germans were right there in the room with them. Uncle Pinchas's lips moved in silent prayer. The soldiers poked around in the wardrobe and then slammed the door shut.

They yelled to Aunt Esther, "Tell your husband not to move from here when he returns from work. We will be back for him."

The Germans left, but the rest of the day was spent in the hiding place, lest the Nazis make good on their threat. That evening, however, the roundup was over, the Germans having collected their quota of people. The family was spared once again.

Chapter 11

It was late in the afternoon, just before curfew, when I reached Aunt Esther's house. Mama had dispatched me to inform her sister that, thank God, we were safe, and to see how Esther's family had fared in the latest German search.

Aunt Esther, expecting the Germans to come back, was frantic with fear to see me out in the street just after a raid and just before curfew. She seemed emotionally drained.

"Thanks to the Almighty we are all here," she said, "but please, Helcia, run back immediately so that you get home safe."

She suddenly realized that my family and I didn't even know that Vrumek was alive, well, and sitting right there in her home. She yelled excitedly, "And don't forget to tell your parents that Vrumek is here."

Now I was stunned. I wanted to ask her what she meant by "here," but she pushed me out the door, again urging me to run fast, adding that everything would be explained tomorrow.

The next morning Vrumek came to the tiny apartment we now occupied on Kadlubek Street. It was an emotional reunion with Mama, Papa, and the rest of us; there were tears of happiness for his homecoming, bitter tears of sorrow for Shlamek, and concern for Heshek in frozen Siberia and for Nachcia interned in a concentration camp.

The first pressing issue was to get rid of Vrumek's illegal bicycle. Uncle Pinchas would offer the bicycle in exchange for food. His peasant contacts still had enough chickens, eggs, milk, potatoes, and vegetables that they were willing to barter for valuables. The bicycle was a valuable commodity, but the trading would be dangerous. Our cousin Sholek Bromberger volunteered. He took off his mandatory white armband and took the bicycle out of town, where the exchange took place. With help from the Almighty he made it home safely, his basket laden with food. Vrumek's two-wheeled liability brought back good luck after all. Only Mama did not partake of the rare bounty of fresh food.

"How can I eat knowing that my son Heshek is starving in Siberia, and my daughter Nachcia, who offered herself to save us, is starving in a concentration camp?" Letters were scarce, but sometimes mail did get through from the camps. Mama was constantly scrounging, saving foodstuffs to be sent to Heshek and Nachcia. She never knew, however, if they received her packages.

The next priority was for Vrumek to get a job; otherwise, his very life was in danger. Vrumek tried the two local shops unsuccessfully, but using his influence with his German employer, Jacob was able to acquire a position for Vrumek with Kleinecke, the German labor commandant. It was a job in civil engineering, but he was resourceful enough to excel at anything that could preserve his life and help his family. Kleinecke was pleased with him and allowed him to get himself an assistant. Vrumek immediately picked Sholek Bromberger, who at the time was also in dire need of a job.

They both had travel passes issued by Kleinecke, so the two cousins often had to resist the temptation to acquire some illegal food from the peasants in their travels. Even though food was so scarce, they knew enough to stay away from trouble.

Yet trouble did not stay away from them. Many times they would be stopped by German patrols; their documents would be investigated while their hearts pounded with fear. When finally identified as Kleinecke's workers, they would be released—most of the time. One time, though, they could not convince an arrogant Gestapo officer to get in touch with Kleinecke's office to verify their employment. They pleaded, but nothing helped. The Gestapo took them to the nearby town of Jaworzno and locked them up in jail. Vrumek was distraught. He was not one to panic, but the situation was so grave, he couldn't see a way out. At least if they had been arrested in Chrzanow, he could possibly get word out to his family, and eventually to Kleinecke. He tried again and again to get the attention of other German officials, pleading for them to contact Kleinecke. All he got was a humiliating beating for being disruptive. Vrumek and his cousin sat there in silence, darkly contemplating their circumstances.

Suddenly, a girl was brought out from inside and ordered to sit next to them on a bench in the front hall. The girl was rather young. She seemed terrified. Her hair was all in tangles, her face red and smeared with tears. Vrumek could not be certain she was Jewish but took the chance of talking to her. If she wasn't Jewish, she probably would not attempt to help them, but she couldn't hurt them either; they couldn't be much worse off than they already were. Vrumek cautiously whispered to her when he got the chance.

"Please, if you do get out of here, I am Vrumek Stapler from Chrzanow. Just try to notify anyone in Chrzanow. Please, even if you don't remember the name, just say two guys from Chrzanow."

Luckily the girl did get out. She was Jewish, and she knew the importance of the message. As soon as she reached her home, she forwarded the message to Chrzanow. Jacob promptly addressed himself to Kleinecke's office. Kleinecke intervened, and the cousins were immediately freed from prison. Vrumek subsequently asked Kleinecke not to send them out of town anymore.

The German raids went on day and night. Without warning, the town was encircled by Gestapo and SS in their green, black, and gold uniforms, stomping their shiny boots through the streets of the town. Swinging their rubber truncheons, beating on doors with them, they terrorized the Jewish community.

"*Raus, Du Judenschwein!*" they would yell: Out, you Jewish swine! Pushing and shoving their captives out of doorways, down staircases, kicking and beating them, they would lead us all to the marketplace, treating us as though we were criminals. The once pleasant marketplace, which had offered wonderful sights, tastes, and smells, had been turned into an arena of terror. Multitudes of people stood there distraught, women clutching the little hands of their painfully apprehensive children. Families huddled together, clinging to each other in a vain attempt to stay together. What did the Germans want this time? Was it the young for labor in their concentration camps? Was it the old, the sick, and the feeble? People milled about, searching for family and friends, taking stock of who was present and who was missing. The Germans spread chaos with the barbaric beating of those deemed less human than themselves.

I stood next to Mama, tightly squeezing her hand. Blimcia and Jacob cuddled together, shielding tiny baby Aiziu between them. Vrumek and Sholek were next to Papa, frantically looking around like trapped animals. Mama scanned the multitude, searching for Aunt Esther and her family. Suddenly she caught sight of her mother, Grandma Chaya, standing there shivering, her gaze blank and empty. Like a lost, terrified child, this elderly woman who had fought life's battles and deserved to spend her final days in tranquillity stood there disoriented among the surging crowd. Her swollen legs barely able to support her, her eyes growing cloudy, Grandma almost slipped to the ground when Mama grabbed her.

Mama and I supported Grandma Chaya as we marched together through the line of SS men who were selecting their victims with the stroke of a finger. Two old women and a child? We were sent to the left. Papa, too, was sent to the left. In a minute we realized that Blimcia, Jacob, Aiziu, Vrumek, and Sholek were all on the other side. They were promptly marched away, and we lost sight of them. We were kept standing in the marketplace for hours before we too were marched away. We were lead down Krakowska Street, marching five abreast, mostly old people, tired, feet dragging on the asphalt road. The Nazis, German shepherds driving their flock to the stockyards, walked along the sidewalks. We plodded on, absorbed in our pain.

Papa was looking around feverishly, trying to find a way to escape. "As long as we are still on the street," he said, "there must be a way. Once they take us indoors it will be impossible."

The German soldier beside him walked up to the head of the column, and Papa felt that this was the opportune time. He wanted to grab Mama's hand and drag her along, but he could not find it in his urgency. He could not let this second go by; the desperate need to gain freedom pounding in his brain, he leapt across the pavement and into one of the houses. Confused, he searched for a place to hide within the dark hallway. He could find nothing. Desperately, he crouched under the steps, cringing. Seconds later, he felt a German boot kick him in his shin. The all too familiar *"Raus du Zaujude!"* rang in his ears as he was dragged back out into the line of marchers.

Mama had been absorbed in her cloud of apathy when she abruptly turned her head to see Papa rush to the sidewalk. She choked back the scream that almost escaped from her throat. Her mind broke away from the lethargy of pain and commanded her to escape. With surprising speed and force Mama yanked Grandma by her hand and pulled her across the pavement, on the other side of the road from where Papa had made his break.

It all happened so fast: Papa running to one side, Mama and Grandma to the other. There I was, alone, marching with throngs of people. I stiffened with fear. My legs kept marching as my head was spinning. My joy at seeing them escape was overshadowed by my isolation. Mama, having pushed Grandma behind a gate, ran back to me. Grandma was too shocked to move. She just stood behind the gate, pressing her clumsy body into a nook. A German saw Mama return but did not pursue her.

Papa had been thrown back in the line and had caught up with us. He was beaten but not defeated. "I am going to try again," he whispered to Mama. Before she could answer, he once again jumped to the curb and ran towards a house. This time, however, he did not even have a chance to hide. A German guard was right behind him, kicking and dragging him back to the road. I was crushed to witness my father so cruelly degraded.

We were all brought to the former old-age home, from which the old people had long been shipped away. People sprawled on the bare floors, tired, thirsty, hungry. The commotion was unbearable. I needed a bathroom badly. Accompanied by Mama, I went outside looking for one. In the yard we saw a long table set up across the end of the yard. At the table sat a nurse in a white uniform. The Germans were all over. Scores of people were with me out in the yard. Behind the table where the nurse sat was a hilly slope that rolled down into wheat fields. We went over to the table. There were other people trying to get the nurse's attention, while the Germans were pushing and shouting.

Mama instantly saw her chance. She pushed me violently behind the nurse's back, making me tumble down the slope. I was not hurt. I knew what I had to do. I sprang up and ran, afraid to turn my head lest I see my pursuers. Through the fields I ran, scared and exhausted, until I finally reached home. From a distance I saw little Aiziu playing by himself in front of the house. When he saw me, he ran towards me, tripping and falling. Panting, I ran to pick him up. The child, frightened and bruised, buried his head against my shoulder, crying hysterically. I cried too, all the agony finally pouring out of my exhausted body. Blimcia heard the screams upstairs and came running down. Overwhelmed by the day's events, she embraced me and her baby, shedding bitter tears of pain. After a short, tearful reunion with Vrumek and Sholek, Blimcia dispatched us to go check on Grandma Chaya and the rest of the family before curfew set in.

The next morning, Blimcia rose early and immediately began efforts to free Mama and Papa. She found out that the people had been transferred from the old-age home to the high school, which was in a district forbidden to Jews. She went to the Jewish community council and pleaded with them to intervene. She then went directly to the Germans, endangering her own life.

"I am on the outside, the only one able to help them. Should I sit back and do nothing when their lives are at stake?"

Some Germans would just chase her away, while others, enchanted by her beauty, would listen to her and make empty promises. Before evening curfew she returned disappointed, but the next day she relentlessly pursued the same agenda. The knowledge that people were still being held at the gymnasium gave us some hope. It gave Blimcia time to function.

She soon discovered that people could be ransomed from the German kidnappers for money. All the jewelry and valuables had previously been turned over to the Germans, and money was in short supply as well. Nonetheless, Blimcia scraped together what she could and brought it to the Germans. Mama and Papa were let go.

Emotionally drained and physically broken, my parents came home to a tearful reunion. In agony Mama listened patiently to Goldzia's horror story. Left alone, she lay petrified in her bed, praying to God for a swift end. Hungry and thirsty while we were gone, she was unable to move her crippled body to help herself. Mama grieved for her child's pain and tried to calm her with kisses. Poor Mama was unable to promise her that she would never leave her again.

But the time for grieving and crying was limited, for new German decrees kept falling on our heads in rapid succession. House raids against the Jews came with ever more frequency and malice. Families were torn apart, with mothers being taken away from small children. Fathers, sons, and daughters were shipped away to forced labor camps. The old and the feeble dared not go out in the streets. Starvation, disease, and death found them in their hiding places. Food was ever more difficult for the dwindling Jewish population to obtain. The Jewish community council was busy caring for as many people as possible, but they were inundated with work for the German authority. There was an infinite amount of registration, documentation, and validation to be done.

There were green stamps and blue stamps and red stamps. The Germans posted announcements that people with a certain-colored stamp had to appear at the appointed hour in the marketplace, where their documents would be given a new stamp. Punishment for nonappearance was deportation, while appearing was likely a registration for the next day's deportation. Not having one's document stamped also deprived a Jew of food rations.

What little news could be obtained from neighbors consisted of rumors, which were bleak and foreboding. No news at all came from the many people who were shipped away. We kept our parents imprisoned at home, watching over them like the most precious possessions. Any socializing had stopped long ago; the bitter despairing populace ventured out only when absolutely necessary. Even our visits to Aunt Esther's became infrequent and sporadic.

It was summer. Summer had once been the time for leisurely walks through the Planty, in the shade of the tree-lined boulevard, with lovers strolling arm in arm. It had been the time for relaxed swims in the cool waters of the Steinbruch or joyous hikes to the emerald riverbanks and enchanted forests, the time to spend lazy hours stretched out in the tall meadow grasses, enthralled by a storybook or by the songs of the circling birds. But such a season was lost in a foggy, distant past.

Little Aiziu was now two years old and went largely unnoticed by the overburdened adults. Smart but subdued, robbed of the joys of childhood, he quietly played alone in a corner. His golden curls shone whenever the brilliant sun managed to penetrate the gloomy interior of the apartment. Aiziu sat absorbed in his favorite game, his game of feeding himself. The spoon in his hand went from the empty pot into his mouth. He then smacked his lips as if real food were in his mouth. At this tender age he knew enough not to cry when hungry. Blimcia would eventually pick him up, sit him in her lap, and feed him his meager supper.

Uncertainty gnawed at Blimcia's nerves, and Jacob seemed pressed by his role of protector and provider in a world where there could be no protection and there were no provisions. And Papa, so tired and aged, lost all his good-natured sensibility. His once gentle eyes were now stern and hard. Mama was passive and withdrawn. Was this the way they'd remain? When the war ended would they be able to come back to life? Was everything as irreversible as our loss of Shlamek?

Blimcia kissed Aiziu good night. The evening was warm and stuffy.

"Maybe you will sit a bit outside?" she asked Papa, trying to cheer him up.

"With whom? With Palka?" Papa asked bitterly.

"No, with Lewi," Blimcia said apologetically.

"Lewi is busy with his family," Papa answered, milder now.

The three Jewish families in the house we now lived in on Zielona Street were each missing family members. Mr. Lewi's wife had been taken away in the last action. A scholarly Jew who had never taken care of household chores, Lewi was now absorbed with laundering his children's clothes and cooking. Mr. Lewi had no time to sit with his neighbors, even to share his misery. Papa, who had loved talking and joking with friends and neighbors, was now sad, lonely, and worried. Papa would sit with a *gemora,* a tractate of the Talmud, in front of him, but one could see his mind was far away. He would remember studying a page of *gemora* with his beloved Heshek on a Sabbath afternoon. Now, instead of the Hebrew characters, he would see the blurred image of Heshek. But if the devastating anxiety destroyed Papa's spirit, he had not yet lost his faith.

"The only one who has answers to our dilemma and suffering is the Almighty," he would state. "This is the time of which our sages and prophets have written long ago. It is the end of days, the kingdom of God, the time of the Messiah. Didn't they warn us that this would be a time of sorrow and calamity, of global war and devastation? Aren't the signs so obvious and prominent? We must accept the Lord's judgment without questions or pleas. Surely in the months ahead the long painful diaspora will come crashing to an end. We are paying dearly for something, something terrible but glorious. May it come speedily and in our days." It was these indulgences of faith that calmed Papa down and radiated sparks of strength and tranquillity into our daily gloom.

There came a day barely two months after the raid in which Blimcia's tireless efforts had ransomed Mama's and Papa's lives. But all of Papa's faith and all of Blimcia's resourcefulness could not help us that fateful summer day. In the early dawn, when the town was asleep, the Germans surrounded the city. Then came the men in the green uniforms with the skull insignia on their hats. They marched through town, entering every building, rapping at every Jewish door with the butts of their rifles. The frightened people awakened suddenly, scrambling to dress in haste. Children cried, people rushed about, women wept as the SS yelled, *"Raus schnell, Judenschwein!"* Out quick, you Jewish pigs! Soon the skull heads were on Zielona Street. Blimcia was the first to hear them when they knocked on Lewi's door. She quickly dressed. Before she had time to wake Aiziu, we heard the rapping on our door. The commotion was terrifying. Within minutes, we were chased into the street, half dressed and whimpering, with the two other Jewish families in our building. We were made to march away, Blimcia cuddling the sleeping baby in her arms. Mama's and Papa's faces were stone white; their hands were trembling.

Under gun and bayonet the Germans marched us through

the sleeping town into the marketplace. Miserable, shivering with fear, thirsty and now fully awake, we stood in the open square with hundreds of people. Some members of the Jewish community council were recognized among the crowd; they were eventually released. Eagerly looking for a possible escape route, Vrumek and Jacob were whispering to each other. Blimcia was absorbed in calming Aiziu, while Mama searched the crowd for Aunt Esther's family and Grandma Chaya.

No movement was permitted. Papa was ready to collapse and sit down on the ground, but Blimcia, flushed with fear lest Papa exhibit a sign of weakness, supported Papa and did not let him slouch. Strong people were still useful in German labor camps, but the weak ones, who knew what their fate would be when they were shipped away? Some people even combed their hair and pinched their cheeks to look younger, healthier, and neater, hoping to be more eligible for the work force. But Papa seemed indifferent, resigned to any fate issued by the Almighty. His only worry was to find Sholek, who had probably been picked up directly from the shop during the night shift.

Mama was murmuring her worries out loud. "What will happen to Goldzia? Who will feed her, give her a drink, turn her back from her night position?" Mama choked with fear for her crippled child.

Meanwhile, the selections were going on. We were made to march through the rows of Germans. Children held on to their mother's skirts, crying hysterically when they were torn from their mothers by the merciless brutes. Wives stretched out hands to their husbands, who were chased away from them. Those trying to run to their loved ones were beaten for their efforts.

Now it was our turn. Mama and Papa marched through together, their shoulders slumped, their faces fallen.

"Left!" And off they were sent. Blimcia followed, cradling Aiziu in her arms. She was sent to the right, with Jacob, Vrumek, and me. There was nothing we could do.

We immediately lost sight of Mama and Papa. Bewildered, we tried to run to the other side of the marketplace to look for them, to be with them, but we were beaten for getting out of our column. Soon we were marched away and ordered to return to our homes or be shot on the spot. We went home brokenhearted, but still Blimcia was eager to repeat her tremendous effort and pluck her parents from the jaws of death.

Another shock awaited us when we reached home: we opened the door and were suddenly faced with Goldzia's empty bed. We mutely stood in front of the bed that had never been empty before, trying to grasp the unbelievable fact that Goldzia was gone. We had heard about sick people being cruelly carried away; now we experienced the horror firsthand. It had still been dark in the house when we were chased out. How frightened she must have been. After hearing the shrill yelling of the Germans, she was left in deadly silence. How had she felt when the thumping boots came up for her? She could not run or hide. They must have hovered over her, roughly grabbing her by an arm or ankle, almost too disgusted to touch her, as if she were contaminated by a plague. The added pain of her loss made us break down and weep uncontrollably. But all the tears could not ease our anguish. We were so helpless.

We felt that maybe the world was coming to an end. We remembered Papa's words, "It is the end of days, the kingdom of God, the time of the Messiah." But we had not died and gone to heaven. We were alive and dangling over the pit of hell.

There was the urgent task of trying to release Mama and Papa. Baby Aiziu needed care, and Jacob and Vrumek were still due to report to work. Blimcia rushed frantically to see the German authorities, to plead with them, to bribe them with the promise of money we could only wish to obtain.

But Blimcia's luck ran out on a fast, efficient German train. Mama and Papa had already been shipped away: Symche and Surcia Stapler, decent, quiet, deeply religious people who had worked hard and raised a loving family. My precious parents, who had never asked much from their Creator, were taken away on that summer day in 1942, taken from all that was dear to them. Grandma Chaya, Great-aunt Channa, Great-uncle Moishe, and thousands of other Jewish mothers and fathers, sisters, brothers, and babies from the town of Chrza-now were taken with them. Their only crime was having been born Jewish.

Blimcia was crushed by her failure to change fate a second time. Only her baby's haunted gaze prompted her to keep on functioning.

Chapter 12

Blimcia now had to work in the tailor shop as well, in order to be entitled to ration cards. I worked the night shift and tended the baby by day while Blimcia was at work.

Vrumek suddenly took sick. He developed a terrible, burning infection in his mouth. His flesh was raw and bleeding and he had a high fever; he was delirious and could not ingest or swallow any food. He stayed in bed, his limp body dehydrating. His sighs and groans filled the air. There was no medicine available, and no doctor could be called. Sending anyone to the hospital was sending him to oblivion. Blimcia sat by Vrumek's side with an eyedropper, patiently squeezing drops of liquid into his dry throat. With a wet cloth she moistened his parched lips and forehead. Neglect-

ing her baby, she clung to Vrumek in a desperate battle for
his life.

After several days Vrumek's fever began to subside. Miraculously, he opened his eyes, looking around as if awakening
from a long dream. He had come back from the world of the
dead. He looked up at his devoted sister, his eyes expressing
gratitude for her courage and perseverance. Slowly, gradually,
he started ingesting liquids and soft cereals. Blimcia denied
herself and her little son, and with the meager food she
managed to obtain she fed her sick brother.

Vrumek had to be transferred to Aunt Esther's house, where
he could be hidden in the room behind the wardrobe to avoid
being deported in one of the continuing raids. Working at his
old job was no option, as several people were taken away in
one of the raids at Kleinecke's shop. When any of the Jews at
the shop reported to work in the morning, the Gestapo would
be waiting for them. They were deported without a chance to
notify their families. Another raid was directed against several
leaders of the Jewish community council who had ceased to be
useful to the Germans.

When Vrumek got well enough to leave his bed, he needed
a new job to earn some desperately needed rations. Any job
like Kleinecke's was too dangerous; we needed to find something safer through connections.

We knew a Mr. Nagoschiner, who was married to a niece of
Uncle Pinchas's; the couple had enjoyed their uncle's hospitality for quite some time. Mr. Nagoschiner suddenly became an
asset to his family when he was appointed as a replacement
member of the Judenrat, the Jewish community council. His
presence in the building did not prevent German raids, but a
cooperative Judenrat member had access to the authorities. He
was a source of firsthand news and could see to it that rations
of coal and other necessities were adequate.

Aunt Esther pleaded with Nagoschiner for a job for her
nephew Vrumek, and the only job available was that of local
militiaman. This unarmed Jewish police force worked under
the auspices of the Judenrat. Equipped with white armbands
and white hats with a blue stripe and a star of David, they were

engaged in keeping order in the Jewish quarter. They were responsible for directing traffic, supervising the food lines, and supervising labor details such as street cleaning, ditch digging, and snow shoveling. The task that Vrumek most dreaded was the service they had to render to the cruel German occupier: the Germans used the Jewish police to help in the raids that carried away the sick, the disabled, the old, and the frail.

It was well known that not all the public servants were equal in carrying out their masters' orders. There were officers of the Judenrat who opposed the vicious German edicts and paid with their own lives. On the other hand, there were those who eagerly cooperated with the enemy in their desperation for personal gain and personal survival. Similarly, some Jewish militiamen were merciful, devoted to easing the pain of their brethren and to trying to make their plight as bearable as possible. But there were those who actually aided the Germans at the expense of Jewish suffering. Vrumek was apprehensive about being branded a uniformed turncoat by his fellow Jews, and he refused to be a lackey for the authorities, but he understood that his own life was in danger while he was unemployed, and he was considered lucky to have Mr. Nagoschiner help him land such a job. The militiamen were nearly exempt from the danger of being shipped away to concentration camps, so Blimcia begged him to accept this job.

Among those shipped away were two prominent members of the Jewish community council, Bezalel Zucker and Mendel Nussbaum. They did not meekly succumb to the Germans, so they were packed away in cattle cars for processing. Soon after their deportation, their families received their ashes as a token from the Germans and a warning to any further Zuckers or Nussbaums who defied Aryan rule.

Vrumek did become a militiaman, promising himself never to use his position to unfair advantage. Vrumek would do his duty, but in his own way. Every morning the men would assemble at the Judenrat, where they were assigned the day's duties. Vrumek would select the more arduous ghetto assignments that involved physical labor, just to avoid tasks requiring cooperation with the Germans. For months he could proudly say that he had never yet helped the Germans in a raid. The chief of the militia knew by now not to insist, to allow Vrumek to serve on other duties. When the Gestapo came unexpectedly to headquarters to get help for an action, Vrumek would manage to slip out the back door. Since he was the latest addition to the force, still largely unknown, he managed to escape. Many times he would come running from the Judenrat, endangering his own life to alert targeted families about an upcoming raid. He would first help them hide and then go back to headquarters to snoop around. It was a sordid job full of tension and danger, yet outwitting and defying the enemy gave him a sense of dignity. Saving a fellow Chrzanower from deportation provided him with the encouragement of having won a small victory in this long, losing war.

Shortly after Vrumek's recovery from his dreadful illness, Sholek came home from the shop burning with fever and complaining of severe headaches. Blimcia gently put him to bed, applying her now familiar remedies of cool compresses and alcohol rubs. But Sholek's condition was getting worse instead of better. His temperature climbed higher. Cramps in his stomach caused him to shriek in agony; his diarrhea was uncontrollable. While Blimcia fought a losing battle, Sholek became delirious. Desperate and determined not to let Sholek die, she went to see Dr. Szymerowa, a Polish woman who knew Blimcia from Papa's store in prewar days. Blimcia had always attended to her with courtesy.

But now there was a dreadful war, and Dr. Szymerowa was Polish. Jews had no right to see a Polish doctor. Jews who were sick were considered parasites to be cleansed away by the German exterminator. Blimcia pleaded with the doctor to come see Sholek. Unwilling to take the risk, Dr. Szymerowa sent Blimcia away.

"You know I am unable to help you," she said unhappily. But Blimcia's tears and pleading aroused her mercy, and the doctor came. The diagnosis was typhoid. Shaken, Dr. Szymerowa pronounced that it was her duty to send Sholek to the hospital. Blimcia adamantly refused to let Dr. Szymerowa even report Sholek's illness. She knew it meant losing her brother for sure. Dr. Szymerowa finally agreed to Blimcia's request and slipped out of the house unnoticed. She reluctantly left Blimcia a prescription for medicine, having warned Blimcia how contagious typhoid is and how dangerous it was to her and her baby.

Once again the responsibility for the life of a family member rested on Blimcia's narrow shoulders. Sholek had spot typhoid, a most contagious variety that was transferable by mere contact. Sholek's bed took up one of the two rooms we now occupied on Zielona Street.

Surrounded by fields and meadows and with only one other house in the immediate area, Zielona Street was far removed from the center of town. It had not been the usual place for Jews to live before the war, being removed from Jewish institutions and houses of prayer and learning. During the war, however, when Jews were chased out of their houses in the center of town, they moved to whatever was available. Sometimes deep in snow or mud, it was not always easy to negotiate the unpaved road to Zielona Street. This was an advantage to the Jews now under siege. There were no other buildings to block the view of approaching Germans, and in the summer, when the wheat in the fields was high, the back yard would provide a hiding place during a raid. The remnants of the three Jewish families who lived in the house grew close from shared pain and persecution. They shared whatever scraps of food or information they had. There were also two Polish families living in the house; they pretended to be friendly, but we could not trust them.

Blimcia had to keep Sholek's disease secret from these neighbors. Protecting the baby, who at his tender age was prone to touching everything, was another battle. There was also the risk of Blimcia herself getting typhoid. She was tired, weak, and skinny, exposed to the contagious disease by her constant contact with Sholek. She boiled and sterilized all the utensils and carefully cleaned Sholek's bedpan, the most dangerous contaminant.

Blimcia never thought of the danger she was in, only of

Sholek's burning fever, parched mouth, aching body, and intestinal cramps. At tremendous risk, Blimcia managed to obtain medicine for Sholek. By the third week, Sholek's fever began to subside. Gradually his fever lessened and his appetite grew. Blimcia concocted soups and cereals, saving every scrap of food for Sholek. Slowly Sholek regained his strength and was able to leave his bed for short periods. Sholek had wrestled with the Angel of Death and survived—thanks to his sister, an angel of mercy.

When he eventually returned to work, Sholek's coworkers helped him make a new beginning. But Sholek was not the same. His body was weak, his spirit low. There were no more songs or jokes. Lively Sholek had finally fallen prey to the most contagious disease of the ghetto—despair.

Chapter 13

When the Germans demanded female volunteers for their concentration camps, Nachcia registered to save our parents from punitive deportations. In the early morning, frightened Nachcia presented herself in the marketplace at the appointed location, with Mama scurrying behind her. Soon the girls were marched down to the railroad station, loaded into trains, and shipped away. Their hometown, which most of them had never before left, slowly disappeared on the horizon.

They huddled together for days in closed boxcars and were finally brought into Gabersdorf, a camp in the Sudetenland, which was now occupied by the Germans. A bitter life of hard factory labor, dawn to dusk, began for the girls. These young girls from warm and loving homes were suddenly thrown into the hell of forced labor, starvation, bitter cold, disease, loneliness, and longing. The meager food supplies they brought with them from home were soon gone, and mail was as rare as a second helping of watery soup. Nachcia did get a letter from Mama telling her about Sholek's disability and return from the labor camp. Nachcia's delicate health and terrible homesickness made her determined to find a way to return home.

Word of mouth had it that the Germans needed and used only healthy, productive workers; it was rumored that others would be sent home, as the Germans did not intend to feed lazy Jewish parasites. Nachcia, then, deliberately presented herself as weak and unable to conform to the hard labor and difficult schedule. She voiced complaints about not being able to see well enough to perform her duties. The Germans at first turned a deaf ear to her pleas, but one dreary morning, Nachcia and two other girls were suddenly called into the Gestapo office. They were instructed to return within half an hour with their few possessions in bundles. No explanations whatsoever accompanied the order. Nachcia's heart pounded with fear. There was excitement, too, promoted by the envious chatter of the inmates: "You are so lucky to be going home." "Give regards to my family, tell them I am all right."

"Who knows where they are really sending me?" Nachcia responded suspiciously. "How I hope you are right! If I get back to our town, I will visit every single family and tell them all about you here. I will tell them not to worry, that you are well and will survive."

Tense and apprehensive, the three girls were marched under SS escort to the railroad station. Hours of exhausting waiting followed, which the girls spent speculating about their fate. Eventually they were loaded into the train, guarded as though they were dangerous prisoners. They could not sleep that night as the cold-blooded German guard, relishing their fear, told them their destination was the dreaded Auschwitz.

Nachcia's thoughts were morbid and remorseful. Why did I complain? she asked herself. Here at least I was together with friendly girls from my hometown. Who knows what awaits us in Auschwitz?

Auschwitz was the former town of Oswiecim, where Great-aunt Channa's daughter had lived. It was not all that far from Chrzanow, but that did not make the camp any less threatening and foreboding now.

"Who knows what the conditions in Auschwitz are like? The rumors from there are horrible. And to be among strangers gives me the creeps," Nachcia whispered to her companions.

"What if the Germans are not even taking us to Auschwitz, but intend to kill us here and now?" rasped her friend in panic.

Nachcia felt a choking in her throat as she thought of Mama and Papa getting the usual message that their daughter perished after contracting a contagious disease. She ached for her parents' grief more than she feared her own death.

They strained their eyes to recognize their surroundings. Before dawn the sadistic German assured them they were nearing Auschwitz. With the first blast of the train's whistle, they recognized the station. They were in Chrzanow.

They were free, they were home. Stunned and overwhelmed, the girls stood at the railroad station of their hometown. Like a runner on the home stretch, Nachcia ran all the way to our new address, not stopping to talk to anyone. She thought only of embracing Mama and Papa, feeling them near, pouring out to them all the accumulated suffering and longing of her months of incarceration. She yearned for her mother's comfort like a girl half her age.

She quickly tiptoed up the steps and knocked on the door. Blimcia had gone to work, leaving me in charge of Aiziu and the household. I was down on my hands and knees scrubbing the wooden floor. While I cleaned and cared for the baby, my first attempt at baking a loaf of bread was in the oven. It was a miserable loaf made of inadequate, illegal ingredients. I was therefore startled and frightened by the knock on the door. The baby burst out crying, and I knocked the bucket over when I ran to open the door. Shocked out of my wits, I saw Nachcia standing in the doorway. I knew Nachcia had been in a concentration camp, so I thought it impossible that she was here.

I stood there speechless while the ghost of Nachcia grabbed me and called, "Mama, Mama, I'm home!"

When no answer came, she pulled away and looked sternly into my eyes. "Where is Mama?" she almost screamed. She shook me by the shoulders and demanded, "Where is Mama?"

I broke into tears, my whole body shaking. After a while I broke the news to her, as we sat on the floor, the way Jews mourn the destruction of the holy Temple. We cuddled Aiziu between us, lamenting the loss of our parents. Sprawled on the floor, we cried our hearts out over our bitter fate. When Blimcia returned home our emotional outburst was repeated.

For days Nachcia walked around in a daze, unable to accept the reality that she was not likely to see her mama and papa again. With her head bowed low, she would murmur, "What good is it being home now that there is no home." Nachcia was oblivious to all but her grief. I had to push her to take on her old household duties.

Winter was approaching quickly. There was not enough coal to keep a fire going. Just when I finally learned to knead bread, there was no more illegal flour to make it with. Other food supplies were scarce at best. Our family was so much smaller now, but there was still not enough food to go around. Jacob tried his best to use his connections to the Gentile population, but contacts were increasingly difficult. The rations were meager and unsatisfying. The work was exhausting, and the German decrees, ordinances, and raids were unending. Uncertainty and fear were our only constants.

The two rooms we occupied on Zielona Street offered no protection in a raid. We spent many hours with our Jewish neighbors trying to find a place to hide. The only possibility was the attic of the building, which was merely a shallow cavity between the roof and the ceiling. The access was a trapdoor in the second-floor hallway between our door and the door of one of our Gentile neighbors. In the attic, there was barely room enough to crawl, even in the middle of the house, where the roof came to its apex. The fellows brought a ladder up the hallway and checked the place out. It was full of cobwebs and bugs. The hallway was small, and there was no way to hide from the Gentile Madeia family when climbing up there. We knew the Gentiles could not be trusted, and we didn't expect any help from them. We could only hope they had enough decency to keep silent during a crisis. On one occasion I heard Jacob and Vrumek whisper that they hoped we would never have to resort to the attic bunker, for they could not imagine how the women would be able to climb up there. The ladder was shaky, and the space under the roof suffocatingly tight. The chances of survival in that place, even if we managed to get up there, seemed slim.

By this time the winter was in full swing and the snow piled up and got stomped down to a crusty, icy sheet. The days were short and the long evenings of curfew unbearable. There was no place to move around in the apartment, and everyone was restless. Came February and I remembered our preparations for Pesach. How fond I was of those times when I would sit and watch Mama prepare the big jugs of Passover wine that she made from raisins. The borscht would ferment for months until the holiday, and the accumulated chicken fat would be set aside for holiday use. Right now nobody thought about the holiday; there was only the present. Where would our next meal come from? What would the next knock on the door bring?

It was February 18. Vrumek reported to duty early in the morning but came back after a short while. We knew there was trouble.

"I did not like what I saw at the headquarters of the Jewish community council," he stated briefly. "There was a lot of commotion. I was sent to call other militiamen to duty. It gave me an opportunity to come home. Something is brewing. I do not know what, but it looks like a major action. I must go back."

Vrumek's face looked grim. We knew what we must do. Quietly we knocked on the doors of our two Jewish neighbors. Mrs. Lieblich commented how lucky we all were to have Vrumek right there at the Jewish community council, where he could smell trouble.

Meanwhile, agile Sholek climbed up and opened the trap-door to the attic. With Jacob helping him, he pulled down the hidden ladder. Hastily yet gingerly, everybody scrambled to the second floor. The men helped the women climb the shaky ladder. We were afraid to utter a word lest the neighboring Madeia family hear us. We hoped they were still sleeping. Sholek, who had helped everybody, did not climb up.

"Why aren't you coming?" Blimcia asked when he pushed the ladder back up.

"No, Blimcia, I am not coming up there. I cannot be con-fined like that. I will run."

Blimcia looked at him sadly. We knew exactly what Blimcia was thinking, but no one dared even to say good-bye. We all knew how unsafe this hole was, but we also knew there was no alternative. Where could we hide? How could we run? And Blimcia with a baby in her arms.

"Go, Sholek," she whispered, "and may God protect you."

We were all praying for Sholek, hoping he could find a place to hide. Then we saw Sholek was not alone. Little Iziek Lie-blich stubbornly declared that he was going with Sholek. Iziek was hardly fifteen, a smart, stocky but agile little boy who had always looked up to Sholek. Sholek closed the trapdoor se-curely and vanished.

In the dirt and cobwebs of the attic, we sat bent over or crouched. We became numb with pain, for there was no room to straighten our legs as the hours ticked away. Tiny, fright-ened baby Aiziu whimpered from time to time but knew enough not to talk or cough or make any noise. The dust choked our lungs, and it was hard to breathe. Time seemed to stand still, as if we had been there for an eternity. Suddenly, we heard voices from downstairs.

"Neighbors, open up. Don't be afraid. It is me, Palkowa."

Our Polish neighbor had discovered us. Full of fear and distrust, we waited in silence, hoping she would go away.

"Don't be afraid. I only want to help. I brought you some water. You cannot stay up there so long without water."

Reluctantly, Jacob pulled the trapdoor open. Mrs. Palkowa handed him a jug and a cup. "Don't be afraid," she repeated.

"Is there anything else I can do for you? Maybe some food?"

"Thank you very much, Mrs. Palkowa," Jacob answered. "It is very kind of you to think about us."

"Oh, what are neighbors for? I will make sure the trapdoor is closed properly," she responded in a concerned voice.

Jacob distributed the water, which we thirstily drank. We blessed Mrs. Palkowa, who proved that some of our Polish neighbors still had some human decency.

We lay there mute and motionless for a while when suddenly we heard them coming. First came the loud German voices, then the stomping of their boots on the steps. Next came the violent rapping on the doors downstairs. We lay still, fear piercing to the marrow of our bones. Even baby Aiziu seemed to hold his breath. We heard them kick the door open downstairs, yelling and ranting; then we heard them come upstairs, our beating hearts echoing each footstep. There was no knocking on the door upstairs—they came directly to our trapdoor. Aghast we saw the trapdoor burst open, beaten in with rifle butts, and the yelling deafened our ears.

"You damn Jew bastards! Get down out of there, you Jew swine!"

With shaking hands Jacob lowered the ladder and, one by one, helped us all down. The enraged, impatient Germans were shoving us off the ladder to the constant shrieking of *"Schnell, schnell! Raus, raus!"*

When Nachcia tried to help baby-laden Blimcia down the ladder, a German slapped her to the ground and flung her down the stairs. Scrambling down the narrow stairs, we were chased out into the street. The icy wind made our eyes tear. We joined the Jews from the neighboring building, who were already there stamping their frozen feet. From these people we learned that it was Mrs. Palkowa who pointed out to the Germans exactly where we were hiding.

Now we understood why our neighbor had been so kind with the water: she wanted to confirm her information, for if she misled the Germans, she would get into trouble herself. That was why the Germans did not even knock on the upstairs door, but went directly to our concealed trapdoor. They might not have found it if it weren't for the help of our trustworthy Polish neighbor.

Through the frozen mud we marched, shivering in our inadequate clothes. In the marketplace we were assembled with a multitude of people. Selections were taking place, and we stood for hours. Nachcia held on to my hand when we marched through the row of SS men.

"How old are you?" I was asked.

"Sixteen," I answered, straining on tiptoe to look taller and older than my fourteen years.

The German hesitated for a moment and then pronounced the verdict: "Right!" Nachcia followed me closely.

Behind us was Blimcia, with Aiziu in her arms. "Left!" he ordered, and Blimcia disappeared among the thousands of weaker people, women with children, and older folks. Nachcia became frenzied, knowing it was not good to be sent where Blimcia had been ordered to go. But we could do nothing. We had also lost sight of Jacob, and we did not know what had happened to Vrumek, or to Sholek.

The Nazis had their bayonets raised high, as if ready for a savage battle charge. The two-legged German shepherds were pushing around thousands of innocent, helpless people. Women and children were being dragged from their husbands and fathers. There were loud cries and broken sobs from the newly bereaved of all ages. The selecting and counting did not stop until late afternoon. The Stapler clan seemed reduced to two, Nachcia holding on to me for dear life. We were then marched to the railroad station and loaded into cattle cars for a long journey.

Our precious, fiercely loyal older sister Blimcia, with her cherubic baby Aiziu, was deported on February 18, 1943, in the action that finally made Chrzanow *Judenrein,* Jew free. The town of Chrzanow once counted over twenty thousand Jewish souls comprising more than fifty percent of the total population. Thus was carried out the final solution to the Jewish problem in the town of Chrzanow, where Jews had resided since the sixteenth century. Here they perpetuated the Jewish way of life while being dedicated citizens of their country. They served kings, petty princes, and elected officials. They served in the Polish army, paid taxes, and labored productively. Now, the only Jews left were the Jewish dead.

Chapter 14

After Sholek had helped the women up the attic ladder that fateful morning, his heart was bursting with bitterness. He burned for the chance to fight for his life. Seventeen years old, eager to live, he could not bring himself to crawl into that grave under the roof to suffocate there like a hunted animal. He was ready to run, to fight.

With his neighbor Iziek behind him, he first thought of running towards the city to Aunt Esther's. But it was too late. From afar Sholek could see the approaching Germans, their rifles at the ready against unarmed Jewish women and children. He was bitter and furious, but if he wanted to survive, he had to hide fast. Seeing the Germans in front of the house, he grabbed Iziek and ducked behind the building, where they disappeared into the fields. From behind a high stack of dead weeds, Sholek saw the soldiers enter the house.

He lay there near Iziek on the cold ground, shivering, praying for the safety of his family.

Sholek's prayers were not answered. He saw the Nazis drag all the people out of the house. He could see that Blimcia, Jacob, Aiziu, Nachcia, and I were all caught. Hot tears rolled down his frozen face. He felt alone and forsaken, lying there with only young Iziek as his companion. Now they were orphans. They saw the Germans march their families away. They heard the last echoes of the cries and sobs, and then all fell quiet, quiet as a cemetery. They were afraid to raise their heads or get up until the SS pulled out and the action was completely over.

They waited until nightfall, and under cover of darkness they ventured quietly back into the silent house. Sholek tiptoed up to the second floor and saw a strip of heavy tape across the door. On it was stamped JUDENREIN. Sholek was afraid to tear open the seal. If the Germans were to come back, they would know immediately that someone was at large, and they would hunt him down. He and Iziek went back to the fields, feeling disconsolate. The night grew ever colder. Their limbs felt numb and stiff. Little Iziek whimpered and kept asking Sholek what they were to do.

"We are going to wait until the Madeias and Palkas go to sleep, and then we will go back to the house," Sholek responded decisively. He was wary of the Polish neighbors, suspecting that they might have turned over his family and the Lieblichs to the SS. When no more lights flickered in the house, Sholek nudged his sleeping friend. Quietly they stole back into the house.

Vrumek reported back to duty at the headquarters of the Jewish community council, where he was subsequently assigned to the Jewish hospital. He was to make sure that no one entered or left the building. Hearing that, Vrumek understood that the hospital was going to be evacuated. He couldn't stand idly by and let helpless people be victimized, and he could not help the German enemy carry out these bestial, murderous acts. He had always managed to escape these dirty jobs before, and he was not about to aid Nazi terror now. For a short time he was the only militiaman in the hospital. He noticed that some of the patients were able to walk on their own. He went over to them and quietly whispered, "There is going to be a major action. If you are at all able to get dressed and get out of here, escape now and save yourselves."

Vrumek did not know what to anticipate, but word spread quickly.

"You are a young hothead," one man said angrily to Vrumek. "You do not realize what you are doing by spreading panic among sick, helpless people. Did you take into account that most of the patients couldn't make it very far?"

"But maybe some will make it," Vrumek answered, convinced that he was right in trying to help the people who might be able to save themselves.

The Germans might even be looking for the renegade policeman who had spread the word and allowed people to escape. Vrumek therefore went through all the rooms and floors, checking all entrances and exits for an escape route. When he heard the Germans coming, he fled to the roof, where he found a tiny laundry room. He buried himself in the dirty laundry and waited. In the commotion that followed, no one noticed him missing.

The Germans employed the Jewish policemen to carry all the patients out into waiting trucks. When it finally got quiet, Vrumek was apprehensive. He knew that if he were discovered, he'd be shot. From his hiding place on the roof, he observed the Germans marching more and more people to the marketplace. Waiting for darkness, Vrumek removed his hat and armband and sped home. He ran through the dark fields, circumventing the city to get to Zielona Street safely. He sneaked into the house, avoiding the Palkas on the ground floor, and scrambled up the stairs. There he was suddenly surprised by the upstairs neighbor, Mr. Madeia. Vrumek stopped in his tracks. At the same time he noticed the fateful seal on the door. He started mumbling an explanation when Mr. Madeia spoke up.

"Mr. Vrumek, you are still here? They took them all out from up there. There is no one left, only Sholek. He was here before. He thought I didn't see him, but I did. I saw him flee from the house."

"When was that?" Vrumek asked.

"Oh, just a short while ago."

"Where did he go?" Vrumek asked eagerly.

"Why, I have no idea," the Pole said in an even, matter-of-fact tone.

Vrumek was shocked and distraught at finding out that he had lost his entire family to the SS purge. With the seal on the apartment and Madeia having seen him here, their home was as good as burnt down. He would have to run and somehow find Sholek. He could not tamper with the seal now, in Madeia's presence. The Pole would probably run for the Germans or accuse Vrumek of endangering his life.

"Thank you, Mr. Madeia," Vrumek managed to say at last. "If you see Sholek again, please tell him that I was here and I will return."

He only risked this statement because he was so desperate to find Sholek. He quickly left the house, then circled around it, hoping to find some solution to his dilemma. He waited for all the lights to go out and then went back into the house. Quietly, he felt his way up the steps in the dark.

Suddenly he thought he heard someone. He paused and listened, wary of Madeia catching him again in the hallway. Coming closer, he could hear someone tampering with the seal upstairs. It was probably Madeia trying to loot his Jewish neighbors' apartment; the Polish vultures always followed the German jackals.

He stood very still, straining his eyes in the dark. No, the figure was too slender to be Madeia. "Sholek," Vrumek whispered.

Sholek spun around sharply. Instantly the two brothers were in each others' arms. Together they opened the seal, only a few feet away from their neighbor Madeia.

Once inside they recounted the day's events and the pros-
pects for escape. They came to the conclusion that Chrzanow
was now *Judenrein,* leaving them like two survivors of a ship-
wreck in a shark-infested sea. They had to flee Chrzanow.
They prayed and thanked the Almighty that at least they had
each other.

"This might be the last time we will be able to pray," Vrumek said, "so let us pray with all our might. We will get some
rest here and leave before dawn."

"You sleep, Vrumek, and I will watch," Sholek offered,
scared that they might be caught in their own house by the
Germans or the neighbors.

Vrumek reassured Sholek that the action was hardly over.
"This is the first night, and the Germans are still busy with
people at the railroad station. And Madeia will probably want
to be sure that the Germans are not coming back before he
comes looting. So it is safe for us here tonight, safer than
elsewhere."

Unbelievably tense and tired, they slept fitfully, rising before
dawn. They picked out some warm clothes, took whatever
money was left in the house, and stole out. Wearing their caps
low over their eyes, they took to the fields and began walking
away from town.

"There is only one place we can go," Vrumek said. "To
Sosnowiec. There are still Jews there." In the predawn darkness, Sholek and Vrumek said good-bye to Chrzanow, the
town where they had been born and raised. The brothers felt
the history of the moment, the finality of this departure and
the additional sorrow of giving up young Iziek, who was nowhere to be found.

They fled without looking back, like Lot leaving Sodom and
Gomorrah; they were afraid they would see the German beasts
following them, like Pharaoh's soldiers pursuing the Hebrews
into the Red Sea. Walking through the fields and back roads,
they hid in ditches when they spotted Germans. They carried
no documents; they would try to pass as Gentiles if caught.

Two little passport photos of Mama and Papa were hidden
in Vrumek's shoe. He did not tell Sholek about the pictures,

not wanting to burden Sholek with his morbid fears, but he could not leave the house without these mementos. He could not even take the smallest prayer book with him, but at least he had saved his parents' pictures. Vrumek felt that Mama and Papa were with him in some way, and that the two brothers should survive for their parents' sake.

In the late morning they reached the city of Sosnowiec and headed straight for the ghetto. Sosnowiec was a much larger town than Chrzanow, and a stranger could get lost in the crowd. But the brothers still had to find a place to stay. They had no friends or relatives in this large city; the only living contacts that could be of any help were the girls who used to shop from Papa at the beginning of the war. Without their addresses, though, Vrumek and Sholek had absolutely no idea where to find them. Besides, they might all have been deported by now.

Finding the Jewish community council was their next step. At least it had a kitchen where the brothers could get something hot to eat. Depressed, subdued, and drained, they were sitting on a bench, lingering over bowls of hot soup, when a man came over to them.

"Aren't you from Chrzanow?" he asked.

"Yes, we are," they answered eagerly. "We are the sons of Reb Symche Stapler from the fruit and delicatessen store on Mickiewicza Street. Are you from Chrzanow, too?" Vrumek asked.

"Yes, I am a Chrzanower. My name is Aharon Schlanger. My wife was from here, but she has been deported, and I am staying with my mother-in-law."

"Maybe your mother-in-law will let us sleep over a night or two until we find a place to stay. We don't know anyone in this city, and we just arrived."

"My mother-in-law is no bargain, but I will try. Come with me," Aharon Schlanger said.

Aharon had come to the committee house to search for anyone from his own family in Chrzanow. Instead, he found two Stapler brothers. Not that he was thrilled with them, but it felt good to have someone around from the same town. They had so many people and places in common.

Upon seeing the two strangers, Aharon's mother-in-law immediately opened with a litany of complaints. "What did you bring me here? Two more mouths to feed? Where am I supposed to put them? There is hardly room for you here, *shlimazel* [one plagued by bad luck]. Who asked you to do *mitzvos* [good deeds] and bring strangers into the house? Do you think these are normal times?"

She didn't throw them out, though. Reluctantly, she allowed them a corner to sleep in. Now that they had a roof over their heads, they kept on searching for their family and inquiring about the transports from Chrzanow. Every day they frequented the Jewish community council house to discover what information was available.

There was a transit camp in Sosnowiec where deportees were brought from the neighboring towns to be reselected. Vrumek, risking his life, snooped around the camp. He noticed two distraught girls running away. He followed them and discovered that they were escapees from the transit camp. From them he learned about a transport of girls from his hometown that had arrived in the transit camp on the day of the Chrzanow selection. They knew of another girl from Chrzanow who had escaped. Pursuing this lead, Vrumek found her and learned that Nachcia and I had come through the transit camp. This is how he gathered that Nachcia and I had been sent to a concentration camp. Vrumek and Sholek now knew that their family had been abducted straight from the attic hiding place with only the clothes on their backs in this bone-chilling winter. With all of their own problems, the brothers considered ways to send us some clothes and food.

Vrumek and Sholek were guests in a stranger's crowded apartment. They possessed no money or food and only one change of clothes for themselves. Still, Vrumek felt he was free, while we were not. His goals were to find out where we were and how to get some food and clothing to us. It was an enormous task, and being a stranger in the city hampered his movements. People were constantly being deported, and actions against the Jews in Sosnowiec went on. With the resourceful Sholek at his side, Vrumek scavenged the apartments of people who had been deported. In one of the abandoned apartments, they found enough women's clothes to warrant a package. With hearts aching that they could not enclose any food, they brought the package to the post office and mailed it to the concentration camp of Langenbielau, addressed to Nachcia Stapler. While they doubted whether their sisters would ever receive it, the mere thought that it might reach some family members was heartening.

Some more dispossessed relatives moved into their host's apartment. Since Aharon had claimed Vrumek as his friend and was willing to share his cot with him, Vrumek stayed on; Sholek, though, had to leave.

In the brothers' desperate search for a place, they tried an aunt's brother-in-law who lived in Bendzin, the next city. Sholek succeeded in winning a roof over his head there, while Vrumek went back to Sosnowiec. For a whole week Vrumek was out of touch with Sholek, but Sholek was able to assure him that he was with friendly people in a house with a good hiding place.

Where Vrumek was staying the household was able to hide in a spare room with a wardrobe concealing the door, much like the setup in Aunt Esther's Chrzanow apartment. With all the women and children in the family, however, Vrumek felt very unsafe in that hiding place. Throughout his stay he searched for a place where the cry of a child or the nose of a German shepherd would not cost him his life.

Vrumek dug a hole in the backyard outhouse, deep in the ground below the waste receptacle. He meticulously covered the hole with a board that had soil and growing weeds on it. He told no one about this new hiding place. Soon the SS staged a major action, and the Jews scurried for their bunkers.

"Where are you going?" Aharon asked.

"I have a better hiding place," Vrumek answered. "Stick with me, Aharon, we have a better chance to survive by ourselves. We are young. We can make it. We will live."

Aharon was tempted to leave the family, but his mother-in-law scolded him for listening to a young hothead.

"You are a married man, Aharon. You should have more sense. This is a good hiding place. Where is he going to schlepp you? Out in the open, where the Germans will smell you out with their dogs? Leave him alone. Let him go where he wants. You come with us. You are my son-in-law. You better listen to me, an older and wiser person, not to this youngster."

But Schlanger was not convinced; his impulse told him to go with Vrumek. They lowered themselves into the hole. In the grave-size bunker they could only crouch close beside each other. Vrumek carefully dragged the board over them from the inside, first making sure that enough earth covered it. As they crouched together in that tomb in the cold moist earth, they heard the Germans come into the house. Everyone was flushed out amid the all too familiar shouting and screaming. The barking dogs and the shrill cries of the women and children sent streams of cold sweat down their backs. The hours went on and the night fell. Some shooting was heard and then it was quiet, but the living corpses didn't dare move from their grave.

The next day the Germans came again, searching with a pack of barking dogs. Once again the two men in the hole heard the Germans chase some people out, throwing them into the trucks amid screams and weeping. Their muscles became stiff and their bodies ached. Minutes turned into hours, and once more night fell. They still did not dare move.

Vrumek meekly whispered to Aharon, "Try to wriggle your toes and fingers; flex your muscles to exercise them. We cannot afford to become paralyzed."

"What is the use?" Aharon retorted. "We will never get out alive anyway. I should have stayed with my mother-in-law. What are our lives worth anyway, with everybody gone?"

"No, Aharon, we must live. They will never find us here," Vrumek said enthusiastically. "Out there it is all over. Here we still have a chance. We still have our freedom. Just keep exercising those muscles like I tell you. When we get out of here, you will thank me."

Numb and weakened by hunger, they often slept. They were awakened occasionally by shouts and loud announcements from the Germans' bullhorns: "All you Jews in hiding, come out. You will not be punished. You will be relocated together with all the others. You will be given work and the opportunity to earn your food. Here you will die in your bunkers and holes. Come out. Save yourselves. This is your last chance. Come out now, and we will not punish you. If you stay hidden, we will flush you out with gas."

All day long the bullhorns blasted proclamations, promises, threats, and more promises. Day and night blurred together for the hunted pair in their hole.

The sound of the Germans would fade away in the distance and then again come close, their heavy boots marching. Suddenly, they felt someone approaching, heading right for them. They thought this was it. They heard the door of the outhouse open and someone come inside. They could hear him relieve himself in the receptacle that was just above them. Only when the German finished and left were they able to breathe again. The outhouse odors that kept the dogs from smelling them out also kept their meager air supply stagnant and rancid. Their lungs craved air, their stomachs food, and their muscles space. It was the fourth day since they had entered their tiny underground bunker. This brutal ransacking of the Jewish ghetto outdid all the previous raids, and the lengthy action prolonged the misery of these two stubborn Jews who would not surrender.

The Fisher family of Bendzin saw in Sholek a link to their lost Chrzanow family. Crowded into their own ghetto apartment, the Fishers found room in their hearts and home for one more person. Sholek slept on the floor in a corner. All day long he hunted for food, which he generously shared. There were two other strangers in the Fisher household, two sisters who had also escaped from Chrzanow. Posing as Gentiles, which was much more easily accomplished by females, the two sisters had managed to reach the city of Bendzin and find refuge in the Fisher household. Sholek wished his older brother Vrumek were with him, as they had a safe bunker in the basement, where a foolproof double wall had been built.

Only two weeks after Sholek's arrival at the Fisher household, there was a Nazi raid. They hastily abandoned the apartment and scrambled into the basement. While they were already somewhat accustomed to the wretched life of hunted people, the raids always caught them unprepared. In the dark, windowless bunker, where air seeped through crevices created in the brick wall, they sat huddled together waiting for the action to be over. Muffled sounds reached them from the outside, so they knew the raid was still in progress. Losing count of the hours, degraded by their lack of toilet facilities, they sustained their dignity and courage with talk of life after the war.

Sholek, the youngest member of the crowd, suffered most from hunger and dizziness, but the fiercest agony was the lack of water. With his mouth too dry to wet his lips, Sholek voiced his intention of going out. It had been three days now that they'd been entombed in the bunker, unable to know what was going on outside. The nights were quiet now, although the days still offered the muffled sounds of shouts and shooting. The Fishers tried to convince Sholek to stay put. The two sisters cried and begged him to hold out. But Sholek felt his body becoming weak, dying a slow death of starvation and thirst. It was against his nature to let death come this way, to succumb without resistance, without a fight.

"Maybe I have a chance," he said. "Maybe I will be lucky. I am young. They will take me to a concentration camp. I will survive. Here I will perish for sure. Another day or so, and we will all be dead."

Sholek was also worried about Vrumek. Maybe they would meet again in a concentration camp. He wanted to try. He wanted to live.

On the fourth day of their incarceration in the dark basement bunker, Sholek removed the secret entranceway bricks and crawled out. With all his remaining strength he meticulously sealed the exit behind him. He put his hands high over his head to show any soldiers that he was surrendering. In the basement the hushed group listened attentively. Instead of the usual muffled sound of gunfire came a distinct, loud bang from close range. Brave, young Sholek met his vile enemy eye to eye but was given no chance. His last thoughts would never be known.

Chapter 15

Like corpses emerging from a grave, Aharon and Vrumek painfully dragged themselves from beneath the outhouse. They had passed much of the time in an unconscious state close to death. They struggled to regain the use of their minds and bodies.

Vrumek was twenty-one years old when, on the seventh day, he emerged alive from that hole in Sosnowiec. His stomach had never been as empty as it was then, his mind never so disoriented. His companion, Aharon, an older man, was hardly any support, but still Vrumek was happy to have the company. Their caps low on their foreheads to shade their hollow eyes and unshaven faces, they began to walk.

"Where are we going?" Aharon asked.

"Back to Chrzanow," was the response. Vrumek felt it was the only place in which they had a chance to survive. It was where he grew up: maybe someone who knew him would help. Afraid to walk through Sosnowiec, they made their way on side roads and through fields. When they could, they stole fruit from trees and dug vegetables from the ground. It felt so good to have something in their mouths that even raw vegetables were delicacies. Before nightfall they were on the outskirts of Chrzanow. Aharon was ready to collapse; they had to find a place to sleep, to hide. In the woods near Chrzanow they found an old tree with a hollow trunk. There was room enough to accommodate them both.

They gathered branches to cover themselves and slept there through the night. In the morning they decided to go into town, but they badly needed a shave first. They could not afford to look like refugees. Not daring to show their faces in neighborhoods where they might be recognized, they went to the Planty, where the Jews had been chased out long ago. There was now a new barber on the Planty, a *Volksdeutsch,* a Pole who sympathized with the Germans. Such a man was an agent for the Nazis, supplying information on dissidents for extra food and supplies. Vrumek decided that this fellow would be their barber. If asked questions, they would pretend to be out-of-towners working in Chrzanow.

Silently suffering from fear and stomach cramps, they sat patiently at the barber's, listening to his chatter and to the news on the radio.

"The last Jewish pigs have been cleared out from Sosnowiec and Bendzin," the announcer crowed, "making these regions *Judenrein* as well."

Now the pair knew they had absolutely nowhere to turn and that no one but the Almighty could help them.

But Vrumek was far from ready to give up. They bought some bread and a bottle of black coffee, which they stuck in their pocket in the manner of Polish workers. At night they went back into the woods; by day they hung around the train yard and searched for food in the fields and the forest. On one of their excursions into town Vrumek suddenly met a fellow student from his old school. He knew the goy to be an intense anti-Semite, so he quickly tried to disappear, but the Pole followed Vrumek and grabbed hold of him.

"What are you doing here, Stapler?"

Unable to get away, Vrumek tried to lead him further out of town so that he could kill him with his bare hands, if it became necessary. Vrumek kept talking to the Pole about making him rich. Vrumek whispered that he would pay an exorbitant price for documents that would identify him as Polish and told his schoolmate that he would meet him at the same spot the next day to consummate the deal. Thanks to the Almighty and to the anti-Semitic notion that even the most desperate-looking Jew has access to great riches, the Pole fell for the ruse and let Vrumek go with a promise on his lips and a gleam in his eye. Vrumek knew that the goy was planning to take the money and then turn them in.

They had escaped the immediate danger, but they knew that when Vrumek was unable to pay him, the disappointed Pole would surely alert the authorities about the existence of two renegade Jews. They stayed in the woods most of the time, and survival got that much harder. They still used the same barber, but they could not risk going to a public bath, where their Jewishness would be immediately discovered. They had to bathe in a nearby brook, even though the water was very cold in late October.

The pair had been in the woods for almost two months when they chanced upon an abandoned, burnt-out house. They sealed the entrance with bricks and made their home in the basement. They would occasionally go into town to a small restaurant to buy some bread or hot soup, risking their lives. An old lady there would sometimes sell them some black coffee, but their money was running low, and danger loomed everywhere. One evening the lady told them not to come around anymore. They couldn't figure out how she'd discovered they were Jewish, but they were grateful that she didn't bring the Germans after them.

They went back to the woods, desperately trying to think of a way to survive. With hunger and fear tearing at them, they were lying quietly in their shelter when they suddenly heard footsteps. The steps were so quiet they never had a chance to escape. They felt trapped when the intruder entered the basement and lit a match. They couldn't see the person, but suddenly they heard a voice.

"*Yidn?* Jews? I am also a Jew."

The stranger had instantly realized that they were Jews in hiding. After the initial scare, they fell upon each other with hugs of shared suffering. The man had a young boy with him, his son. In whispers they recounted their awful story and were astonished to hear of Vrumek and Aharon's prolonged survival in the woods. The father and son had been thrown out from the home of a Gentile, who had hidden them for as long as they had money to offer. The man told Vrumek and Aharon to try to get out of Poland, to head for Czechoslovakia and then Hungary. As long as they were not interned in a concentration camp they must try to move beyond the German advance.

That night they once again heard footsteps, but this was the heavy tread of German jackboots. Vrumek and Aharon jumped out of the shelter and ran away into the thick forest. They could not see whether the man and his child tried to run too; all they knew was that they could not come back to that hiding place again. The Germans had tracked them there. They never got the name of the man who so briefly stayed with them, but to them he was a godsend, like Elijah the Prophet. He opened their eyes to their goal—to run westward to freedom. They presumed the man and his son were caught, because they heard the Germans yelling and their dogs barking. Once again the two fugitives started off on a journey to the unknown.

It was almost the end of November, and quite cold. Summoning their reserves of strength and willpower, they walked all night and slept during the day, hidden in fields, abandoned buildings, or deep within haystacks. They dug up potatoes and ate them raw, but sometimes they had to settle for bits of grass or garbage. Occasionally they stopped in small-town railroad stations to consult a train map; this was their only way of making sure that they were heading in the right direction.

When they encountered freedom fighters or partisans they asked if they could join. Invariably, a Polish anti-Semite among them would suspect the two fugitives of being Jews and would not let them share the partisan cause, nor their bread. With no money or weapons to offer them, Vrumek and Aharon would be chased away by the partisan bands.

They pushed on, their isolation weakening their spirits as their hunger weakened their bodies. Eventually they reached the small town of Zwardon on the Czechoslovakian border. The town was teeming with Germans, making the chances of escape across the border quite slim. Again they turned to the fields, lying low, hugging the frozen earth and observing the movements of the border patrol. The night was dreary; a cold rain soaked them to the bone. The two units of the patrol were moving a couple of hundred yards in each direction. When the soldiers were at a fairly safe distance, Vrumek and Aharon made their move. Crouching low to the ground, they ran to the border fence and crawled under the barbed wire. Catching their breath, they waited for it to be safe to get up off the ground and ran on as fast as they could, to get away from the troop-infested border. They were one country away from Hungary and freedom and already had hopes that the Czechs would be less hostile to them than the Poles had been.

By the time the sky was graying with dawn, they were approaching a town. Now they were faced with a new predicament: they did not have any Czech money, did not speak Czech, and did not even know how to look Czech. Luckily they could understand some of the language, as Polish and Czech are both Slavic. They risked going into a train station, and tried to buy tickets by pronouncing only the name of the town they wanted to get to. Vrumek pulled out his largest bill, but the conductor asked him a question that he did not understand. Vrumek pulled out other banknotes, but this made the conductor angry. A crowd began to gather, and the two refugees had to slip away before they attracted the attention of a German official.

There was no forest in which to hide. There was no place to stay, and so the only alternative was to move on toward Hungary, which was not occupied by the Germans. They traveled on back roads, occasionally getting a lift on a farmer's wagon. Soon they reached a river—with a bridge full of Germans. The water was deep and icy cold. For hours they searched for a way to cross the river.

Eventually they found a place where the river was narrow and there were some large rocks and trees on the banks to help them negotiate the crossing. They were moving from branch to branch when suddenly the old tree limb Vrumek was climbing on cracked and he plummeted down into the freezing stream. With the last ounce of his strength he grabbed on to a rock to avoid being carried away with the ferocious current. Aharon helped a hurt and wet Vrumek up on the other side of the river.

They were now in Hungary. But the pair of fugitives were too exhausted to celebrate outwitting the Nazis. Not knowing the Hungarian language, having no food, no local money, no place to stay, and no documents of any sort meant that they remained illegal refugees. They were subject to arrest and perhaps deportation. Vrumek managed to change some money, get some food, and get them a train ride to Budapest, where they could seek out the Jewish community.

While the local Jews helped them with food, clothing, and offers of extended shelter, they did not heed Vrumek's warning that they should all pick up and flee, to get as far away as possible from the rolling Nazi death machine while they still could. Vrumek did not plan to stay any longer than necessary to prepare himself for further travel. He did not pay attention to the Hungarian Jews' assurances of safety. His intuition and bitter experiences told him not to be lulled by the fact that the Germans were not yet there.

He managed to get some funds through the good hearts of the Jewish community and the Mizrachi organization, which he had belonged to at home. Vrumek and Aharon smuggled themselves into Rumania just before the Germans occupied Hungary. Vrumek winced at the thought of his recent benefactors being subject to the dreadfully familiar routine of Nazi decrees leading up to selections and deportations. He aggressively tried to arouse the Jewish community in Rumania to the peril that faced them. He warned his skeptical brethren of the doom that he foresaw for all of Europe's Jews. Tolerant of the exaggerating alarmist in their midst, the Rumanian Jews tried to convince the pair to settle down.

Vrumek and Aharon were almost seduced by the relative paradise of prewar Rumania. Commerce between Gentile and Jew was still commonplace. Food was readily available. For the two homeless refugees, freedom from daily terror and hunger was intoxicating indeed. They were warmly welcomed by the Jewish community, given endless hospitality, and offered an abundance of food. But having spent so many months scratching for survival like animals, fiercely battling a savage enemy, their survival instincts were too sharply honed to be overcome by all the sudden ease.

Tormented with concern for their families, they felt they could not betray them by enjoying any respite. Rather than fill their shrunken stomachs and lose their haunted memories, they were eager to move on. Still fearful of the Nazi danger to their own lives, they strove to continue on their way to freedom. From the Mizrachi organization they learned that a small, illegal vessel would be carrying two hundred people from Rumania to Palestine. They pleaded and fought to be included on that boat.

In the four months they had spent in Rumania, they met refugees who by the mercy of the Gentiles survived their escape from the ghettos. Most of these Gentile benefactors kept up their hospitality only as long as the Jews' money held out. Some of these Jews who survived the final deportations managed to escape Poland and eventually reach freedom in Rumania. A group of these Polish Jewish survivors banded together to grieve and to hope.

Despite Aharon's constant objections, Vrumek successfully worked to obtain permission for them to be among the two hundred passengers on the illegal boat out of Rumania. This small freighter, packed to capacity, was hired by the Mizrachi at great cost and risk. Most of the passengers were Rumanian Jews, traditional Zionists struggling to get to Palestine, the Promised Land. They paid enormous amounts of money to assure a place for themselves and their families. Lacking the money, Vrumek worked hard for the organization to secure a place for himself and Aharon. Wishing he had Sholek at his side and some news of his scattered family, he boarded the vessel to start another journey into the unknown.

Packed like herrings in a barrel, the two hundred men, women, and children set out to leave the massive Jewish graveyard that Europe had become. It was the winter of 1944. The high waves of the stormy Black Sea tossed the small freighter about. Seasick people vomited; children cried; the religious prayed. There were rumors of underwater mines placed by the Germans. There were dark nights when the freighter was suddenly lit up by the searchlights of gigantic battleships. They sometimes had to hide in treacherous, uncharted waters. They had to fear both Germans and other cooperating authorities who might discover the Jewish refugees and sink them, as they had already done to another boat, the *Patria*.

Sick and shivering, they finally reached the port city of Ankara, Turkey, where a delegation from a Jewish agency awaited them. They distributed some oranges, which were relished by the grateful passengers. The exotic taste of oranges was a symbol of Palestine, a sweet taste of hope and freedom. From Ankara they were transported by train to Lebanon, where they were challenged by the British authorities. They spent days in a bureaucratic purgatory before permission was granted for them to travel on to British Palestine.

Vrumek knew no one in Haifa that he could count on for any help. Now that they had finally reached freedom and security, Aharon and Vrumek parted ways, each one trying to find his own place in the pioneer Jewish settlement of Palestine. Vrumek was lonely, afraid for his family and tormented by nightmares. But there was no time to brood. Here he was alive and well and free. Even though penniless, homeless, and emotionally exhausted, he was able to start life again. He contacted people from his hometown of Chrzanow through organizations like the Mizrachi, and he was able to get a job and a place to stay. With the help of the Neichofs, who were also from

Chrzanow, he began work in a light bulb factory. His pay was meager and the work hard, but he was bothered little by these inconveniences. He was too worried about his family. He hounded agencies like the Red Cross for any news from Poland, but nothing other than military news of the raging war came through.

Chapter 16

In the hellish chaos of that cold winter day, the eighteenth of February, 1943, when the town of Chrzanow became *Judenrein*, Nachcia and I clung to each other, filled with horror. She shielded me with her body. The Nazis constantly kept selecting, tearing apart the last remnants of families. We stood in the marketplace until nightfall, frozen with pain and fear. Then we were marched to the railroad station, the same station from which my cousin Gucia and I went to spend our vacation in Bielsko with my brothers. It wasn't until we were packed into cattle cars that we suddenly found our cousin Hania Bromberger. Hania did not know where the rest of her family was either.

It was pitch dark in the bare boxcar, with nothing but the

warmth of our closely packed bodies to keep us from freezing. We had only the clothes on our backs. We were mostly young women, girls, and children pretending to be older. The train clanked heavily on the rails, jolting to a stop every so often. All we could hear through the bolted doors were German yells of *"Schnell! Schnell!"* before the train proceeded again. We did not know where we were being taken. The uncertainty, coupled with the hunger and thirst, added to our misery.

Hours passed before we were finally unloaded and marched into a big building surrounded by high walls. With dawn we found out that we were in a transit camp in Sosnowiec. We were roughly herded into a yard where thousands of women stood in rows while another round of selections began. The German SS, with their bayonets extended, marched back and forth among the prisoners. The higher-ranking German butchers strolled with broad smiles on their icy faces. With a stroke of their whip they selected: "Right. Left. Right. Right. Left." We shivering cattle only knew which line to follow, not what each line meant for our chances of survival.

Nachcia kept me behind her back in the second row to protect me from the vicious German eyes. She quickly pulled me along when she was sent right or left. Cousin Hania also stayed as close as possible to us. Several contingents were being sent back to the building, while the German in charge once more scanned the rest of us. He leaned over behind Nachcia's back and, pointing to me, ordered me out of the row and over to the left. Nachcia had just opened her mouth to protest or beg when the Nazi drowned her out by yelling, "March!" Nachcia was marched into the building with many other women, and soon she was upstairs with most of the others. She desperately pushed her way to the window and spotted me still standing in the yard in a smaller row of women. She became hysterical, wanting to run down and be with her little sister, but the doors were locked.

After I was pulled out from behind my sister's back, I immediately lost track of Nachcia. My heart pounded as I stood in the row alone, trapped and helpless. What am I going to do without Nachcia? I wondered in desperation, as I scanned the yard and building for a glimpse of her or Hania.

Suddenly, I caught sight of Nachcia's face in the window a second before it disappeared. Knowing where my sister was, I knew I must get up to her. I spontaneously darted over to a line of people being led into the building. Like an arrow I shot into the building, running up steps, weaving through the crowd. I finally found Nachcia and we flew into each other's arms. Nachcia was stunned, holding on to me with all her might.

There were two more days of selections to tear at the nerves of us frightened girls. Food was given to us only once, some black coffee and a slice of bread. We had no sleep at all, for the selections lasted day and night. In the middle of the fourth night we were finally marched away from the camp, Hania, Nachcia, and I still somehow together. Under heavy German guard, with a sea of bayonets shining in the pale moonlight, we were marched to the railroad station.

The suffocating cattle cars did not reveal the light of day. Hours dragged by with the clacking, screeching steel wheels. We had no fresh air, light, food, water, or sanitary facilities. In a heavy rain in the pitch dark we reached a stop near a camp called Gogolin. Emotionally drained and physically exhausted, we were marched under constant prodding with the *"Schnell! Schnell!"* of the bestial Germans in our ears. From the railroad station we marched to a camp of barracks surrounded by barbed wire. We were led into a barracks that held several rows of three-tier cots. The cots seemed like heaven after our long, exhausting ordeal, and we dropped into a dead sleep.

We were roused at dawn by our barbarous captors. During the night our clothes, bodies, and hair had been invaded by large white lice; our faces and bodies had been bitten while we were too exhausted to feel anything. Stunned and unable to fight this terrible plague, we were given no time to think. *"Raus, raus! Schnell, schnell!"* was the order barked over and over again as we were assembled in the freezing yard for hours of further selection. By evening we were let back into the barracks after being given some black coffee and a slice of limy bread, our nourishment for the day. Now we had time to think about the pestilence. We found out that this was a transit camp where thousands of victims passed daily, so contagion was easily spread. There was a doctor, a Dutch Jew, who was assigned to the camp. When he came into the barracks we pleaded with him for help. The only advice the doctor offered his scared, heartbroken charges was a gesture showing us how to squeeze the lice between our fingernails. Killing the lice was as useless as it was difficult and disgusting. The creatures were nestled in the seams of our garments, and in the hair of our heads, armpits, and privates.

Nachcia, who had always combed, washed, and braided my long hair, now cried bitterly at the necessary cropping it with rough and crooked chops. On Sunday the Germans allowed the "dirty Jews" to delouse themselves. Water was boiled in a big tub and we threw our clothes in. We sat in our underwear while our dresses were boiling and drying. Unfortunately, my dress was all wool, and it shrank to an unbearably small size. It ripped when I tried to squeeze my body into it.

By Tuesday we were set to be shipped out. We stood at attention for another selection, with a fat German counting us. Stopping exactly at Nachcia, he said, "Sixty, enough!" He separated the column between the two of us, Hania and Nachcia on one side and me on the other. We began crying and begging the cruel German please not to tear us apart. Motionless, unmoved, he stood there smiling broadly, enjoying our misery. When our tears and his game ended, he finally let me join my sister and cousin. Once again we were marched away to the railroad station, to leave the louse-ridden transit camp of Gogolin.

Sprawled again on the dirty, cold floor of the cattle cars, we suffered silently, while the train slowly dragged along. Occasionally someone would unbolt the doors and slide a pail of water across to us. Like animals, we drank thirstily. Anything, any destination would have been better than the endless ride in the cattle cars.

Shivering in the winter air, we were again unloaded and marched away. In the predawn hours we traveled a hard, snow-covered road to a camp that wasn't much more than a large, empty warehouse. There were big lofts with bare walls and wooden floors; large glassless windows let the howling wind in. We were led a short distance away to a railway line, where wooden boards that were to be assembled into three-tier cots were unloaded. It would be our responsibility to assemble the cots without the aid of nails, hammers, or any tools. Under the constant German whip we quickly unloaded the chunky wooden boards, and with our bare, frozen hands, we dragged the rough wood from the trains to the upstairs hall, assembling the cots as best we could. It wasn't until the next day that we could finally rest on the strawless bare planks of the cots.

Five o'clock in the morning we were woken by shouts of *"Raus, Du Judenschwein!"* accompanied by the barking of German shepherd dogs. We were rushed to the yard downstairs, to a row of icy faucets. Under the constant guard of a pack of fierce dogs and a tall young German in shining high boots who held a whip, we were made to strip and wash. That accomplished, we were marched to our respective work groups. There was a group that hauled coal from the trains and loaded it onto smaller wagons; the girls were then harnessed to the wagons to draw and later unload the coal. There were also groups pumping water and dragging it in iron barrels to the camp. Other work details shoveled snow, heaping it into big mountains.

Nachcia and I were marched to another warehouse, a tall round building with a narrow winding staircase. Our task was to bring old building materials up from the ground floor to the top floor. These included long heavy logs and beams full of large rusty nails, and rusted sections of railroad tracks. In the freezing cold, the girls were stationed up and down the steps to pass the material up from hand to hand. The stairs were narrow and winding, making it impossible for the long planks to go up without twisting and turning them from side to side. The frozen steel stuck to our skin, and the rusty nails ripped our hands and arms open as we pushed and lifted. Lagerführer Kiski and his hound kept running up and down to press our pace with whips and commands to his dog to "get the lazy Jews."

From predawn to past dusk we worked, hauling and pushing the heavy, dirty logs and rusty beams. Our hands were bleeding, our backs were breaking and we were terrified of the dog's teeth and the Nazi's whip. In the freezing cold, we were marched back to camp, where we lined up for hours for some warm soup in a rusty metal bowl. The soup was a concoction of hot water with beets and vegetable peels. Dinner was hastily eaten while standing outside, and we were then sent to the warehouse for the night and allowed to lie down on the bare, hard wood of the three-tier cots while the wind whistled through the open windows.

We were a group of strangers from different cities, of all ages, newly separated from husbands, children, parents, and siblings. Our only crime and common denominator was our being Jewish. We several hundred women were provided with only a single pail for bathroom facilities. The pail would soon overflow, causing us to wallow in filth, to sleep with fetid odors, and to scream at each other.

And so our nights too were filled with agony and strife. In the beginning of the night I would force myself to stay awake, so I could be among the first ones to use the urinal pail. I would then exhaustedly fall asleep until the cold wind chilled my frail body. Waking up, I would again need a toilet. I would sleepily go to the pail, which was overflowing by then, to face the terrible choice of urinating and being yelled at or holding it in to bursting.

In the morning the girls who had hall duty for the day carried the overflowing pail out, leaving a trail of stinking waste. They were also the ones to clean up the mess in the hall. There was no time for getting acquainted, as no talking was permitted in the assigned work details. Each frightened person simply tried to obey and to stay out of the way of the guards. In the hall at night the lights would go out before we had a chance to get into our cots. There was little communication except among the few relatives who succeeded in staying together. Nachcia, always protective of me, would give me the bottom cot, taking the one above me and giving the top to Hania. She knew the bottom would be easiest for me, since I needed the pail so much. She regretted that she could not help me in my backbreaking work. The labor camp was hardest on those who had always been protected and spared from hard physical labor.

While most of the girls stayed out of the way of the German SS men, there were those who wanted to be noticed. Of course, the Germans picked their capos from the ambitious, aggressive ones who were capable of sadistically abusing the other prisoners, taking out their own rage on their helpless victims.

One such girl was Chaika. Naive enough to think that helping the Germans would assure her own betterment, she believed that the vicious German Kiski actually liked her. Arrogantly sure of herself, she did all she could to curry favor with the Germans. Chaika was responsible for lining up the prisoners in the morning, marching with them to work, and speeding up production. Chaika gained certain freedoms for herself, marching where she wanted and not performing any labor. She ran up and down the stairs to reinforce Kiski's supervision, making sure the logs moved rapidly between the swollen hands of the prisoners. Trying to please Kiski, she urged and prodded with her own cruel methods, relentlessly demanding unreasonable efforts. Having known Chaika in their hometown, certain girls particularly abhorred her. Feeling their resentment, Chaika would single out those girls for mistreatment. She did not hesitate to squeal to the vicious German about those who tried to rest a minute in his absence.

Chaika once brought Kiski up and pointed her finger at a girl named Ruzia, whom she accused of disobeying her and slacking off. Kiski felled Ruzia with one hideous blow, throwing her head against the rails. As the vulnerable girl lay there, the German pounded her with his heavy boots, leaving her bleeding and virtually unconscious. With Chaika's help Ruzia was made to stand up and resume her work. Several girls who tried to interfere received their share of blows from the ferocious German.

Our quota was produced daily and increased periodically, and meeting it extracted from us the last ounce of our strength.

Totally exhausted, we would be marched back to camp to endure more indignities and suffering.

Here in the labor camp of Faulbruck, our spirits were broken. There was no time to think or to grieve over our severed families. The hourly fight for life was all-consuming. Those who were able to mechanically carry on were the lucky ones; they could best preserve their lives and sanity.

Fela was one woman who could not bear the recent trauma of having her little daughter torn from her. At night she would relive her tragedy, talking to her child, crying and laughing. Girls sat with her to calm her, but Fela could not be consoled. She would talk to her missing child, fight to keep her from the SS, and cry out in pain when replaying the moment that her baby was taken away. Her agony became our own. We finally realized that Fela had lost her sanity, and for days we kept protecting her from the wicked captors, helping her in her work, dragging her along, trying to calm her at night, and, when necessary, shutting her up by force. Fela's hysterical cries eventually did bring the Germans up one night, and she was taken away, tearing the hair out of her head, screaming the name of her child.

The cold winter frost chilled our weak bodies to the marrow; the slave labor nearly broke us. We endured with only the thought of not being separated from one another, not being sent away. We got up in the morning with our stomachs painfully empty and our bladders painfully full. The one objective was to escape Kiski's whip, his dog, his boots. The winter was endless, and the logs and beams became heavier.

In those dangerous, contemplative moments I could hear Papa telling us at the Seder table that we should try to imagine being slaves in Egypt. Where are you, Papa and Mama? Where are you, Moses and Aaron? When will children solemnly sit around a table remembering what it was like to be Hebrew slaves in Europe?

We were constantly lined up to stand for hours in the cold air, stomping our frozen feet. Like heads of cattle, we would be counted up and marched away, some never to be seen again and some driven back to the loft. In one such assembly a group of two hundred fifty prisoners, including Nachcia, Hania, and myself, were counted up. We were marched to the railroad station and again packed into the cattle cars. Our hearts pounded with anticipation in the dark. This time, upon reaching our destination, we were marched through the streets of a big city with spectators all around us. We were led into the yard of a factory with heavy iron gates that locked us in. After a lineup and several hours of counting in the chill of a blustery day, we were finally led into the factory. The warmth of the indoors engulfed us and gave us the illusion of an improved situation. The conditions had changed, but not our status. We, the slave girls, were posted throughout the factory, each one assigned to operate several machines.

Hania's beauty won her a station where the German constable did not constantly watch her, leaving her in the hands of the factory staff. Nachcia and I were shown four weaving machines each to work. I stared blankly at the huge yarn wheels, loops, combs, and spools, frightened by the deafening noise. With difficulty, a tall skinny German in dark overalls showed us how to make the machines run.

That night we prisoners were housed in our new quarters in a building adjacent to the factory grounds, which was surrounded by heavy iron gates. Not that anyone had any notions of running away—where would we run to? The factory yard looked strange; the barbarians outside jabbered in a strange dialect and pointed at us during the day. We were in a prison, deprived of our basic human rights, but we were consoled that the environment was not as cold and bare as the murderous labor camp in Faulbruck. The factory's windows did keep the wind out, and the miserable pail was replaced by a real toilet. All two hundred fifty of us women and girls were crowded into the top floor of the factory building, the lower floors housing the spinning facilities. There was a constant cloud of dust rising from the spinning machines to the upper floor, causing additional pollution of the already stagnant air. Chaika's mother was chosen to be the *Judenälteste,* the Jewish leader of the group. Older and wiser than her teenage daughter, she was more sensitive to the suffering of the inmates.

There were no SS men to guard the prisoners, since we were never out of the perimeter of the factory. The German *Lagerführerin* was a woman. Young, tall, blond, and quite pretty, with a frivolous fondness for luxuries and men, she thoroughly enjoyed her status as queen bee of the little Jewish slaves. She had the national gift for sadism and demanded that we extend our homage to her fat white cat, Mici. With our eyes bulging and stomachs churning with hunger pains, we had to feed Mici her milk and delicacies. Petrified of Fräulein Babin's severe punishments, no one would dare withhold any food from Mici. Always nonchalant, the German camp leader would relegate underlings to beat the girls and withhold their food rations.

In the morning we would be lined up in the yard, while the local population arrived to work. These were mainly women and a few men who were either older or unfit for military service. We desperately eyed their lunch boxes. With the ring of the bell at precisely eight o'clock, the power was turned on and the machines started clanking. The inexperienced prisoners encountered severe difficulties with the machines, which required coordination and much physical strength. Vastly undertrained, we nevertheless caught hell when material ripped or machinery malfunctioned. Every time a machine had to be restarted, we broke out into a fearful sweat. If a machine stood idle, the German mechanic, the *Meister,* would see to the problem, rudely grumbling and insinuating that the prisoners were committing sabotage. The material we produced was called *fallschirmseide,* a thin, strong nylon material used in parachutes.

The factory was divided into sections. Nachcia's *Meister* was an old heavyset German man with a round, bald head. The fingers of both his hands were missing past the first two knuckles. It was said that he lost them there in the factory. He resented anyone who had fingers, and he relished pounding the girls over their fingers. With his half fingers he was able to perform his job of fixing the machines. The *Meisters* were technically not allowed to beat or punish the girls, as we were the exclusive property of the Wehrmacht. The factory personnel were supposed to bring all complaints against the prisoners to the attention of the camp wardens. The *Meisters* took their wrath out on us nonetheless, fully aware that no one would complain. When beaten for difficulties at our machines, we didn't dare lodge a protest.

With her nearsightedness, Nachcia had trouble threading the machines. She was therefore beaten and yelled at more than most. She stiffened in fear whenever Paluch, or "Fingers," the nickname given her *Meister,* came near her. Too often she was chased around the machine and beaten mercilessly on her fingers.

The *Meister* in my section was nicknamed Bezdupny, "Assless," because he was tall and skinny as a stick and his clothes hung limply on him. He was fiercely intimidating; he had a taut face, protruding cheekbones, and a murderous look in his eyes. Even from far away his piercing gaze made me cringe. He would kick with his bony legs, and he often reported me to the camp police for lack of discipline.

Twice a day the prisoners were allowed to go to the bathroom if they received formal permission from a tall supervisor named Knauer. She was an uneducated small-town factory girl who was suddenly graced by the Nazi regime with the authority to allow or deny bathroom privileges to hundreds of women. She gloried in her power and status. Glancing at her coworkers, so they'd notice her exercise of executive decision making, the petty queen of the bathroom expressed her agreement or disagreement with a stately nod. Denials, of course, enhanced her aura of power and gave her the opportunity to see her underlings squirm in discomfort.

The bathroom was a row of toilets in a poorly lit and foul-smelling room. Yet the opportunity to relieve oneself and to rest a bit from the unrelenting pressures of our work gave us the greatest pleasure we could know. The girls would sprawl or sit on the dirty floor, discussing our shared misery while one girl stood watch.

Most of the German workers were older women or disabled men, and almost all of them were abusive to us Jewish slave girls. One exception was Puckel Knauer, the hunchbacked brother of Fräulein Knauer. Perhaps his deformity lent him a measure of sensitivity. He seemed embarrassed by his sister's enjoyment of our degradation.

Among the girls was a pretty, dark-haired fifteen-year-old named Chanale, who looked like a midget among her four giant weaving machines. Every time her machine would stop, the sweat on her brow would dampen her locks of jet black hair, her cheeks would burn, and her dark piercing eyes would grow moist with alarm. She meekly directed her begging eyes to Puckel Knauer at the neighboring machine. Carefully looking around first, Puckel hopped over, skillfully took Chanale's hand, and together they pushed the lever to restart the machine. Chanale's face lit up in a grateful smile, her unspoken words hanging in the air, while Puckel sneaked back to his machine. Chanale shared the incredible news with her friends.

"There is a German who does not hate us!" she revealed to the astonished girls. "He even helped me."

The story spread like wildfire among the prisoners.

Twelve o'clock heralded lunch break. The German workers would reach into their lockers for their lunches. Out came sandwiches and bowls of soup, and stew pots to be warmed on the factory stove. The smell of food made our mouths water and our stomachs growl. Our empty bellies were painfully knotted with hunger spasms. We prisoners were rationed a hot, slimy soup of water and flour. The girls lined up for the precious bit of food, eyes trained on the hand with the ladle. Every drop of that poor liquid was hungrily gulped down, or slowly sipped to make it last. The tiny portion only made us hungrier than if we had had no lunch at all.

Soon it was back to work pushing the heavy bars of the weaving machines, using up all of our strength to keep them noisily clanking away. As the hours dragged on we would sometimes get lost in thought about our families, even though if we were caught slacking off we would be accused of daydreaming and dealt extra blows.

I had waking nightmares about my machine killing me. I worried about Nachcia's suffering my loss. And how would she explain my death to Mama when they finally met again?

Could Mama, who had already lost her son Shlamek, survive the loss of her youngest child? How Mama used to pamper me. Where is Mama now? I asked myself over and over. Is she suffering now too? I remembered Blimcia's wild look when, her baby Aiziu clinging to her, she was sent away to the other side during the selection, suddenly losing contact with her family. Blimcia, our pillar of strength, looked so forlorn, so helpless, so frightened.

What did the Germans do to her? Is she also working in a factory like this or lugging chunks of coal somewhere? How is she able to care for Aiziu? How is her husband Jacob, who said he would not live without her? And what of Papa, Heshek, Vrumek, Sholek, and Goldzia?

My hands mechanically worked as my mind milled my tragedy into verse. Clank, clank, clank! I repeated and memorized, weaving, spinning my pain into parachutes of poetry.

Finally the bell would ring, at exactly six o'clock. The Germans would pack up their belongings and leave, while the prisoners were assembled in the factory yard to be counted and marched into their cells in the adjoining building. There on the top floor we lived, several hundred Jewish women of all ages, descriptions, and backgrounds. Those from wealthy families suffered the most from the hard labor. Their good manners allowed others to push in front of them in the food or toilet line. Those from poor homes were used to hunger and strife. They had the guts and skills to occasionally sneak back into line for an extra bowl of soup. They used loud, coarse voices and foul language to vent their suffering.

Day after day the prisoners were awakened in the early dawn to rush downstairs to the yard for the morning lineup. Counted and recounted, we would be handed some black, sticky brew made from a coffee substitute, its bitter taste like a Passover symbol of our lives. Then we were marched into the factory. Day resembled day. Any changes were dreaded, since they could only mean a worsening of our situation. The winter was almost over when we first saw our new *Lagerführerin*.

"I am Lagerfuhrerin Kaufman," she spit at us, slicing the air with her long whip. We shivered to see the sadistic figure in front of us. She was a stocky woman of about fifty, her thick blond wavy hair worn shoulder length. Her stern face unmistakenly belonged to a prison guard. She wore high black boots and a long black leather coat like the Gestapo men. Her gloved hands clutched a sturdy leather whip, which she used to punctuate her loud, shrill sentences. Her *Judenälteste* was to perform like a soldier. The poor *Judenälteste* scrambled around counting the girls feverishly as Frau Kaufman stiffly stood there with a satanic grin on her face. Once inside the factory we were the sole property of the *Meisters,* who were just as sadistic but less poised than our *Lagerführerin.*

One day in May, with the German workers in spring clothes and I still squeezed into my shrunken winter dress, I stood at the machine tormented by a toothache. The monotonous pain drilling in my head affected my work and my sleep. There was nothing my sister Nachcia could do for me, and the pain was growing more severe. I could not even eat my miserable portion of soup, which I gave to Nachcia, who always insisted on sharing her own meager portion with me. There was no medication of any sort in camp; the *Judenälteste* could only render a report to the Germans that she had a sick prisoner. The fate of a sick prisoner was uncertain, and Nachcia was afraid to seek help for me. I eventually succumbed to the pain, staying in my cot when unable to drag myself downstairs. Horrified of what might happen to me, Nachcia had no choice but to hurry down herself for morning roll call. She trembled at her machines that day at the thought of not finding me when she returned.

All alone in the vast hall I cringed in my cot, trying to sleep away the pain, when suddenly I woke to see Frau Kaufman standing in front of me, her sleek black leather coat shining in the light, her whip at her side. I could not decide if my fear were stronger than my pain, but I wished to be dead and rid of both. Still, I sprung to my feet when Kaufman addressed me. Her voice was not as shrill as usual when she declared that I would be sent to a dentist the next day. I kept lying there after Frau Kaufman left, trying to convince myself that I wasn't going to be sent away somewhere and never see Nachcia again.

A relieved Nachcia shared my hope that I might actually get treated. If I were to have been taken out and eliminated, the efficient Germans would have done so that morning. After drinking Nachcia's soup, I spent the night pretending to sleep. The excruciating pain did not allow me a moment's rest. I could hear the girls stirring, snoring. The piercing scream of someone having a nightmare occasionally broke the stillness. I wanted to scream in pain, but some of the girls would probably strangle me. I lay on my cot whimpering softly like a wounded animal.

When the girls hurried out to roll call at daybreak, I started praying. I begged the Almighty to spare me, if only for Nachcia's sake. I was alone again in the large, frighteningly quiet hall densely packed with wooden three-tier bunks. In the forest of bunks, my mind spun back to playing hide-and-seek in the woods with my brothers. Should I hide between cots when they came for me now? All my thoughts were interrupted when the door opened and the *Judenälteste* called for Stapler to go downstairs quickly. Usually a prisoner would be addressed by a number, or more commonly, "You Jewish pig."

Dressed and ready, I scrambled down to the yard, where an armed male guard in a green uniform commanded me to march in front of him. My heart hammered away, and my knees buckled as I marched. The fresh air was shockingly refreshing, but it did not lessen my pain or fear. Was he really taking me to a dentist, or was he bringing me to the railroad station to be shipped away? We reached the railroad station and boarded an ordinary passenger train. He sat across from me, observing me watchfully. He did not utter a word throughout the journey. We soon disembarked in a town with small residential houses surrounded by gardens. The air was warm, but I shivered with pain, exhaustion, and fear. I kept my eyes on the road, avoiding the people who stared at the prisoner. I was a marked person, wearing three stars of David sewn onto my dress: one on my chest, one on the back of my left shoulder, and one at the bottom of my dress near my knee. I would be easily recognized and apprehended should I try to escape, but I lacked the strength and destination to make an attempt anyway.

I was led into a barbed wire compound with female prisoners, where I was turned over to the local guard. I was then taken into a big room and made to sit on a chair. An inmate there was introduced as the dentist, but someone whispered to me that the ''dentist'' was only a woman who'd learned a few things from her dentist father. I saw the prison dentist take up a pair of dental tongs for pulling teeth. She had five prisoners hold me down, while I opened my mouth. She grabbed hold of the aching tooth with the dental pliers and pulled. The tooth was not yielding. She turned the tool, tugging and wrenching, pulling, jerking, and twisting. I felt as though she were tearing my head off my shoulders. Eventually, the tooth was yanked out, with a fountain of blood streaming from my mouth. With rags stuffed into my mouth to stop the bleeding, I rested several achy minutes before being turned over to the constable for the trip back to the factory. The stinging pain was gone now, but the throbbing in my head did not stop. I could not swallow my soup ration, but I was back in the factory with my sister and prayerfully optimistic that my pain would go away. For the first time in many nights I fell into a deep sleep.

I woke up feeling that I was choking. In the total dark I crawled out of my cot fighting for breath. Groggy with exhaustion, I touched my hands to my mouth, suddenly becoming aware of a solid substance filling my mouth. Had someone stuffed something into my mouth to choke me? In the dim light of the bathroom I saw that my hands were covered with blood. I stood over the toilet bowl ripping out piece after piece of coagulated blood that filled the whole cavity of my mouth. I stood in the little toilet room with hot tears of frustration and pain mixing with the blood that smeared my face. I decided not to wake poor Nachcia, who was weak from denying herself food so she could give it to me. I slunk back to my cot, feeling the warm liquid seeping into my mouth. I spat and swallowed it and soon fell back asleep. Before dawn, when we were awakened, I had a mouthful of blood again. I slipped to the toilet and cleaned myself up. During the day in the factory I managed to keep the blood from coagulating by swallowing and spitting. Nachcia was terribly worried when she saw that I could not even eat my soup that night. I fell asleep exhausted, only to wake up several hours later choking again from blood. For two more weeks I suffered from severe bleeding and from the abuse of the cruel *Meisters* because of my resultant weakness.

Chapter 17

I had finally recovered when we were all made to move again. The order came with no preliminary preparations or prior instructions. After the day's work was finished and the roll call completed, the usual order to disperse into the loft did not come. Instead, the gates of the factory yard were opened. Placing one guard in front of the row and one in back of it, Kaufman shouted the order to march. Pacing up and down the column of prisoners, liberally dispensing lashes with her whip, she marched her troops in a straight line, five abreast, down the main street of Reichenbach. On both sidewalks people lined up to watch the *Juda Mädla,* Jewish girls, in the local dialect. No one waved or smiled to us circus animals on display. Apprehensive about our fate, we left the city perimeter, marching along a main road through fields and gardens. Whenever a passing car forced the marchers to the roadside ditches, Kaufman was there whipping us back into a perfectly straight line. The sinking sun dropped below the horizon, and a gray dusk signaled our obscure future.

Into the dark night we marched, finally reaching a camp. We were stopped in front of a gate. An armed guard opened the gate, which led to a dark yard with searchlights flashing from a center tower. We were divided into groups of forty and led towards the barracks.

Langenbielau, a small town hardly on the map of Germany, became home to over a thousand Jewish female prisoners. Stumbling over each other, we were rushed into barracks, where cots had been erected by previous prisoners. We tired girls scrambled into the cots, quickly settling among ourselves which berth to take. In hushed voices we speculated about our new surroundings and how they might affect our lives. The murmurs gradually dissipated into exhausted sleep.

Before dawn we were awakened by the shrill sound of a whistle, and by harsh German voices which drove us out into the yard. The sky was ink blue, but we could discern the shapes of women coming out of the barracks on all sides. We stood in the middle of the yard for roll call as floodlights lit up the open gate. Groups of prisoners were being marched outside. Sleepily, we marched into the rising dawn. We kept on marching as the local population rose for the day's activity. Here and there people appeared, riding their bicycles, their lunch boxes stashed in attached baskets. Rushing to their work, they would still stop a moment to stare at the Jewish slaves.

Soon we reached the city of Reichenbach, whose streets were filled with eager onlookers. We had marched to the same factory we'd been working at, we discovered, it was just our accommodations that had been changed. We were marched into the yard, before the factory bell rang. Lined up at attention, we stood until the eight o'clock bell announced the beginning of the shift. In we promptly went to begin our day's slavery.

It was not until Sunday that we saw our new home camp for the first time in daylight. Similar to our first camp in Gogolin, the transit camp, this was a large rectangular lot cleared in the middle of a forest. The barracks were erected in single rows all around the lot, facing the center. There were four barracks shoulder to shoulder on the short sides, eight on the long sides. On the outside of the gate was a small house, which served as quarters for the *Lagerführerin* and her watchmen. On the inside near the gate was a barracks housing the few privileged Jewish prisoners. These included the *Judenälteste,* the cook, the dentist, the nurse, the shoemaker, and the seamstress. Surrounded by barbed wire, the camp was watched and patrolled by armed SS. In the middle of the uneven ground of the camp were the lavatories and washrooms, primitive outhouses with long rows of metal pipes and faucets sticking out over deep bins. They probably had previously served as animal feeders. Thirty-nine to forty-two women lived in each barracks, sleeping in three-tier wooden cots. In the middle of the room stood a rough wooden table of unfinished boards; there was just enough space to pass between the table and the cots. Next to the table stood an iron potbellied stove. Two windows in the room looked out on the fence and the camp grounds. The bare windows facilitated the guards watching the prisoners even in their barracks.

A wagon of straw was hauled into camp by the prisoners, and sacks were distributed. We were allowed to fill the sacks with straw for use as mattresses. The open sacks were a constant nuisance, spilling straw onto the floor. Every Sunday the sacks had to be brought outside the barracks to be aired so that "the dirty Jews do not contaminate the place." The cots had to be scrubbed down, and the last two girls on cleaning duty had to scrub down the table and floor. Even though we were not marched to work on Sunday, the prisoners would wake up before dawn to grab hold of the only pail and brush. From that moment on there was anxious waiting to get hold of that precious pail. We had to wash our hair and our underwear and get our cleaning duty done, so we would all beg and yell and cajole and fight for the one pail.

On Sunday mornings when the whistle would sound for roll call, we would all have to scramble into our places even if we were wet or half naked. For long hours we were kept standing in the baking sun or pouring rain while the barracks were inspected. As in the army, our straw sacks had to be flattened straight and even like a tabletop. A blade of straw found on the floor could mean that the whole camp would be left standing for an extra two hours, or the entire barracks made to kneel for several hours.

If we were lucky and an inspection proved faultless, we were permitted to line up in the early evening in front of the kitchen window to get our soup. Then we were free to go back into the barracks. It felt like a holiday to suddenly be able to sprawl on the straw, luxuriously stretching out our aching bodies, going to sleep early or just lying there quietly thinking. Some would talk about their homes, their parents, their siblings, and their shattered lives.

Of course, Nachcia and I were a unit. There were four other girls, not related but all from the same neighborhood, who formed a family. Hadassah, at the tender age of fifteen, was the mother figure who took charge. Her short dark hair bounced on her head with every aggressive, nimble move. Her round face, pink cheeks, and lively eyes radiated authority and decisiveness. She was in the middle bunk next to ours. On the bottom was Sabina. Tall, with long, ever growing limbs, she was a tough tomboy. Her thick, golden blond hair gave her something of an Aryan look, but it did not help ease her constant hunger. Hadassah had to keep her bread portions safe from Sabina's mouth. Petite Rachelka was on the top bed. She was mature for sixteen and served as our mentor and peacemaker. The fourth girl, on the cot above Nachcia and me, was the fragile young Bronia. Always protected by her friends, the sweet, smart, and childish Bronia walked limply on broomstick legs with swinging, ropelike arms.

The aisle between the two cots, about two feet wide, had to accommodate six girls, so it was important to cooperate. With all of us rising in the morning, returning, eating, and climbing up for the night all at the same time, activities had to be closely coordinated. Luckily there were no problems in aisle number one.

"I wonder how long they will keep us here in this camp," I said, laying on my cot, not addressing anyone in particular. Sabina sprawled on her stomach in her lower berth, only a foot away, her hands hanging out, swooshing back and forth on the floor.

"What is the difference where they take us? If we only had a little more to eat, so we would not starve before they shipped us away."

Poor Sabina, Rachelka thought, she is suffering so. "I wish I had something to give you. I remember your mother, Sabina," Rachelka commented to change the subject. "She used to come and pick you up from school. I never saw her without white gloves. She would walk with you arm in arm; you could see how proud she was of her daughter."

"Were you an only child, Sabina?" Nachcia asked.

"Yes," Sabina answered, turning now to lie on her back. She stared straight up, staring into the boards of the upper berth. The one naked light bulb that hung in the middle of the room did not shed any light on the lower cots, and Sabina was immersed in semidarkness. Painfully aroused by Rachelka's comment, she talked about her mother. She remembered sitting in the parlor and practicing the piano. Her mother was seated on the sofa with embroidery in her hand, putting her head back to enjoy the sweet tunes. Her mother always listened to her playing, and often, when Sabina had finished practicing, she would play a small duet with her. Sitting close to her on the piano bench, Sabina would feel the warmth of her mother's body, her soft caressing hand and her supporting arm. Instead of the padded piano bench, she was now here on the hard, cold cot, darkness surrounding her from without and from within.

It was not until we were well settled into the camp at Langenbielau that we found out about the proximity of the men's camp. Some of the people at Langenbielau had relatives in the men's camp. There were even some women from our hometown of Chrzanow who had fathers or brothers there. Occasionally some men were brought to Langenbielau to perform menial jobs that could not be performed by women. Only the staff that remained in camp had a chance of getting messages through to them. Sometimes a woman would find a way to send her bread ration to her husband at Sportschule, the men's camp. When someone complained how worried she was about her father, she would be reprimanded.

"Don't complain. At least you know that he is alive. You might even get a chance to see him if he gets into a work detail that comes here."

Many times a loved one came to the women's camp on the pretense of being a woodworker or bricklayer. Sometimes the women leaving for work in the morning encountered a detail of men being marched to Langenbielau. If a relative was sighted in the group by one of the girls, we were all happy for her. Our day passed by more easily knowing that someone was lucky.

We were allowed no contact with the outside world, not even eye contact, but on our way to work we would encounter different people. A prisoner staring back at a German spectator was swiftly lashed and made to march on. A prisoner losing the marching rhythm was driven on by a rifle butt.

One day on our journey to the factory, a man dressed in a trench coat stared at the women. Being ordered to move on only spurred his desire to observe us. He moved away, only to reappear at the next corner, watching us intently. The following day he was there again. Avoiding the SS guard, he tried to get close. None of the prisoners wanted to talk to him and risk getting beaten up, just because a German was somehow interested in her—none, except for Bina, a woman in her forties. She figured that an interested German is worth the risk. It could not hurt to discreetly make contact. Maybe one day he could be of help. When Mr. Trench Coat appeared she smiled at him boldly. He smiled back and quickly disappeared. The next day when we reached the city limits on our march to work, Bina searched the street, but he was nowhere to be seen. She even earned a kick for falling out of line, so carelessly did she pursue her search. Suddenly, he appeared at the corner. He gazed directly at Bina, smiling and winking. He advanced to the next corner to face her again when she marched by. He swung by very close for a second and managed to say, "My name is Karl."

Every day now Karl waited for us to march by. He learned Bina's name and started bringing her some gifts of food. A sandwich packed in a brown paper bag would be thrown onto the road a few feet before Bina would pass the spot. She would bend down to pick it up while the other girls would avert the guard's attention. When she was unable to pick it up, another prisoner did and passed it on to her.

Soon everybody knew about Karl. Sometimes he included a sheet from a newspaper or a personal note. In his letters he called her sweet, affectionate names and made plans for when the war was over. At the day's end the girls would crowd around Bina to hear what he had to say. Karl became not only one woman's platonic lover, but an important source of information for all.

Nachcia struggled to keep up the pace of the daily marching. She was never in the best of health, and the labor camp ordeal weakened her. Her weak legs, empty stomach, and eyes strained by working the machines only compounded her severe headaches. I vainly tried to appeal to the *Judenälteste* on her behalf, as I could not stand seeing my sister suffer so.

There were now close to a thousand women housed in the labor camp of Langenbielau, divided into different work details of several hundred prisoners each. Every day each group was marched to one of the factories. We produced war material under the threat of German guns. But the camp was not yet full. One evening when we returned to camp, we saw a terrible sight. In the middle of the yard stood a small group of people, less than a hundred, who wore dresses yet looked like men because of their shaven heads. They were dressed in coarse, gray, prison smocks, their bare feet in wooden clogs, and they ravenously gulped the soup that was given to them. As hungry and tired as we were returning from our day's toil, we considered ourselves more fortunate than these miserable victims, who seemed totally deprived of any vestige of femininity.

We were eager to exchange information. The newcomers wanted to know where they were, and how long we had already been here. We wanted to find out where they came from and what was happening outside the walls of our camp. But there was no time to make contact or get acquainted. Each group was promptly directed to its own barracks, with hardly enough time to do our evening chores before lights went out. Only on Sunday were we finally able to get together.

The disappointment was great when we realized that we were unable to communicate. The newcomers were from Hungary and spoke only Hungarian, whereas the majority of us were from Poland, speaking Polish and Yiddish. In part sign language, part broken Germano-Yiddish, the Hungarian women told of their having been recently taken from their homes and shipped to a camp called Auschwitz. There they were torn from their families and stripped of all their possessions. Shrouded in their prison dresses their heads shaved, they were shipped here, confused, forlorn, shattered. Some friendships were eventually established between the Polish and Hungarian girls, but the majority of them kept to themselves.

Letters from a prisoner's family were rare and sporadic. On occasion, even a package of food or clothes got through. Occasions like these were usually shared by all the inmates of the barracks. A letter would be read aloud, interpreted, and studied for any obscure meanings. People who received packages were certainly lucky, although the contents held mostly sentimental value.

One Wednesday evening Nachcia, Hania, and I returned from our day's labor to get the surprise of our lives. Mama, Papa, Blimcia, and Jacob had been taken away long ago, Heshek was somewhere in Siberia, yet we were called into the *Judenälteste's* quarters to receive a package. With queasy stomachs, heads spinning from excitement, we undid the rope and heavy brown paper, our hands shaking.

Inside were four pairs of underpants, four pairs of black

stockings, two tops, two skirts, three kerchiefs, and two un-
dershirts. Stunned, we sat staring at the clothes, speculating
about their origin. Not a word was enclosed, or, more likely,
none had been allowed to get to us. It was a sign from the
Almighty, at any rate, that someone was alive in our family.
Our emotions ran wild. We imagined Blimcia somewhere hidden by Gentiles—that could be why there was no return address, for she was endangering her own life to help us. And
Mama and Papa? Where were they? Had Blimcia been able to
help them too? How did she know where we were? Maybe it
was not Blimcia. What about Vrumek? Could he be hiding as
a Gentile? After all, Vrumek had found a way to come home
from Bielsko after the war had begun. It could not be Sholek:
he had run into the fields, penniless and homeless. Where
would he be able to get clothes to send us?

I began dreaming about the members of our family. I saw
them struggling, wrestling with the Germans. I saw them
being torn from each other. I would wake up crying, moaning.
Nachcia would come down from her cot and sit next to me,
holding me, our bitter tears mixing in our embrace. We would
quietly whisper again and again the possibilities of who might
be alive in our family.

The clothes we received were very large, about size 52, yet
they were cherished. Nachcia wore one of the blouses and
skirts while Hania received the other outfit. The light cotton
skirts and blouses were drab and worn and did not afford much
protection from the chilly weather. Still, they were a welcome
addition to our nonexistent wardrobe. I took the underwear
and the stockings, which I wore tied around my waist and legs
with string.

I had befriended a Hungarian girl named Lili. She was tall
and slim and looked distinguished despite her shaven head.
She did not walk bent humbly like the others, she walked with
her head held high and seemed a little arrogant. Her face was
beautiful, with deep black eyes, a high, wise forehead, and a
dainty nose, and when she smiled, a dimple appeared in her
cheek. She spoke a good clear German with a heavy Hungarian
accent. What attracted me to her was her assertiveness and

confidence. Lili told a group of us the story of how a German woman in the factory attacked her and insulted her by demanding that she wear a kerchief on her head.

"Aren't you ashamed to appear like that in public? You disgust me with that shaven head of yours. Cover your shame," she ranted.

In total defiance, Lili looked the woman straight in the eyes. "I should be ashamed? I should cover up? It is you who should be ashamed. You Germans have done this injustice to me. You shaved my head to humiliate me, degrade me, and defile me. And even if I wanted to cover up, what could I use to cover my head? This prisoner's dress is now my only possession. You cowardly thugs have pilfered all we had."

"I knew I was asking for trouble," Lili continued her story, "but my outrage was so great that I became oblivious to the consequences. I stood there bold and challenging, ready to receive a slap or blow, but the German woman just abruptly turned away."

I was immensely impressed. That is exactly how I would have wanted to act if I had the courage. I always feared them punishing me or taking me away from my sister Nachcia. But oh, how I yearned to defy them, to stand up to them like Lili. I became friendly with Lili and managed to spend some time with her on Sundays. I tried to be like her and at the same time tried to help her. Lili was much worse off than I, as she had no one in her family with her. She was friendly with another Hungarian girl, Estee. They shared their food like sisters. I also admired Lili's ability to love and share and be compassionate in this sea of ugliness, violence, terror, and competition for survival. The first thing I did when I received the package was give Lili a pair of underwear and some stockings. It was the only thing I had to offer.

The camp routine involved waking up before dawn, lining up for roll call in the dark yard, being marched for two hours to the factory, trekking back to camp after a ten-hour workday, lining up for a ladleful of soup, and then doing some evening chores. But there were also many terrifying breaks in our routine. There were new arrivals coming to camp now and then, and there were selections taking place in which people were sent away. These added additional tension and anxiety to our lives. Who would they take away next? Even in our free hours we could not relax, we could not forget where we were and the dreadful fate that might await us. Because of that constant fear, we tried to cheer each other up, to persuade ourselves that we were still normal people who could cry and laugh. We were persecuted and hated, yet we strove to remain capable of love. There were those of us who fought over crumbs of bread or pails of clean water. There were ugly words, vicious name calling, and curses pronounced. But in the midst of it all there were devoted friends, loving sisters, and cherished relatives who cared and sacrificed for each other.

Whenever there were selections Nachcia would stand in the front row hiding me behind her back. One day the fat German SS man who unexpectedly appeared while we were lined up for roll call pointed his finger at Nachcia. The *Judenälteste* told her to march over to the other side. Her face flushed red, her heart pounded, and her knees buckled, but before she panicked there were other prisoners being ordered to stand with her. Soon there were about fifty women left standing in the yard, while the rest of us were ordered away in the usual shrieking manner by the *Lagerführerin*.

I was distraught—suddenly I was so alone. My heart banged in my chest. I could not let my sister be taken away. Nachcia stood there in the middle of the yard, forlorn, petrified. Mustering all of my Lili-inspired confidence, I told Nachcia not to panic in sign language. I ran to Fanny, the *Judenälteste*. I pushed my way through and unrelentingly clung to her, pleading, crying, begging her to help get my sister out of the group standing in the yard. Fanny raced back and forth ranting and screaming, but I insisted. I followed her every step, chasing after her.

"Please, help me! I cannot live without my sister. I will perish, and my sister is going to die wherever she is sent. Please get her out!"

The Germans who had made the selection were gone, and

only the local constables were around. The selected girls stood at attention for hours. When they were finally marched towards the gate for their departure, Fanny simply pushed Nachcia out of line. In the commotion I grabbed my sister's hand and pulled her along into the barracks. We hid, crouching in the corner on our cots, and sat there stunned for hours. With bitter weeping we poured out our anxiety and gratitude to God for this one more time that we had been spared.

Two years had passed since we were first incarcerated in this labor camp. Our limbs grew weaker, the labor felt harder, our stomachs were emptier and the emotional suffering became more severe. Hardest hit were the Hungarian girls, who were totally without resources. To still their hunger pangs, they scavenged through the garbage, picking out whatever was edible. Sometimes some were lucky enough to find peals from potatoes or other vegetables prepared in the camp kitchen for the staff. The few less moral prisoners cheated by going on the soup line twice, often not being noticed in the line of over a thousand people. There was a danger of taking away the portion of the last one on line, so no decent individuals tried to get doubles.

After food, clothing was our greatest problem. Our shoes were wearing out from all the marching. Business deals developed, and the going currency was our bread ration. A discarded belt from a factory motor would be concealed and carried back to camp. It might be bartered for three portions of bread. Another portion would buy the services of the prison's shoemaker, who would use the leather belt to resole a pair of worn shoes. Now the girl would have the shoes to save her feet, but it would have cost her stomach four days of bread rations.

Others were not so lucky. Their shoes were gone altogether by now, and the camp provided them with clogs. Those thick wooden soles with cloth uppers offered poor protection for their weary feet. Heavy and abrasive, they made marching a torture. During the summer many prisoners carried the clogs over their shoulders and marched in bare feet, but in freezing winter weather this was impossible.

The long march in the heavy clogs was devastating for Nachcia, whose original shoes had been rendered useless. Nachcia's general situation was worsening. Her headaches were severe, and her eyesight was so impaired that she could not properly handle the machines. She was getting into constant trouble with her *Meister,* Paluch. I was panicky for my sister's welfare. Again I went pleading to Fanny to do whatever she could for my sister. My imploring finally brought results when Nachcia was placed in the kitchen. It was a glorious morning when she was marched away together with the kitchen staff. Nachcia felt grateful to me for my courage; she knew she could never have secured the job for herself. She finally appreciated her little sister's newfound aggressiveness.

The kitchen work itself turned out to be harder than the factory work. From before dawn till late into the night, Nachcia was in the kitchen hauling barrels of water, carrying pails full of potatoes, and scrubbing the big pots, sinks, and floors. For hours she sat hunched on a low stool, cutting potatoes. She hosed them down and transferred them into pots for cooking, but she was not allowed to be close to the cooked food. She was not the one ladling out the portions at the window when the girls lined up for dinner. Although Nachcia's job involved hard physical labor, she thought of herself as lucky to be out of the factory. Her gratitude toward Fanny was immeasurable, and her faith in God was stronger than ever. The Lord had spared her the long marches and the sadistic *Meisters* and was leading her to safety, holding her under his protective wing until that time when she could safely return home to Mama and Papa and her family. In return, Nachcia pledged to help others the best she could, having been placed in the vicinity of that precious life-giving substance, food.

Winter was fast approaching. The days were shorter. We again stood at attention in the pitch-dark morning hours with the wind cutting through our meager clothes. The long march over the dark roads in the pouring rain was debilitating. Now

I was marching alone, without my sister. Stumbling in my clumsy clogs, soaked to the bone, I was now hit much more often by the German whip. Nachcia was not there to shield me from the German boot. By the time we reached the factory, my cold wet body ached all over. With no chance to change or get dry, I would rush to start the machine as Bezdupny hovered over me like a dark demon. I shivered with discomfort for hours. Finally, I would go to Fräulein Knauer to ask permission to go to the toilet and rest a minute. But I often had to rush back when another girl would come in with the horrible news that Bezdupny was again at my machines, looking for me. I knew immediately that I was in trouble. A few blows from the *Meister* on my return crumbled my remaining reservoir of resistance. Totally devastated, I would push the machine's lever into the slot with all my strength, only to fail and create a *Schützenschlag,* a tear in the material. Now Bezdupny would get enraged. He would kick me and threaten to report me.

Devastated after such a day, I would drag myself back to the camp wanting to be dead. I simply could not endure any longer. Tears would be choking me when I finally saw my sister at night, but I knew I must not cry. I must not let Nachcia see my suffering. Having gone through the search at the gate and the long line at the kitchen window, I would go to Nachcia in the kitchen when all the other prisoners were finally in the barracks. Nachcia would be sitting hunched on a little stool, her hair mussed, her clothes wet and dirty. She was feverishly cutting the horse beets into tiny cubes.

"I have two more barrels to do," she would say apologetically. "Go to sleep," she urged me. "I will come when I am finished. It will take a while. I still want to hose these down. I cannot stand what they feed our people. These beets are for animals anyway, and on top of that we have to put them in with the skin and dirt and rotten parts. I cannot do that. I cut away what is rotten, so it takes me longer. I also hose them down more to remove all that heavy dirt and soil."

She was apologetic to me for not doing her job faster and having more time to be with me. I would see her sad eyes and tired face, the fingers of her swollen hands slowed by pain. I was exhausted myself, but I could not leave my sister. I loved her too much to let her sit there by herself. She kept me alive; she was all I had to hold on to.

"No, Nachcia, I am not going. We will finish together and go to the barracks together."

Nachcia knew I was frightened to be without her, having to get through the day now on my own. She did not send me away.

"Sit here beside me, then," she said. "And wait until I finish."

"I did not just come because I'm afraid," I protested. "I came to help you."

Together now we worked cutting, washing, until the required thirteen barrels were full. It was just minutes before curfew when we ran together back to the barracks, with just enough time to slip into our cots before inspection. We fell asleep immediately, exhausted after a wearying day. In my sleep I could feel the ticks crawling on my face, biting my skin. Too tired to open my eyes, I just brushed them away, scratching my skin until it bled.

In the dim morning light Nachcia would see my bitten, scratched-up face. Like a loving mother she would kiss my swollen face before rushing away for another grueling day of kitchen work.

During the day, when all the prisoners were at the factories and the camp was empty, the kitchen staff was able to move around. Nachcia would wait till after barracks inspection was over to work on her scheme. It was a big and dangerous undertaking, but she had promised herself to help others, since God had spared her. She herself nibbled and picked at whatever she could get in the kitchen. She hid things for me in the kitchen under the pile of potatoes or beets that she was working on. I now came daily to help her after my own day's work. Nachcia would smuggle her own soup ration out of the kitchen. Carefully watching out for German guards, she would shoot over to the barracks and hide the bowl under the bed. If a constable ever found the soup under our bed, all six occupants of the aisle would be punished.

When I showed up after work in the evening, Nachcia quickly dispatched me to the barracks with instructions. Nachcia gave the extra portion of soup to different people each night. Even though the soup was ice cold and often had bed bugs floating in it, it was a blessed treasure. The recipient would praise Nachcia, gulping it down hungrily. The feeling of alleviating the gnawing hunger of her friends helped Nachcia bear her own hunger and torment.

There were often fierce fights over the distribution of the bread rations. After the prisoners returned from work and got their meager soup supper, they all piled into the barracks to obtain their *kaltverpflegung,* their dry food portion. There would be five round loaves of dark bread, which would be divided equally into forty portions. Everyone stood around the table where the *stubenälteste* (eldest person in the room) measured them out. There were loud complaints and quiet murmurs about how she favored friends with larger pieces. There were also exchanges between good friends and relatives, with the older ones giving the younger ones the larger piece. Crazed by hunger, we bickered over every crumb. One set of sisters actually fought and insulted each other, to the profound embarrassment of the rest of us. Sometimes a spoonful of jam or a cube of margarine was distributed with the bread ration. Every prisoner had a strategy for her precious bit of bread. There were those who slowly licked off the jam in heavenly delight and then hid the bread for the following day. Others just wolfed it down fiercely, trying to quell their hunger now, although it meant having to fast all the next day.

It was now the winter of 1944. The hard frozen earth beyond the camp's barbed wire fence was blanketed with snow. It was a known fact, murmured among the prisoners, that those dark fields held a gigantic treasure—potato storehouses. The potatoes were stored in a large pit covered with soil. In hushed voices, girls talked about risking their lives to steal potatoes from the field. It would be a most hazardous venture, as the camp was surrounded with barbed wire and armed SS guards. By ten o'clock curfew the whole camp was in pitch darkness, with a single searchlight trained on the gate. After bed inspection by the German guards, the room became silent and dark.

One night after the guards left, two brave girls waited for absolute quiet. Sabina and Bronia slipped on their coats and listened at the door for the marching footsteps of the German guard. When they heard him pass the barracks, they noiselessly sneaked out of the room. They ran across the yard like frightened mice, hunched close to the ground in the pitch dark, managing to reach the other side of camp before the constable did. They hid in the dark alley between the barracks, pressing their bodies against the wooden planks.

Their hearts in their mouths, they panted for breath. If discovered they surely would have been shot on sight. Hearing the guard march past, the two scurried along the barbed wire fence to find the hole that had been made by previous prisoners. They raised the wire over the hole, and crawling on their bellies like snakes, they pushed themselves through without getting snagged.

They were outside the camp. They carefully covered up the hole with the protruding wire. Then they made their way across the field in the deep snow, erasing their footsteps with their hands. Finally, they reached the location where they had hungrily imagined making their death-defying potato dig. With their bare hands, they dug out the heavy snow. The earth beneath was frozen solid. Like wild animals, they scratched the hard earth with their numbed fingers, their hearts thudding in their chests. When they finally felt potatoes in their hands, they wanted to scream with excitement. Slipping the potatoes into the linings of their coats, they carefully filled in the hole they'd dug and tried to replace the snow to cover any traces of their work. They now had to make the terrifying return journey back to their barracks. Totally spent, they staggered into the dark room. There they found Hadassah and Rachelka standing at the door, shivering, crying, and praying for their safety. There were hugs and kisses from Nachcia and me as well, and a united effort to conceal the potatoes in the sacks of straw that were our mattresses.

It wasn't until Sunday, when we weren't marched out of the camp, that the girls could cook the potatoes that they had gambled their lives for. There was no fuel for our old potbellied stove, so the girls who worked in the coal detail had to smuggle bits of coal back to camp. The precarious cooking venture had hardly started that Sunday when the password, *zex*, was sounded. This meant that Germans were on the way in. The precious fire had to be extinguished, the hot potatoes hidden, and the barrack quickly aired out. The brief inspection passed without incident and soon the clandestine cooks were at it again. Plenty of nerves were stretched to gain us each one half of a potato.

The next Sunday, however, everything went wrong. Sabina and Bronia had each taken three potatoes with them to roll call, afraid to leave them behind in their straw mattresses. We stood numbly in the cold, stamping our aching feet as the barracks inspection went on, taking an unusually long time. We were worried. The sun shone without warmth on our frostbitten faces. Fanny, the *Judenälteste,* was excitedly running in and out of the barracks with the Germans. We nervously murmured among ourselves. The barracks inspection finally ended, and the Germans began searching the prisoners—something not normally done on a Sunday.

Nachcia, as usual, stood in front of me. Sabina and Bronia were hidden behind Hadassah's and Rachelka's backs. Our hearts pounded when the Germans went to the back line. The girls in the front row were not allowed to turn their heads and see what was happening. Bronia's hood was suddenly ripped off her head, and her potatoes thudded to the ground. Sabina's face flushed; the German's hand was on her head. Her headgear was ripped off too. A strong slap to Sabina's face shot through the stillness.

My heart sank with pain for my friends. The Germans then barked for all of us to kneel. We knelt for several hours while Sabina and Bronia cried. No one consoled them, not knowing the extent of our punishment. Our limbs were frozen, our bodies tormented in the kneeling position. Finally, several Germans marched towards us and ordered Sabina and Bronia to the middle of the yard. While facing the entire inmate population, their heads were ceremoniously shaved down to their bleeding scalps. The spectacle was over and we were marched back to our barracks.

Bronia was devastated, and Sabina felt defiled. They somberly sat on their cots, not capable of responding to our attempts to comfort them. We completed our chores in a brokenhearted and grave state of mind and brought our pain to sleep. The spirits of our two intrepid friends seemed permanently broken. Nachcia chose them more often to have the bowl of soup she distributed, and they were grateful. The friendship between the potato smugglers and the two of us became stronger.

My clothes were in miserable shape by now, my clogs a source of great agony. My feet were full of blisters from marching in the snow, which would stick to my clogs. At times the snow was knee deep. Learning from others, I took courage and stole leftover spools of yarn from our machines. Trading my soup, I procured knitting needles made from the barbed wire fence. The factory yarn had to be disguised, and Hania had access to dye. On a Sunday when the stove was lit, we were able to heat some water and dye the yarn. With instructions from the girls I knitted a pair of heavy stockings. The work could only be done on Sunday nights. The unfinished product had to be hidden for weeks before it was ready to be worn. It was stashed deep in the straw of my mattress, and prayers were offered daily for the project not to be discovered.

Fräulein Knauer became *Lagerführerin* of the women's camp. Advanced from her post as factory worker and supervisor of the factory toilets, she plunged with delight and vigor into her new position of authority. She relished punishing us and thought of different ways to make our lives miserable. New edicts would be announced daily, and new punishments invented. Searches became more frequent and beatings more recurrent and severe. It was now about January, 1945, not that we prisoners knew the date or what hour of the day it was. All we knew was scrambling out of our bunks the moment we heard the whistle. In a mad rush we ran to the toilets and the icy water faucets.

In no time the whistle sounded again to announce that it

was time to line up for roll call. In the morning the inspection and countdown were fast, and we were marched out of the gate five abreast, the different columns of women for the different labor assignments. Young and old, tall and short, we were all emaciated, the rags hanging on our bodies. We all limped in our ill-fitting wooden clogs, dragging ourselves along to the constant accompaniment of jabs from rifle butts, kicks, and lashes.

Then came the grueling day at the machines, my four giants devouring the spools that I constantly kept pushing down their throats. The three highlights of the day, the soup for lunch and the two times we got permission to go to the toilet, marked the passing of conscious time. Another lineup, another countdown, another march, another search, another punishment, another curfew, and another day passed—another day had been survived. And for what? Were we another day closer? Closer to what? There was no light at the end of our endless tunnel. There was only nonstop struggle for every minute, every hour, every day. There was no time to think, there was only the instinct to fight on, only the fear of failing, of stumbling, of being the one who does not make it, of being picked out of the lineup, of being shipped away in a boxcar to oblivion.

Fräulein Knauer's punishments were as ingeniously barbaric as the culture that had nurtured her. On Sunday, our day off, she made us haul our straw sacks outside to be searched. Her ferocity boiled over if she found anything that displeased her. She would make the entire camp kneel till evening, running in and out of her office to check on the guards and the prisoners. Any slouching or supporting oneself on one's hands, any murmur or sigh was met by a savage beating from her.

One Monday morning, in the fierce January wind, Fräulein Knauer appeared in sunglasses, but they could not conceal the black blotches on her face. That day in the factory Puckel Knauer hopped over to Chanale's machines.

"Did you see my sister?" he asked. "I can no longer stand the atrocities she is committing. She might be your *Lagerführ-*

erin, but she is just my rotten sister. She argued with me, called me a Jew-lover. I am a Communist, you know; to me all humans are equal. And, besides, I love you. All my bitterness I took out on her. I promised next time to cripple her, ruin her perfect posture. She should feel what it is like to be a cripple. Being crippled all my life, I can feel for the unfortunate. But she? She is so healthy and beautiful and upright that she can only be cold and cruel. Did you see her black eye? Maybe now she will understand. If she does not stop beating you, she will get it again, until she comprehends.''

But Fräulein Knauer did not stop—on the contrary. She became even more ferocious. Chanale had to beg Puckel Knauer to stop his counterproductive lessons in mercy.

Tragic news from the men's camp in Sportschule reached us through the trickle of men who still came here to the women's camp to work. One girl's father was sick, another one's brother was ill, and still another one's husband had died. There was a typhoid epidemic decimating the men's camp. Sanitary conditions were dreadful, hospital care or medicine nonexistent. Whoever could drag himself to work would do so, terrified to remain in camp and be exposed to the infection. The men were dying by the hundreds. The women were in a frenzy. The little food we had we would give to the men in the work parties to smuggle through to the men's camp. Our only living link to fellow Jews, to family members in some cases, was being wiped out. We wondered when the plague would reach our camp.

The cruel winter cold was another enemy we were unarmed to fight. It was March now. My cherished stockings were in shreds, and my clogs were falling apart.

On Saturday we cleaned the machines in the afternoon. It was a gigantic job, but it meant that tomorrow was Sunday. There would be no marching to the factory, a brief reprieve for my tormented feet. Unfortunately, this Sunday turned out to be more ghastly than any march. Once again at roll call fifty women were picked out, and Nachcia was among them. Shivering, she stood there among the selected prisoners, contemplating her grim fate and her slim chances of surviving alone.

I was mad with fear of losing her. Frantically, I ran again to Fanny. I knew I had no chance this time. The same trick would not work twice. But what choice did I have? I had to fight to rescue Nachcia—I had to succeed.

For hours the fifty women stood at attention while Fanny ran around ranting and shrieking orders. Fräulein Knauer was busy with the higher-ranking Germans who had come to pick up their prey. The prisoners were lined up in front of the kitchen. Nachcia looked around. She remembered my telling her how Papa had run away from the marching column when they took him, how Mama had pushed Grandma Chaya into the yard behind the gate. Papa had not managed to escape, but Grandma had. What did she have to lose? She was as good as dead anyway. Nachcia crept back, then bolted into the kitchen, crouching behind a big barrel. A moment later the women were marched away.

Not having seen her escape, I was lamenting bitterly at my cot when Nachcia came into the barracks. We embraced and wept together. We had cheated death again.

Chapter 18

One morning, we had cleared the miles of slush and were again marching down the streets of Reichenbach when our angel Karl appeared. He was the first to bring the news. The Germans were losing the war. But even daring Karl was now more cautious and apprehensive; it had become even more dangerous to have any contact with the Jews. The Germans were nervous, their wrath more in evidence. They did not hesitate now to shoot people on the spot. Rumors were rampant. "The Germans are going to evacuate the prisoners," went one version. Another bit of information that leaked in to us was that the entire perimeter of the camp was being mined. We were scared.

It was May 7, 1945. Something very unusual happened:

there was no morning whistle to awaken the prisoners. Since we were not summoned to come out, we stayed in the barracks. We huddled together, nervously looking out of the window, eager to spot any movement. All was quiet. Restlessly, we speculated, hoping for the best yet fearing the worst. No one dared set foot outside the barracks door.

By midday the girls watching at the window noticed the German guards entering their quarters. Fräulein Knauer was among them. They were dragging along hand-drawn wagons. The girls watched attentively from the corner of the window so as not to be noticed. The Germans were scrambling up and down the several steps in front of their house, their arms laden with packages, cartons, garments. All were loaded into the wagons. Stupefied, the prisoners watched the Germans harness themselves to the loaded wagons and rapidly pull them away. Glued now to the window, we waited to see what was going to happen next. Before long, the Germans returned to reload and left again in a hurry. Until dusk we could see them coming and going.

The camp gates were locked, as they had been the night before. Nothing moved inside the camp, neither was the usual guard patrol in sight. We were frightened. We lay on our cots, too apprehensive to sleep. We murmured about being blown up soon by the explosives around the camp. The Third Reich would wipe out all traces of us, we feared. Nachcia prayed for me, that my young life should not be snuffed out so brutally.

When would the end come? Before dawn, we peeked through the window again. All was still. We waited, pinned to our cots with indecision and fear. No one wanted to be the first to suggest opening the door. It was almost midday when we suddenly heard the noise of bicycles going by. Soon we heard voices coming from the woods behind the camp. We strained our ears to hear. The strange voices did not sound German, but somehow familiar. Perplexed and excited, we pushed against the window to listen. Astonished, we saw three men get off their bicycles right in front of the window.

"Hadassah!" We yelled. "Hadassah, look! Come quick."

Bewildered, Hadassah pushed through the crowd. When she reached the window, she stood there unable to utter a word.

"Hadassah!" called a man who was feverishly cutting the barbed wire. It was Mendek, Hadassah's boyfriend. The girls shouted, laughed, and cried. Hadassah wept uncontrollably.

Mendek and the two boys who were with him furiously ripped open the barbed wire fence. "Come out!" they shouted to the girls. "Come out! Don't be afraid anymore. Come out."

No one moved. We were paralyzed with fear. Only when the boys came into the barracks, when we saw Mendek embrace Hadassah and we could touch these unguarded, free Jewish men did our terror begin to subside.

"Don't just stand around," the boys urged. "We need white cloth to make a flag of surrender, to avoid being bombarded." Someone quickly pulled out a nightgown. Another girl ripped the stick out of the broom. They fiercely tore open the night-gown and tied it to the broomstick. The boys climbed up onto the roof, with a few brave girls trailing behind them. They succeeded in tying up the flag, raising it as high as they could. More prisoners became aware of what was happening and they slowly started coming out of the barracks. They encircled the three boys, wanting to know exactly what was going on and what had happened to the Germans. The girls wanted to get to the men's camp or send messages to their fathers, brothers, husbands, or fiancés.

The news spread like water overflowing, as prisoners spilled out from their barracks onto the camp grounds. They restlessly moved about, listening, speculating. The majority of the prisoners went back to their barracks, afraid to be outside, afraid to be killed now in this wartime commotion by Nazi land mines, the incoming bombardment, or just spiteful shooting from the defeated German home guard. But some others could not wait any longer. They were free; they wanted to eat. They did not want to die of starvation now that their imprisonment was over. I, too, wanted to go out. My older and wiser sister would not hear of it.

"It is too dangerous outside. We must wait and see what happens."

All of Nachcia's appeals to my mind did not meet with my stomach's approval. Disobedient and trembling with fear, I followed Big Bronka to the fence. Through the new opening in the barbed wire we exited into the fabled potato fields. We ran hunched over into the nearby woods, afraid to stand up straight. In total disbelief we whispered to each other, "Are we walking alone? Isn't somebody ordering us? How can we march without following orders?"

Our feet felt like lead. The singular silence, the lack of the usual vulgar marching orders in screeched German accompanied by lashes from whips and blows from rifle butts made us oddly lame, unable to move. Slowly, suspiciously we proceeded, crouching every so often to listen. We trekked through the woods until we reached the unfamiliar streets of the town. We carefully advanced along the deserted streets, occasionally spotting other prisoners going in and out of abandoned buildings. Encouraged by the sight of fellow prisoners, we ducked into the back yard of a house. We found a small hand-drawn wagon and made off with it like scared thieves.

We came across a bakery with the doors ajar. The aroma of fresh-baked bread made us dizzy with hunger—we wanted to sink our teeth into those fresh-baked loaves and swallow enough down to fill our bellies to bursting. But there was no time even to taste a crumb. The bakery was filled with prisoners tumbling over each other, grabbing, pulling the hot loaves from the shelves. Big Bronka and I feverishly loaded loaves of bread onto our wagon, not stopping until the wagon was full. Tired but as excited as gangsters with bars of gold, we ran, pulling our wagon through the streets of Langenbielau, bequeathing a trail of fallen bread loaves for lucky prisoners to find.

In one of the streets we encountered two girls from our camp dragging a large side of pork behind them, holding on to the leg. The two had obviously found the local slaughterhouse. We greeted each other excitedly and raced together back to the camp, where we could share our lifesaving bounty.

Suddenly we heard the rumble of oncoming vehicles. Stowing away our goods, we ran for cover behind some roadside trees and lay there motionless in the underbrush.

"German tanks, and they are coming this way!" Big Bronka whispered.

Why didn't I obey Nachcia just once more? I asked myself. Why was I so stupid, so adventurous at such a dangerous time? We have survived so much together, why did I have to abandon my protective sister now? I whispered to Bronka, "I can hear the soldiers' voices. It is all over for us. They will find us here and shoot us in the ditch. The girls will find us later. My poor sister, my Nachcia."

Bronka, whose father was a Jew and her mother a Gentile, was brought up as a Catholic. The big strong peasant girl quickly crossed herself and covered her head with her hands, ready to receive the bullet that would end her life.

"Pray!" she ordered in a commanding mutter.

I remembered the seven martyred Jews in my hometown of Chrzanow, and their final utterance of *Shema Yisrael!* Hear O Israel! when they were hanged by their necks. I silently repeated this holiest Jewish prayer as the tanks thundered closer. The muted voices that wafted by were growing more distinct, and we suddenly realized that the language was Russian. Instantly alive with new vigor, we jumped to our feet, running towards the road. We waved and shouted *"Zdrastvicie!"* Hello! The helmeted soldiers in the tank turrets waved back and smiled broadly. The tanks kept churning away until they vanished in the distance.

Exuberant but still shaken by the experience, we pulled our booty into the camp and took it directly into our barracks. We then divided the spoils between us and each had a small mountain of bread on our cots. I caressed the pile of bread with my eyes, finally feeling free of the demon hunger. I did not care at all about the Russian invasion of Germany, only of Helcia's defense of Breadloaf Mountain. I sat at the edge of my cot with my back blocking the bread from hungry eyes. I luxuriously spread my hands across my crusty treasure, feeling an unfamiliar tranquillity and sense of control. Nachcia, too, looked contentedly at her baby sister who had provided them all with a lifegiving treasure.

But not everyone was engrossed in gastronomical gains. Inmates were milling around the yard near the main gate. A red carpet strewn with flowers was spread in front of the wide-open gate. Girls were holding bouquets and awaiting the arrival of our liberators, and one dark-haired beauty had somehow put on a red blouse. The lookouts soon ran into camp yelling, "They're coming, they're coming!"

Presently, soldiers wearing *rubashkas*, tunics buttoned along the side from the neck down, and round red-banded caps disembarked from their trucks and marched through the gate. The girls went berserk with excitement. Some threw flowers at the soldiers, others hung on to their arms, hugging and kissing them. The girl with the red blouse flung herself onto a soldier's neck and kissed him on the mouth. She let go of him and went through a line of others. The soldiers were exuberant, laughing and loudly greeting everyone with triumphant cries of *"Zdrast-vicie!"* Welcome! Hello! Some girls pulled at their sleeves, tugging and dragging them into the barracks. Some soldiers were carried in on the girls' shoulders. More and more soldiers were now pouring into camp; they were brought into almost every barracks. The girls tried to communicate in Polish or broken Russian.

Soon the soldiers pulled out their bottles of vodka and began celebrating their victory the only way they knew how. They wanted to share the vodka with the girls, but few of the under-nourished inmates ventured a try. Some girls were more interested in feasting on third-rate Russian army rations; others were too intoxicated with their newfound freedom to care for food or drink.

Vodka flowed freely, and the soldiers drank themselves into a stupor. They climbed onto our cots, only to plummet down with a crash of broken boards. The dramatic day was coming to a close. The brilliant May sun hid behind the wooden barracks as the pale dusk descended on the tired camp. The girls were exhausted, spent; the laughter had all died down. The drunk soldiers were sprawled all over the barracks. Awakening from their stupor, they now sought to satisfy their other needs and desires. They wanted women. Enticed by the warm welcome they had received just hours ago, they now eagerly pursued the girls, trying to lure or push them into bed. Unwilling to accept the girls' refusals, our Soviet heroes became aggressive, angry, and insulted.

"We are your liberators. We freed you from your bondage. You just shouted that to us. You tore wildly at us to come to you, to free you from this prison, and already you are so ungrateful as to refuse us."

The girls tried in vain to explain how tired they were, how malnourished and ill. The older women begged them to leave the girls alone. They tried to explain that they were truly grateful but were emaciated prisoners; they desperately needed rest and nourishment to recover their health. But all was in vain. The Russians became brutal and forceful, preferring to be conquerors than liberators. The girls became hysterical, running from their barracks, afraid to return. The older women cried and pleaded. They searched among the troops to find Jewish soldiers to appeal to their conscience. They begged them to take their Gentile associates away peacefully. But even those soldiers who claimed to be Jews only wanted to use it as a privilege.

"I am a Jew," they would say, "so come to bed with me. Surely you are not going to refuse a Jew."

It was long past dusk and the soldiers in our barracks were still there, loudly claiming their right. With the girls pleading with them to leave in peace and with one high-ranking officer on our side, the soldiers one by one capitulated. Some of those who left came back later. It was almost dawn when the girls finally managed to get rid of the last one. We quickly dragged over several cots to barricade the door. Impatiently waiting for daybreak, we speculated about where we could go. We could not stay here in camp another night: we were too easy a mark for the rapists who had saved us from the murderers.

Nachcia worried about us, as other little groups formed and left together. Some had a father or a brother or a husband from the men's camp in Sportschule. Those with male escorts were out in the early morning. Some searched for a place to stay; others took advantage of the chaos to gather some clothes for themselves from abandoned stores and apartments. The older people and wiser ones knew enough to go for the good stuff: money, jewelry, watches, and other tangibles that could be bartered for food and other goods.

The Russian soldiers were prowling the streets in pursuit of much the same. One could see the more inebriated Ruskies walking the streets of the town, wearing long lacy nightgowns over their uniforms. Some wore ladies' dresses and elegant hats adorned with feathers. But watches were particularly desired by the Russians. Soldiers wore wristwatches from their wrists up to their shoulders, in all sizes, shapes, and styles. They even wore alarm clocks hanging from their coat buttons. As far as we were concerned, our liberators had far too much time on their hands.

Nachcia and I were too distraught to enjoy our liberation. There was no place to go, and our barracks were unsafe from skirt-scavenging Soviets. Help came from our friends in aisle number one. Hadassah had her boyfriend Mendek, with his cousin and a close friend. Of course, Hadassah was not alone. She was part of the "Holy Four," as her clique was called, consisting of Hadassah, Sabina, Rachelka, and Bronia. When Mendek came to pick the girls up early in the morning, Hadassah turned to Nachcia.

"I know you have nobody," she said, "but you can come with us. We are going to look for a place, and whatever we find, we will have room for the two of you as well."

Nachcia embraced Hadassah with grateful tears in her eyes.

"Don't worry, Nachcia," Hadassah reassured her, "I'll always remember what you did for all of us here in camp. You always shared with us. Now whatever we will have we will share with you."

It was exasperating to leave most of the bread I had stashed away in my cot, but we had to hurry and follow the boys. I grabbed two loaves, reluctant to leave my aromatic hoard of bread, which smelled of security and survival.

The boys found an abandoned house and immediately took

possession. It was a two-story, one-family house with enough bedrooms for everyone. We girls settled in the upstairs bedrooms, and the fellows slept downstairs for protection. The Russians visited every night, banging loudly on the door.

"Open up!" they would shout. "Where are the women?" they demanded. They were mostly drunk and looking for wicked fun. As soon as the banging started, we frightened girls would scramble into hiding places under beds, in the closets, in the hamper, or wherever we might avoid detection. The fellows would open the door and claim that they lived there alone, just the three of them, but sometimes the soldiers wouldn't leave. They would linger around the kitchen table, inviting the boys to go drink with them. They were rowdy and loud, and so the girls upstairs dreaded to even think about what would happen if the soldiers discovered them.

Even during the day, we girls were afraid to go out much. The fellows supplied the food and the girls kept house. The fellows brought home whatever news they heard. One day they instructed us to come out. We were surprised. They gave us the distressing news that we had to head back to camp to attend a funeral. We found out that we had to bury a friend of ours, a camp inmate who had been shot to death by Russian soldiers when she could not follow their orders to carry heavy suitcases loaded with loot for them. Such were our saviours.

The Russians were plundering and raping, going wild in the streets of the town. It was too dangerous for the girls to be outside. When we ventured out, it was on the arm of one of the guys, who, if stopped, would claim the girl to be his wife. Being somebody's wife was the only protection from being attacked by a soldier.

We had some male protection now, and we did not lack food and beds, but the girls all wanted to go home. Nachcia and I wanted to go home to Mama and Papa, to see Blimcia and Jacob, to squeeze little Aiziu to our hearts. We wanted to hug Heshek and Vrumek and Sholek, and we wanted to know what had happened to poor Goldzia. We yearned for Mama to hold us close in her warm lap, to sit and listen to Papa recount all that had happened to them. We wanted to pour out our bitter hearts and tell our beloved family how much we suffered and how much we missed them.

The boys felt that it was too early to travel, but Nachcia and I could not wait any longer. At the first opportunity, we went to the neighboring city of Reichenbach, a larger city where there were many former inmates. There we met Janek Fishgrund, a friend of Blimcia's from Chrzanow. He took us to an apartment he shared with other former prisoners. We had been there only one night when the Russians barged in and rounded us up. There were no shouts, kicks or whips, but we were led out of town into what seemed to have been an army camp.

In total astonishment, we found ourselves being interned again in barracks surrounded by a fence, with a soldier stationed at the entrance gate. Rumors were rampant, the most prominent being that we were going to be shipped into Russia for labor. Again we were prisoners, our bare hands our only defense against armed soldiers. We were allowed to take along a bag of our meager belongings, an extra pair of shoes and some clothes the boys had helped us accumulate in Langenbielau. I sat in the barracks on top of my bundles. There were Golda and Tila Grajower, the two sisters from Chrzanow, and there was our cousin Hania. Nachcia and I lamented our fate after the heartbreaking promise of liberation. We talked among ourselves, unable to come to any conclusion. I, the youngest among us, voiced the strongest protest.

"I am not going to be imprisoned again. We must find a way out. We must not let them ship us away."

People were congregating in the yard, speculating, whispering, talking. I snooped around among the throng of prisoners and listened to every rumor. I even dared to talk to the Russians. These were soldiers on duty, so I was not afraid of them. I prodded them with questions about our fate. I observed the soldiers and learned that they all congregated at the front gate, far more interested in pretty girls than in watching their post.

I then convinced my friends that we must run away, promising to make their escape possible by distracting the guards. To Nachcia's distress I stood at the gate talking to my soldier "friends," averting their attention while motioning to our friends to disappear behind my back. And so Golda, Tila, Hania, and finally Nachcia slipped past me and the guardhouse and into the night. It then occurred to me that I was now utterly alone with several Russian soldiers at the gate. I could not perceive how in the world I was going to get away without being shot at. I waited until their attention was drawn from me; an altercation developed between them, and I acted in a split second. I abruptly turned and slipped into a shadow behind the gate, and from there to freedom.

We had all arranged to meet at the house. There we found new arrivals, other homeless refugees. Now we knew we must leave town. We wanted to go home. But how could we travel to Poland without any possessions or money? The few articles we had collected after liberation were in our backpacks in the camp barracks we had just fled. To attempt a return to Poland empty-handed was not wise at all. Who would help us on our way? It was too dangerous now for girls to be out alone searching in abandoned buildings for clothes and other articles.

I offered to go back to the camp and see if we could somehow get our bundles back. Nachcia did not want to hear of it; she scolded me, saying I was too young to understand the danger. I was forbidden to go anywhere. Nachcia had no plans, only hopes that we would eventually get back to Poland and to our family.

But I could not wait for eventualities. Secretly I spoke to Hania, Golda, and Tila, trying to convince them we should get our possessions back from the camp. No one yielded, but after a while Tila called me aside.

"I'll go with you," she whispered.

We quietly slipped out. It was high noon when we reached the camp. The surrounding fields were calm. As we approached we saw that the camp was deserted. The gate was open, and there were no guards or prisoners to be seen. We meekly ventured inside, a queasy feeling in our stomachs. Through the window we could see our former room, empty but for five bundles sitting forlorn in the middle of the floor. The windows were closed. The door handle had been removed on the outside. If we could only open the door, the bundles would be ours again. If we only had an instrument to pry the door open. A simple handle would do. We decided to go back, get some tools, and return for our bundles.

We had started on our way back when suddenly we noticed three Russian soldiers walking towards us from far away in the field. They were pushing bicycles, talking loudly and laughing. There was no place to hide in the open field. We wished we could have vanished somehow, but there was nowhere we could turn. Trapped as we were, we managed to keep our cool. We just kept walking briskly, even though we would pass each other on the only available path. The closer we came to them the louder our hearts beat. It was hard not to look at the soldiers since we almost had to touch to pass one another on the narrow path. We tried to avert our eyes.

"*Zdrastvicie!*" the soldiers greeted us, looking straight into our eyes. We did not answer but kept walking. The soldiers turned their bikes around and began following us. We did not discuss it out loud, but we knew we could not run: surely the three young soldiers with bicycles could outdistance us.

The soldiers stopped us and wanted to know what we were doing here in the fields, where we had come from and where were we headed. "We were taking a walk in the fresh air," we claimed, and started walking again. Soon the fields were behind us and the five of us had reached the city limits. Then the soldiers insisted on accompanying us to headquarters, where we could explain everything. I felt remorse for having gotten Tila into this bind; I whispered to her to make herself disappear while I kept the soldiers busy.

I launched into a tirade. The soldiers paid no attention to the departing Tila, who was much too old for them anyway. Now I was left alone with three young Russian soldiers. All I could think of was that I needed a miracle. I fervently prayed to God to help me in my distress. I felt his presence hovering over me, and I suddenly felt an inner strength. I turned abruptly to the soldiers and said, "I am going to bring you my working papers."

We had just reached the neighborhood where we were staying. Having promised to produce my papers, I ran into a nearby house. I expected them to follow me in and arrest me, so I ran around to the back yard and hid, crouching in a thick clump of bushes. It was just after dusk. My head was throbbing. I could not forgive myself for disobeying my older and wiser sister. I stayed in the bushes until it was fully dark and I was certain that the soldiers had given up on me. My sister lovingly embraced me when I finally came upstairs to our room. Happy to see me, she forgave me like a mother.

Chapter 19

The trains were taking refugees back east. Before dawn we tiptoed quietly through the deserted streets, avoiding the main thoroughfares, making our way to the railroad station. Relieved to see no boxcars, we boarded the train that soon arrived. We were empty-handed and exhausted, but we were glad to be leaving that hateful city and that hated place where we had known so much pain. We hoped that we were finally on our way home.

The journey was a perilous one. Hundreds of people crowded into trains that were not following any orderly schedule, but traveling and stopping at random. Russian soldiers were everywhere. They were bothering passengers, especially the girls. In their desperation, three females would cling to a male on the train, each claiming to be his wife. The Russians would snidely say, "You have three; that is two too many. You keep one, and two go with us." In our struggle to avoid being raped, we girls often had to abandon our places, sometimes jumping out of a moving train. We hid until the Russians left, having to wait for hours on end for another train. We developed codes to alert each other to impending danger. We learned to recognize our own people and to use the accepted password *amcha,* "your folk." If the person were Jewish, he or she would know to respond *amcha.*

It was a warm summer day when we disembarked from a train in the city of Katowice. From there we had to make our own way to Chrzanow, about forty-eight kilometers away. We were in a large plaza and people were milling all about. We noticed a big truck with a small step ladder attached to it. People were piling in, stepping over each other in haste, pushing, shoving, forcing themselves into the truck. Nachcia urgently grabbed my hand and dragged me along, pushing us through.

We were very lucky to have made it into the truck, where we were squeezed in among a crowd of women. At least there were no soldiers to bother us, and the truck promptly jolted and jerked and was on its way. Soon we were out of town, standing shakily in the fast-moving vehicle.

Suddenly, the truck swerved off the road, stopping sharply in a clearing beside the forest. The driver, a young Pole, came out of the cabin, opened the back of the truck, and said, "Everybody out!"

We all scrambled out without a word of protest. Presently the man stationed himself beside the little ladder and held out his palm. Those women who paid the required fare were allowed to stagger up the ladder and back into the truck. The women dug deep into their bosoms to produce zlotys for a place in the truck. When we approached to climb the ladder, the man barred our way.

"Where is your pay?" he demanded.

"We have no money," we started to say, wanting to explain where we were coming from. But the man had no patience to listen. Shoving us away, he snapped, "You don't have money, so you don't go."

As soon as the last passenger was on board, he removed the ladder, jumped into the cabin, and took off with a roar. Stunned, we stood at the side of the road at the edge of a dense forest, watching the truck disappear in the distance.

We were alone and destitute, but we could not afford to despair now. We had come a long way and were determined to reach Chrzanow. Somberly, we began walking in the chilly air along the winding forest road. The sinking sun hardly penetrated the tall trees. Exhausted, we realized that we would never make it to Chrzanow before nightfall. We decided to try flagging down a passing vehicle but they just zoomed by. When one finally stopped, we ran towards it, only to find that it was a Russian military truck. The soldiers were happily waving to us. Terrified, we ran into the forest to hide.

When the truck was gone, we resumed our search for transportation, trudging onward. Soon a gigantic truck stopped. We were relieved to see that the military truck was merely loaded with metal oil drums tied down with chains. With only one soldier in the truck, we felt it safe to ask for a ride. The Russian soldier sitting in the cabin laughingly told Nachcia to climb up in the back and motioned for me to come inside the cabin next to him. We begged him to let us both be together, but the driver would not hear of it. Only when we walked away did he finally agree to let us both climb up with the barrels. We hung on to the chains high atop the oil drums, frightened that at any moment we might tumble down, together with dozens of rolling barrels.

It was after dusk when we finally reached the town of Chrzanow, the town of our birth, of our childhood. Our hometown now looked terribly strange. We recognized the houses, but there seemed to be an alien chill coming from them. Passersby turned unfriendly faces to us with a curious hostility, seeming to say, "You too are alive? There are too many of you left." We walked by the store we used to own, afraid to approach it, and then down to Zielona Street where we had last lived.

Quietly we stole up the steps, our hearts pounding hard, and knocked at the door, listening attentively. When an answer came, we opened the door hesitantly. In the middle of our former kitchen, where Goldzia's bed had been, there was a big plain table. Around it sat about seven or eight men dressed in overalls, heavy boots, and old worn hats. The room was filled with smoke from the pipes they were smoking.

An eerie feeling possessed us. We had stumbled into hell. "We are sorry," I stammered. "We knocked on the wrong door." We swiftly turned and ran down the steps, wanting to be anywhere else but there. Walking back to the center of town, we whispered to each other.

"Where are we going to go now?"

"We must stay to find out who is alive."

"Were Mama and Papa able to survive? And Blimcia, would she have given away her child, her Aiziu, so that she could stay alive?"

"Goldzia? What about Goldzia? Did she have any chance? How did Goldzia die? Will we ever know?"

Shlamek was dead. We knew that. But Heshek, Vrumek, and Sholek were young and strong. They certainly had had a chance; surely they were alive. They would come back here to Chrzanow, we decided. This was the only place where we could meet. We had to stay here and wait.

But we had nowhere to go. Here we were in Chrzanow where we had had so much family and so many friends. Should we try Great-aunt Channa's house, Uncle Nachman's, Grandma Chaya's, or Aunt Esther's, which, after all, was always our second home? But there would be no one familiar in any of these houses. The whole town seemed foreboding and haunted.

We heard people talking about us, making comments like, "So much of that filth is still around."

Eventually we met other Jews who had returned. We found an abandoned apartment in which the stoves were destroyed. The Poles had demolished all the stoves in Jewish homes, looking for valuables that the Jews might have hidden there. Other survivors were congregating there, so we felt it was safe to sleep there too. That first night when I got up to go to the bathroom, I staggered a few steps and then fainted. When I came to, Nachcia was standing over me, spilling some cold water onto my face; there was nothing else she could offer me.

The next day we went to the Planty, where a soup kitchen had been set up by survivors who had returned some weeks ago. Our cousin Hania was there, and we found out that her brother Sholek had returned very ill from a camp. Through the good graces of Mrs. Lask, an older Jewish woman who had survived in Chrzanow, Cousin Sholek was placed in the hospital. Together with Hania, we went to see him. Sholek's body was all swollen, filled up with water, his lungs only partially functioning. We sat by his bedside for two days, but he was unable to communicate with us. After dusk on the second day, Sholek died.

Hania was hysterical. Nachcia and I had to tear our cousin away from her brother's corpse. We arranged for a simple funeral. We slowly walked behind a horse-drawn cart, Sholek's body in a white sheet resting on its planks. The cart rolled through the streets of our hometown from the hospital to the Jewish cemetery. Sholek's body banged against the wooden boards of the wagon as it rolled down the cobblestone road. Now there were only the three of us from our large family.

The next day we went back to the soup kitchen, praying to catch sight or word of someone in the family, and our prayers were answered. Hunched over his soup and looking terribly aged and ill was our brother-in-law Jacob. We wept in his arms, slowly rocking back and forth in our grief. It was not easy for Jacob to talk, but over several hours his story emerged.

When Jacob first heard the German rifle butts banging the boards covering our hiding place, his heart sank. In seconds the trapdoor was opened and rifles poked at our feet.

The physical pain from being cramped beneath the low roof was now joined by pangs of anguish. He was the man, the one to protect his lovely Blimcia, his precious baby Aiziu, his sisters-in-law Nachcia and me, who needed him now as a father. He had failed us all.

"Raus schnell, Du Judenschwein!" barked the soldiers.

There was no time to wallow in guilt. Jacob lowered the

ladder and helped everyone down. His mind spun with turmoil as Nachcia was brutally struck and Blimcia struggled down the ladder with Aiziu in her arms. He was reeling from kicks and slaps, trying desperately to find Blimcia's hand. There was a swirl of noise and a throbbing pain in his head during the swift march to the marketplace. He was jostled in a sea of agonized victims crying out for loved ones torn away. Where was the wife he loved more than life? Where was little Aiziu?

Barely conscious, Jacob realized he was with a group of men and boys. He tried to locate the women's group, to at least discover their destination, but the men were all pushed into cattle cars. The dark car was packed solid. People were passing out from suffocation and could not be revived. Feeling the wall behind him, he instinctively pressed his face to a crack in the boards to suck in some fresh air. Jacob was convinced that suffocation and thirst would kill them all before the train finally stopped.

After an endless, deadly journey, the doors were flung open. The lights of the camp blinded them, as the living were chased out like sheep to a clearing fenced in by barbed wire. At each corner of the camp stood a guard tower with a machine gun. The prisoners, now devoid of human dignity, were made to strip and line up for inspection and to have their heads shaved. They were issued a pair of striped pants and a striped shirt and cap, plus a pair of wooden clogs. Jacob would remain in Markstadt labor camp for a full year, beginning in the winter of 1943.

They were awakened every morning before dawn by the shrill sound of whistles and the bellowing of the cruel capos. They were lined up for roll call and pushed into exhausting maneuvers before being marched away in different work details. Jacob was assigned to the Krup munitions factory, producing pipes and parts for antiaircraft and torpedo rockets. He became emaciated and broken-down by the starvation rations and the endless hours of forced labor; and his spirit sank lower with each day. After their first year of slavery in the factory came a change—a change for the worse.

Markstadt was closed down and the prisoners were shipped to Fünfteichen. The SS made them construct a barracks for their living quarters. The meager ration of soup got thinner, the slice of limy bread got smaller, the icy winds cut more sharply through their flimsy striped suits, and their wooden clogs bruised their feet even more deeply on the long marches to reach their work at Krup. The resolve to survive for Blimcia's and Aiziu's sake kept Jacob alive.

In February of 1945 the camp was evacuated. The inmates were loaded like so much cargo into open coal wagons. The trains inched forward for days on end, then stopped in the middle of nowhere. For twelve hours they witnessed the bombardment of Dresden. Totally exposed to the icy wind, the starving prisoners warmed and fed their souls with the twelve hour downpour of fire and brimstone that thundered from the sky upon their wicked foes.

When the human cargo was finally unloaded at Gross Rosen, one third of the prisoners had to be shoveled out. Still among the living, Jacob was then lined up for the infamous death march to Buchenwald. When the American army arrived and liberated the camp, the Americans wanted to place Jacob in a sanatorium to nurse him back to health, but Jacob wanted only one thing: to return to Chrzanow and find his wife and child.

After a perilous journey, he did reach Chrzanow, but he did not find Blimcia and Aiziu, nor any indication that they had survived. As powerful as his will to live for them had been, so was his determination not to live without them. He blocked out the world and would not be consoled by us or anyone else. We left Jacob with our own spirits bleak, but with the driving need to find some of the other ten souls that had comprised the Stapler family.

It was weeks later that we discovered that Jacob had been placed in an American hospital. He refused all medication and food. He had survived a hundred wartime hells only to die shortly after liberation.

*   *   *

On the next day's walk to the soup kitchen, I suddenly noticed something peculiar about some laundry I saw hanging on a line. It somehow looked so familiar. When I examined it closer, I found it to be my family's laundry: there were my brothers' monogrammed shirts and my sister Blimcia's lacy nightgowns with her *B.S.* embroidered on all of them.

Who was using our family's clothes? I had to find out. I began removing the clothes from the line, and sure enough a woman stuck her head out of the window, yelling, "What do you think you're doing, stealing my laundry?"

I recognized Mrs. Madeia, the shoemaker's wife who had been our next door neighbor on Zielona Street. I promptly went upstairs. Upon entering I felt faint again, as though I were a ghost haunting my former home. The Madeias had apparently moved to the more affluent Planty, where the Stapler furnishings fit better. Somewhat taken aback, Mrs. Madeia now brought out a pillow that stunk from little Krisia's urine. She offered it to me saying, "I know you have nothing, so here is a pillow for you to sleep on."

I looked around the room; everything was eerily familiar. The furniture, the linens, the tablecloths, even the white enamel water barrel. Displayed on the dresser was Shlamek's beautiful box for his shaving gear, the one he received from the army as an award. The set's mirror was open to adorn the room.

My heart was breaking. Mrs. Madeia still stood there, the generous offering in her hand. "I don't want anything," I declared. "You can keep all our furniture and our clothes and linens. Where would I go with it anyway? But this box belonged to my brother Shlamek, who died fighting for this country, for Poland. I don't know about the rest of my family, but I know that my brother Shlamek is never going to return. And I want this box to keep as a memento."

Mrs. Madeia put the pillow away and adamantly said, "And what do you suppose I will have as a souvenir of your dead brother? Certainly I need something to remember him too."

I just turned and walked out and down the steps. Nachcia and Hania were waiting, waiting for God knows what. We only knew that we had to leave this town, this country, this continent that had forsaken us.

Only in the years ahead did we discover what had happened to our family, and to a million other families in the hell that came to be known as the Holocaust. Our bodies and souls were seared for life, but we came to be known as survivors. The only other survivor, the third Stapler left of the twelve of us, was Vrumek in Palestine.

It has been fifty years. I am now the last of the Chrzanow Staplers. I offer these pages, these memories, to my children and to yours.

Stapler, Sara Miriam	Mother	Perished in Auschwitz.
Stapler, Symche	Father	Perished in Auschwitz.
Rauchwerger, Blimcia	Oldest sister	Perished in Auschwitz.
Stapler, Shlamek	Oldest brother	Killed on the battlefield.
Stapler, Heshek	Second brother	Died in Siberia.
Stapler, Goldzia	Third sister	Killed by the Nazis.
Stapler, Sholek	Fourth brother	Killed by the Nazis.
Rauchwerger, Jacob	Brother-in-law	Died upon liberation from Markstadt Fünfteichen Buchenwald.
Rauchwerger, Yitzchak	Blimcia's son	Perished in Auschwitz.
Laufer, Chaya	Grandmother	Perished in Auschwitz.
Bromberger, Esther	Mother's sister	Perished in Auschwitz.
Bromberger, Pinchas	Esther's husband	Perished in Auschwitz.
Bromberger, Sholek	Esther's son	Died upon liberation from Markstadt Fünfteichen Buchenwald.
Bromberger, Chamek	Esther's son	Perished in Auschwitz.
Bromberger, Gucia	Esther's daughter	Perished in Auschwitz.
Laufer, Nachman	Mother's brother	Perished in Auschwitz.
Laufer, Lieba	Nachman's wife	Perished in Auschwitz.
Laufer, Sholek	Nachman's son	Perished on death march from Markstadt to Fünfteichen Buchenwald.
Bachner, Channa	Chaya's sister	Perished with her seven children and twenty-six grandchildren in Auschwitz.
Bachner, Moishe	Channa's husband	Perished in Auschwitz.
Enoch, Ruchele	Father's sister	Perished with her husband and two children in Auschwitz.
Stapler, Pinkus	Father's brother	Perished in Theresienstadt.
Stapler, Elsa	Pinkus's wife	Perished in Theresienstadt.
Stapler, Freddy	Pinkus's son	Perished in Theresienstadt.
Stapler, Dolfi	Pinkus's son	Perished in Theresienstadt.
Schein, Sabina	Cousin	Perished with her husband in Auschwitz.

My Mother's Tears

Was she clutching at her heart
When from Father, they ripped her apart,

Was her stare savage wild,
When they took away her child,

Was her throat choked with tears,
When she faced the Nazi beasts,

Could she handle her distress
When they told her to undress,

Were her tears already dry,
When she said her last good-bye,

When she stifled in gas in fume,
When she knew we were all doomed,

Will I ever in passing years,
Know about my Mother's tears.